John Penry and the
Marprelate Controversy

TO HARRY GODDARD OWEN

in recognition of his efforts to improve the standards of teaching and scholarly research in the College of Arts and Sciences of the Men's Colleges of Rutgers, The State University of New Jersey, during his tenure as Dean (1945 to 1965)

by DONALD J. McGINN

John Penry and the
Marprelate Controversy

RUTGERS UNIVERSITY PRESS

New Brunswick   *New Jersey*

Author's Foreword

On March 22, 1593, John Penry, the Puritan pamphleteer, born in Wales and educated at both Oxford and Cambridge Universities, was captured by pursuivants of the Crown. On April 5 he was examined at the Sessions House in Old Bailey Prison, on which occasion he refused to take the oath *ex officio mero*, which required an accused person to answer all questions put to him before he knew either the identity of his accusers or the basis of their charges against him. Five days later, on April 10, again at the Sessions House, Penry was questioned on his religious convictions. On May 21, at King's Bench Court, he was formally accused of contempt for the Queen and for attempting to overthrow religion, as well as of treason and rebellion.

For reasons impossible to ascertain at this late date his trial did not actually begin until May 25. On that day, again at King's Bench, the earlier accusation was not mentioned, but instead he was charged with publishing seditious writings. Finally, on May 29, he was hastily removed from prison, dragged on a hurdle to a gallows set up at St. Thomas a Watering, and there hanged.

The legality of his sentencing has been questioned on the ground that the charges against him were based on the Act of Uniformity (passed during the first year of Elizabeth's reign), which did not embrace felony or capital punishment. The few historians who have attempted to vindicate Penry's execution cite a statute made in 1581, "An Act against slanderous words and rumors, and other seditious practices against the Queens Majesty." But this act was never mentioned during the proceedings.

For the first accusation against Penry on May 21 the evidence consisted of certain private papers removed without his knowledge or consent from his lodgings in Scotland, where in 1589 he had fled for asylum after the capture of the printers who were secretly printing another incriminating manuscript written by him. An indication of the hostility of Her Majesty's Government toward him appears in the Queen's application to James IV of Scotland, later James I of England, to banish him from Scotland. In response to the Queen's request, James IV issued an edict for him to quit the realm, but it was never enforced. The Scottish presbyterian clergy, who admired Penry, apparently were on his side. The new evidence brought forward at his trial on May 25 consisted, in part, of excerpts taken from one of his Puritan pamphlets, *Reformation No Enemie*, published in Scotland in 1590.

This was not the only writing of Penry's that had called down on his head the wrath of the authorities. His first pamphlet, the *Aequity*, purporting to be an appeal to foster the preaching of the Gospel in Wales, was so outspoken in its criticism of the episcopalian form of church government that no sooner was it published in 1587 than John Whitgift, Archbishop of Canterbury, ordered five hundred copies seized. Penry was summoned before the Court of High Commission presided over by Whitgift and severely reprimanded by the Archbishop himself. After this examination Penry was committed to prison for twelve days. Moreover, the remainder of his signed pamphlets, all of which were secretly printed, in defiance of the law, became more and more violent in their denunciation of the civil magistrate who meddled in ecclesiastical affairs —an allusion to the Queen as the supreme governor of the Church of England—and of the episcopalian hierarchy, whose names and offices, according to Puritan doctrine, were "relics of popery."

Another fact that tended to alienate the good will of the authorities was Penry's conversion to separatism. Upon returning to London in the late summer of 1592, he had abandoned presbyterian-Puritanism and had joined the separatists, whose chief propagandists were Henry Barrowe and John Greenwood. In spite of several years of imprisonment these two men, followers of Robert Browne, the most eloquent of the separatists, had continued to write and had succeeded in smuggling their writings to the outside world.

The increasing activity of the separatists induced the Parliament of 1593 to review another act of 1581 originally directed against Catholics who violated the Act of Uniformity by refusing to attend the services of the Established Church. This act in its progress through the House of Commons was variously described as the "Bill for Obedience to the Queens Majesty against the See of Rome," the "Bill to retain the Queens subjects in their due obedience."

On February 28, 1593, a Puritan member, Henry Finch, expressed his fear before the House of Commons that the bill as amended might be interpreted as including "those that came not to Church by reason of the mislike they had of the Church Government," in other words, the presbyterian-Puritans. On March 12 this bill was scrapped, and in the new bill substituted for it it is clear that the intent of the legislators was to include the Protestant nonconformists, particularly the Brownists and the Barrowists; nevertheless, on April 4, after further amendments had been made, Finch pointed out that the bill "pretendeth a punishment only to the Brownists and Sectaries, but throughout the whole Bill, not one thing that concerneth a Brownist." He contended that it would affect not only papists but all those "who spoke against non-residence, excommunication, or any other abuse in the Church." Following these criticisms, appropriate committees of both houses conferred "for the better effecting of a convenient Law to be provided for meeting with the disordered Barrowists and Brownists without peril of intrapping honest and loyal Subjects." On April 7, 1593, the new bill with some additions and amendments was read the third time and passed upon the question. The penalty for the convicted was banishment from the country.

On the previous morning Barrowe and Greenwood had been executed at Tyburn. They had been convicted under the Act of 1581 "against slanderous words and rumors, and other seditious practices."

Penry's close association with these two men could hardly have enhanced his position in the eyes of the officers of the Queen; however, granting the generally hostile climate of opinion prevalent in 1593 against separatists, an ulterior reason for the harshness of Penry's sentence was his active participation in the Marprelate Controversy of 1588–1590, one of the fiercest attacks ever made on the Church of England. That Penry played a lively part in this controversy was well known, but on the crucial point of whether he was the mysterious literary genius who signed himself Martin Marprelate, or mar-bishop, to a series of inflammatory pamphlets, the evidence was purely circumstantial and was not introduced at his trial.

The seven major pamphlets signed by Martin Marprelate boldly demand that the episcopacy be replaced with a presbyterian system of government and are filled with scandals about prominent persons, particularly those in high positions in the Church of England. So vivid is Martin's personality that it shines through everything that he writes. From his first pamphlet the reader might think him a mere gossipmonger eager to take personal revenge upon the bishops, but his subsequent pamphlets become more earnest and reveal the courage of a man who knowingly endangered his life in order to defend his religious convictions. At the same time his evident zest in contending with the high ecclesiastical authorities suggests that exercising his own wit was almost as important to him as defending his doctrines.

Although the Martinist pamphlets are completely Puritan in doctrine, their violence places them slightly out of the main stream of presbyterian-Puritanism, which was striving to achieve a political reformation of the Church of England. Indeed, the bitterness of Martin's attack on the government of that Church is closer to the writings of the separatists, Robert Browne, Henry Barrowe, and John Greenwood.

The grave challenge of the Martinist pamphlets to the power of the establishment was not lost on Whitgift, who in his younger days as Vice-Chancellor of Cambridge University had been Thomas Cartwright's formidable opponent in the first Puritan controversy. In an effort to stem the tide of nonconformity Whitgift enlisted some of the best minds among the episcopalian clergy: his own chaplain, Richard Bancroft, who later became Bishop of London and then Whitgift's successor in the see of Canterbury; John Bridges, Dean of Sarum; Thomas Cooper, Bishop of Winchester; Robert Some, Rector of Girton and in 1589 to be elected Master of Peterhouse College, Cambridge; Matthew Sutcliffe, Dean of Exeter; and last, and perhaps most famous, the theologian Richard Hooker, whose *Ecclesiastical Polity* is generally recognized to be the standard defense of the Established Church. In addition, Whitgift succeeded in persuading George Gifford, an active Puritan, to write a series of devastating pamphlets against the separatists, who were becoming more of a threat to the Establishment than were the Puritans.

Martin's witty rhetoric, his colloquial style, and his seeming good humor have won him high praise as a satirist. J. Dover Wilson classifies his writings as "a little body of tracts which are, admittedly, the chief prose satires of the Elizabethan period." Martin was "the great prose satirist of the Elizabethan period and may rightly be considered as the forerunner of that much greater satirist whose *Tale of a Tub* was a brilliant attack upon all forms of religious controversy."

The more immediate imitator of his racy style was Thomas

Nashe, the young "Juvenal" of England as he was called by his literary companion Robert Greene, who also learned from Martin through Nashe. To "olde Martin Makebate," Nashe, the most modern writer among the Elizabethans, was greatly indebted for abandoning the stale euphuism of his first literary effort, his *Anatomie of Absurditie,* and adopting the lively style that made his *Pierce Penilesse* the most popular Elizabethan prose pamphlet. Nashe's successful imitation of "Martinizing" was followed by the pamphlets of Thomas Dekker and Samuel Rowlands and thus established the pamphlet as a literary genre.

To this day the question of Martin's identity is one of the enigmas of the Elizabethan period as far as legal proof is concerned, for no new documents have come to light in the intervening centuries. Literary historians have taken violently opposed positions on the basis of the circumstantial evidence, and the same sharp disagreement is characteristic of comparisons of the literary style of John Penry and Martin Marprelate. Whether or not all the documentary evidence, both legal and literary, has ever been adequately examined in its full historical and theological context is yet another matter in question.

Convinced that no completely satisfactory account of the Marprelate Controversy or of Penry's part in it had yet been written, and unable to resist the challenge in Ronald B. McKerrow's statement in his edition of the *Works of Thomas Nashe,* "there are in the whole range of English literature few characters more interesting, more curious, and it may be said, more completely bewildering" than Martin, I set out to do some detective work. I was spurred on, of course, by memories of the unfavorable reception given in certain quarters to an article that I wrote in 1944 identifying John Penry as Martin. I undertook to retrace my steps and to examine all relevant controversial literature both attacking and defending the Church of England in the last quarter of the sixteenth century. Little by little the set of depositions made by persons suspected of complicity in the Martinist conspiracy took on new meaning for me. Further close reading of the pamphlets signed by Penry and Martin and a comparison of their literary style and allusive content led on to inspection of the printing until finally the case for Penry was overwhelming. Neither John Udall nor Job Throckmorton, the other candidates most frequently suggested to establish the identity of the mysterious satirist, fitted all of the known particulars.

At this point I shall merely add that I have tried to interpret the Marprelate Controversy in the framework of related conformist and nonconformist literature of the period and to maintain a position free from bias in appraising both my primary and my secondary sources. I have not attempted a point-by-point analysis of the involved arguments of the scholars who have previously written on the subject.

I express my gratitude to my good friend Rudolf Kirk, Professor Emeritus of Rutgers University, who has constantly followed the progress of this study and urged its completion. To the Research Council of Rutgers University I am indebted for a series of yearly grants that have helped to defray the expense of purchasing microfilms and supplies and of obtaining secretarial aid. For permission to quote from the rare pamphlets I wish to acknowledge the kindness of the following libraries: British Museum, Folger Shakespeare, Huntington, Lambeth Palace, Union Theological Seminary, University of Wales, Yale.

DONALD J. McGINN

Rutgers University
New Brunswick, New Jersey
September, 1965

About the Author

Professor Donald J. McGinn did his graduate and undergraduate work at Cornell University and has been a member of the English Department at Rutgers University since 1936. He is also the author of *The Admonition Controversy*, an account of the first literary clash between the Puritans and the defenders of the Church of England (1572–1577), and of *Shakespeare's Influence on the Drama of His Age* and *Literature as a Fine Art* (with George Howerton).

This book was set in Caslon Old Face type, printed by letterpress on 60# Publishers' Imperial Text, and bound in Bancroft Oxford Linen.

Contents

John Penry and the
Marprelate Controversy

Chapter I

The Year of Decision

In the mid-fifteenth century Johann Müller of Königsberg, better known as Regiomontanus, a mathematician whose astronomical tables were used by Columbus and his fellow navigators, drew a picture of the heavens as they would appear in the year of our Lord 1588.[1] In his astronomical forecast he predicted an eclipse of the sun in February, two total eclipses of the moon, one in March and one in August, and finally a conjunction of the three planets Saturn, Jupiter, and Venus with the moon. Interpreting this unusual celestial activity, he prophesied, if not the end of the world, at least all kinds of physical upheavals and political changes for the fateful year.

If his "scientific" explanation were not enough to convince everyone that this year was to be one of dire portent, the horrifying interpretations of the prophecies in the Apocalypse, or Book of Revelations, made by the eminent Protestant theologian Philip Melanchthon would have added the finishing touches. On the hypothesis that all history was divided into cycles, each of which was marked by some catastrophe or other, Melanchthon noted that the final cycle of ten times seven years, which in the Old Testament was the length of the Babylonian Captivity, began in 1518, immediately after Luther's nailing of his theses on the castle church doors in Wittenberg, and would end in 1588. Melanchthon therefore predicted that in that year, according to the prophecy of St. John, the seventh seal would be opened, Antichrist (the Protestant term for the papacy) would be overthrown, and the Last Judgment would take place.

Those prophets who would not go so far as to predict Doomsday at least were convinced that the year 1588 would bring forth all sorts of disturbances in the physical universe, including earthquakes, violent tempests, terrible floods, hail and snow in midsummer, darkness at noon, bloody rain, and even monstrous births. These prodigies were to persist from the beginning of the year until August.

To circulate these predictions a popular sixteenth-century literary form, the almanac, was used. Oddly enough, though in Holland a great many almanacs appeared, in England, where the almanac was also extremely popular, little reference was made to the prophecy of Regiomontanus. Garrett Mattingly suggests that the Queen herself may have forbidden it.[2] Noting that an almanac by one of the most distinguished students of astrology in England, Dr. John Harvey, ridicules the prophecy and condemns the horrendous interpretations of it, Mattingly offers the further suggestion that the Queen, conscious of political threats to her kingdom, may have invited Harvey to issue his refutation.

However that may be, just as today the *Farmers Almanac* frequently succeeds in correctly forecasting the weather for a particular period, the predictions of stormy weather during the first half of the year proved accurate. In May and June hailstorms ravaged fields and orchards in Normandy, floods overran the meadows of Picardy, and during the period from May 9, when the Spanish Armada set sail from Lisbon, Portugal, until it arrived at the mouth of the English Channel on July 29, Western Europe was buffeted by gales more typical of December than of May and June.

For several months immediately preceding the appearance of the Armada off the coast of Britain rumors of its approach had spread like wildfire throughout Southern England. On one occasion a false report had sent some of the more timid inhabitants of the coastal towns flying inland to London, to the great embarrassment of the Queen and her Government. In June, 1588, while the Spanish fleet was beating a slow path up the Atlantic against inclement weather, rumors of another, more subtle, threat to the Queen's power were passing from mouth to mouth in the little community of Richmond, a few miles from London. A mysterious personage living at the home of a well-known Puritan named Thomas Horton was engaged in writing a book on behalf of John Udall, the Puritan minister of the nearby community, Kingston-on-Thames. Though apparently of the least significance in comparison with the prospect of armed invasion, the incipient activity in Richmond was destined in time to prove more destructive to the monarchy than the ill-fated Armada.

Contrary to the point of view made popular by such nineteenth-century historians as James Anthony Froude and John Lothrop Motley, and to a lesser extent by Mattingly himself,[3] the Puritan threat to royal power was essentially as "treasonous" in the eyes both of the Queen and of her Privy Council as were the exhortations of Father Robert Parsons, S.J., and Dr. William Allen, founder and president of the English College at Douai, co-founder of the English College at Rome, and eventually Cardinal. Both of these priests, exiled from their native land, were indeed urging English Catholics to rebel against Elizabeth, who on February 25, 1570, had been declared a heretic by the bull *Regnans in excelsis* issued by Pope Pius V. And even though in 1580 Pius' successor, Gregory XIII, by permitting English Catholics to obey their Queen in civil matters, had qualified the bull of excommunication, the original papal action had rendered all English Catholics suspect, with the result that active persecution of their numbers was intensified. Likewise the Puritan writers, while protesting their loyalty to the Queen as civil magistrate, had as early as 1572 begun to question her authority as supreme governor of the

Church of England. Just as the seminarists sent by Allen to England were charged to exhort their flocks to separate themselves from the heretics, so the Puritan preachers maintained that only one person who did not accept the presbyterian interpretation of the Scriptures would contaminate the entire congregation and hence must be excommunicated from it.

Thus the year 1588 was a critical year not only for the English Government but also for the Church of England. For Elizabeth I, monarch of the realm and supreme governor of the Established Church, this year was doubly fateful. Ever since her accession to the throne in 1558 after the death of her half-sister Mary, the wife of Philip II of Spain, the relations between England and Spain had been unfriendly. With the increase in the frequency of English raids on Spanish ports and on Spanish possessions in the New World, Spanish tempers were rising, and Philip was hard at work with his advisers on plans for an invasion of England, which in the spring and early summer of 1588 would attain their fulfillment. Beside the flamboyant spectacle of great naval battles that ushered in a new age,[4] the clandestine operations of a Puritan press attacking the Church of England and its supreme governor may seem undramatic. Fortunately for the monarchy, the patriotic fervor aroused by the threat of invasion had the effect of increasing Elizabeth's popularity among her subjects. On the contrary, the dissemination of Puritan pamphlets not only caused considerable embarrassment to the Queen herself but also added fuel to the growing antiroyalist sentiment that would in time culminate in the execution of her successor, King Charles I.

Almost immediately upon mounting the throne, after the martyrdom of the leaders among those Edwardian Protestant divines who had elected to remain at home under Queen Mary, Elizabeth was confronted with the demands of the returning exiles who had taken refuge in the Protestant strongholds on the Continent. Thoroughly indoctrinated with Calvinism and grimly determined to carry out an ecclesiastical reform that in their opinion would complete the work begun by Henry VIII, clergymen like Edwin Sandys and Edmund Grindal, who became bishops and then archbishops under Elizabeth, never completely conformed. Their goal was to change the government of the Church of England, which to them too closely resembled that of Rome, into a model of the ecclesiastical polity of Geneva. Thus, in the years leading up to 1588, the twofold burden of avoiding war with Spain and of treading a precarious middle path between Geneva and Rome was placed on the young Queen's shoulders.

In the very opening years of her reign she had set out on this *via media* when in 1561 she had combined the strongly pro-Catholic First Edwardian Prayer Book with the equally strongly pro-Genevan Second into the Elizabethan Book of Common Prayer. But as the political antagonism developed between Protestant England and the Catholic powers on the Continent, the more zealous among her subjects began to question as anti-Christian anything remotely associated with the liturgy and the rites of Catholicism. Of course, the fact that the chief enemy was Catholic Spain naturally increased the antipapal sentiment in England. As the Pope became identified with the Spanish King the religious extremists, searching the Bible for symbols of tyranny, found them in the Book of Revelations, whence Melanchthon derived his prophecies of disaster for 1588. The Whore of Babylon, the destruction of whose empire built upon seven hills would, according to St. John, precede the coming of Antichrist, was taken to represent the combined forces of Rome and Spain.

Vigorously condemning the Catholic sacrifice of the Mass, the more ardent of the reformers began to attack everything associated with it—vestments, sacramental crossings, and kneeling at communion. Sponsors in baptism were considered unnecessary, and the use of salt and oils in its administration was condemned. Indeed, all sacraments except baptism and communion were to be eliminated. Thus all of the ancient rites and customs that had grown up in a Church a millennium and a half old were stigmatized as "relics of popery" and therefore to be cast out.

Eventually through a series of bitter controversies, consisting of nonconformist attacks and episcopalian defenses, the extremists arrived at the decision to separate from the Church that under Henry VIII had made its original break with the Mother Church in Rome. Of the many clashes between the nonconformists and the Establishment the two most decisive were the Admonition and the Marprelate Controversies. The first of these (1572–1577) represents the initial attack on the government of the Church of England and signals the rise of Puritanism; the second (1588–1590) dramatically marks the decision on the part of the mysterious writer at Richmond to bring about a showdown between presbyterian-Puritanism and episcopalianism. Since the logical outcome of the efforts of this anonymous spokesman for nonconformity who called himself Martin Marprelate (that is, mar-bishop) could only be a complete break with the Establishment, any consideration of this second controversy must include the evolution of the psychology of sectarianism, or separatism.

Now in the mid-twentieth century Christians of every denomination are beginning to contemplate the possibility of reversing the trend toward the multiplication of sects and of searching for a common ground of understanding, first, among those who call themselves Christian and then among Christians and non-Christian religions. It has been authoritatively stated that the controversy between the presbyterians and the episcopalians never really advanced beyond the lines drawn up in the Admonition Controversy of the 1570's.[5] Similarly, it is no exaggeration to add that the causes that led to separation from both episcopalianism and presbyterianism have not multiplied since the 1580's. Accordingly, in view of the present efforts on the part of churchmen of the various faiths to establish a spirit of brotherhood throughout

Christendom, it is, perhaps, a propitious moment to reexamine these divisive causes. It may well be that they will have considerably less validity for the ecumenically-minded mid-twentieth century than they had in October, 1588, when Martin Marprelate's first pamphlet burst upon the English reading public.

Chapter II

The Rise of Puritanism

Historically the Marprelate Controversy represents the last desperate effort on the part of the extreme reformers to rally public opinion in order to effect a peaceful change in the government of the Church of England from episcopalianism to presbyterianism.

The first literary attack on the episcopacy occurred in 1566, when an anonymous pamphlet entitled *A briefe discourse against the outwarde apparell and Ministring garmentes of the popishe church* ushered in the so-called Vestiarian Controversy, in which the main target was the use of vestments in the Church of England. The author took the stand that vestments, symbolizing "popery," are not conducive to the edification of the church of Christ as set forth by St. Paul, II Corinthians xiii, Ephesians ii and iv, and I Corinthians xiv; moreover that the magistrate, whose duty is merely to execute God's commands, has no right to demand conformity. These two objections to vestments were soon to become the two fundamental principles of nonconformity, later to be elaborated upon by Puritan controversialists: first, that the Scriptures set forth the complete plan for the building of God's church, and second, that the magistrate is subservient to the authority of the church.

This initial attack on episcopalian authority elicited a reply entitled *A briefe examination for the time of a certain Declaration,* in which the author states, first, that vestments are "indifferent things" and hence not essential to edification, and second, that in returning to the usage in the church in the time of the Apostles the writer is misled by what was done in times of persecution rather than in times of peace under a godly magistrate. From these two arguments are derived the fundamental episcopalian defenses against the extreme reformers, namely, that whereas the Scriptures contain all doctrines essential for salvation they leave the details of polity to the church, and that these details in peaceful times under the godly magistrate Queen Elizabeth differ from those in times of persecution.

The nonconformists came back with another tract, *An answere for the tyme, to the Examination*. While inserting objections to crossing at baptism and to baptism by women, the author concentrates on denying that vestments are "indifferent" and on defending the scriptural interpretations given in the original nonconformist pamphlet. And like the first writer he contends that the magistrate's only duty in the church is to defend it, not to rule it: "Kings and Quee[n]s shold be Nurcies of the Church, but not Lordes of it, nor of our consciens." At the same time the Answerer levels the first attack on episcopalian authority: "Yet shall the porest mynisters, euen euerie vicar, curat, and parrish priest . . . haue as great authoritie, in the ministration of the word, and Sacraments, in his Church, as any of these prelates." But no suggestion had as yet been made regarding the displacement of the episcopacy by a presbyterian system of government.

At once recognizing that the refusal to conform to episcopalian authority was closely associated with limiting the power of the Queen as supreme governor, the bishops responded with another plea for conformity entitled *Whether it be mortall sinne to transgresse ciuil lawes, which be the commaundementes of ciuill Magistrates*. To this defense of the established order were attached statements by noted continental reformers recommending conformity and a tract entitled *A briefe and lamentable consydera-*

tion, of the apparell now vsed by the Cleargie of England, in which the author denies all arguments based on Scripture forbidding the use of vestments.

Only obliquely, in demanding equality of ministers, did the nonconformist pamphlets in this early controversy attack the episcopacy. Four years later, however, Thomas Cartwright, Lady Margaret Professor of Divinity at Cambridge University, in a signed statement of his theological views specifically called for the abolition of the names and offices of archbishop and bishop and in their stead the establishment of the offices of bishop, to be renamed minister, and of deacon, as he himself from his reading of the Scriptures interpreted the functions of these two offices. Cartwright's signature of this document was demanded by the authorities, who were cognizant of the fiery sermons delivered by him from his pulpit at the university.

In Cartwright's plan the government of the Church was to be taken from the episcopalian hierarchy and given to the presbytery consisting of seniors, or elders—a transfer of authority for the purpose of instituting the principle of equality among ministers. In addition to attacking nonresidences and pluralities, established practices in the Church of England, permitting a clergyman to receive an income from a parish or parishes which he did not serve, Cartwright demanded a change in the order of calling and making ministers. In subsequent writings Cartwright spells out what he apparently had in mind in his insistence upon this change. Instead of the traditional method of ordination by the laying on of hands by the bishops, along with the words, "Receive the Holy Ghost," he insisted that a minister's ability to instruct must be "tried," whereupon the "church" would be asked whether or not they objected to the proposed candidate.

At this point in the gathering nonconformist revolt occurred two developments destined to have great significance in all future opposition to episcopalian authority. First, in order to implement Injunction 51, requiring strict censorship of all printed matter, the High Commission, originally established by the Queen to serve as an advisory body of clerics and laymen for the determination of ritual, doctrine, vestments, and discipline in the new Establishment, published a decree from the Star Chamber setting forth a series of restrictions. Any book either printed or published against the Queen's injunctions, ordinances, or letters patent was liable to forfeit, and any printer or publisher responsible for such a book as this was to suffer three months' imprisonment and was not to be permitted to print again; the selling, binding, and stitching of secretly printed books were likewise prohibited; finally, the wardens of the Stationers' Company were given power to search all suspected places, to seize all books printed against the Queen's ordinance, and to arrest anyone involved in their printing, binding, or sale.

The second development in the growing dissent, probably the result of the enforced curtailment of pamphlets appealing directly to public opinion, was the attempt to bring pressure on Parliament to reform, or altogether to abolish, the Book of Common Prayer. Between 1566 and 1572 a number of bills intended to remove offensive rites and ceremonies and to legalize the use of the Genevan Prayer Book were introduced into Parliament by members sympathetic with nonconformist demands. Finally, on May 22, 1572, a command from the Queen brought to an abrupt halt all efforts to reform the Book of Common Prayer through parliamentary action.

A few weeks later appeared a deliberate attack on the government of the Church of England and on the Book of Common Prayer, the anonymous *Admonition to the Parliament*, followed almost immediately by the *Second Admonition*, both of which developed Cartwright's doctrines as preached at Cambridge. The authors of the first *Admonition*, presumably John Field and Thomas Wilcox, condemn the names and offices of "lordly lords, archbishops, bishops, suffragans, deans, doctors, archdeacons, chancellors, and the rest of that proud generation"—indeed, the whole episcopalian hierarchy—as contrary to the Word of God, and instead demand equality of ministers in order to "restore the church to his ancient officers." In place of the episcopacy the Admonitioners would establish the Genevan system of elders, who along with the ministers would exercise ecclesiastical discipline. Cartwright in his *Replies* defines this discipline as "the election or choice and the abdication or putting out of ecclesiastical officers," the "excommunication of the stubborn or absolution of the repentant," and "the decision of all such matters as do rise in the church either touching corrupt manners or perverse doctrine."

The author of the *Second Admonition,* probably Cartwright himself, in somewhat greater detail renders the program for reorganization and, in addition to reinstating the office of "doctor" discarded by the first *Admonition,* carefully distinguishes this title from that of "oure vniuersitie doctors," which is "for vayn glory sought and graunted." He also adds another order to the four already mentioned, namely, that of widow.

But it was left to Cartwright, who has aptly been designated the arch-Puritan,[1] to become the champion of nonconformity by publishing his three *Replies* defending the two *Admonitions* and thereby laying the foundations not only for English presbyterianism but for English nonconformity in general. Designating Cartwright's *Replye to an answere,* his *Second replie,* and *The rest of the second replie,* along with John Whitgift's *Answere to a certen Libell* and his *Defense of the Aunswere* as the "textbooks" for all subsequent controversy between Puritan and episcopalian, the church historian W. H. Frere declares, "Much was added in bulk and volume, but the Puritan controversy did not really advance an inch beyond the point reached here." [2] The accuracy of Frere's statement, at least for the remainder of the sixteenth century, is attested in every Protestant pamphlet appearing before 1600. The word of the "puritans T.C.," as Martin Marprelate reverently calls him,[3] is final in all arguments for a presbyterian system of church government; similarly, Whitgift's monumental *Defense of the Aunswere* contains the standard episcopalian replies.

In defending the antiepiscopalian viewpoint of the two *Admonitions*, Cartwright introduces the idea that in the Scriptures, set forth complete to the least detail, is the plan for the Christian church, which, insists Cartwright, is presbyterian rather than episcopalian in government. His assumption is based on his *personal* conviction that if God had appointed "the form, the length, the breadth, the height, the wood, the kind and sort of wood" for the Ark of Noah, which was the figure of the church, certainly he must have done the same in the New Testament for the church itself. This assumption he reinforces by citing God's specific directions to Moses for the construction of the tabernacle and to Solomon for building the temple. Whitgift's objection that the figures of the tabernacle and the temple apply to ceremonies rather than to government Cartwright brushes aside with the question, "Is it a like thing that he [the Messias], which did not only appoint the temple and the tabernacle but the ornaments of them, would not only neglect the ornaments of the church but also that without the which (as we are borne in hand) it cannot long stand?"

The principal authority for the presbyterian form of government Cartwright derives from the following texts taken from the Epistles of St. Paul:

I Corinthians xii.28: And God hath set some in the church, first apostles, secondarily prophets, thirdly teachers, after that miracles, then gifts of healings, helps, governments, diversities of tongues.

Ephesians iv.8: Wherefore he saith, When he ascended up on high, he led captivity captive, and gave gifts unto men. . . . 11. And he gave some, apostles; and some, prophets; and some, evangelists; and some, pastors and teachers. 12. For the per-

fecting of the saints, for the work of the ministry, for the edifying of the body of Christ.

In order to answer the argument of the episcopalian apologists
that certain of the offices mentioned in these scriptural passages—
namely, apostles, prophets, and evangelists—have not been heard
of since the time of the Apostles, Cartwright arbitrarily divides
"all the whole ecclesiastical function" into "extraordinary, or
those that endured for a time"—that is, apostles, evangelists, and
prophets—and "ordinary, which are perpetual," that is, those
governing the whole church, whom he calls elders, and those taking charge of only one part, or deacons. The elders, in turn, he
separates into two categories: first, the pastors, whose function is
preaching, and the doctors, whose function is teaching; and
second, the elders proper, or seniors, who along with the pastors
according to Matthew XVIII.15–17 exercise not only the election, or choice of, and dismissal of ecclesiastical officers but also
the private disciplining of the members of the congregation
through admonition and reprehension:

> Matthew XVIII.15: Moreover if thy brother shall trespass
> against thee, go and tell him his fault between thee and him
> alone: if he shall hear thee, thou hast gained thy brother. 16.
> But if he will not hear thee, then take with thee one or two
> more, that in the mouth of two or three witnesses every word
> may be established. 17. And if he shall neglect to hear them,
> *tell it unto the church:* but if he neglect to hear the church,
> let him be unto thee as an heathen man and a publican.

It was upon this last step in the "discipline" of excommunication,
usually referred to as *Dic ecclesiae* (Tell it unto the church), that
most of the controversy was centered.

Whitgift defines the *ecclesiae*, or church, as meaning "such as
have authority in the church": "Therefore when you complain to

my lord's grace, lord bishop of the diocese, or their chancellors, commissaries, &c., you tell the church, that is, such as be appointed to be public magistrates in the church according to the very true sense and interpretation of that place."

But little did Whitgift, the conformist, realize what interpretations were to be given the word *church* in the years ahead. The first of these Cartwright provides in his rebuttal, foreshadowing those yet to come:

Now I would ask who be meant by the church here? If he [Whitgift] say by the church are meant all the people, then I will ask how a man can conveniently complain to all the whole congregation or how can the whole congregation conveniently meet to decide of this matter? . . . Well, if it be not the people that be meant by the church, who is it? I hear M. Doctor say it is the pastor; but if he will say so and speak so strangely, he must warrant it with some other places of Scripture where the church is taken for one, which is as much as to say as one man is many, one member is a body, one alone is a company. And besides this strangeness of speech, it is clean contrary to the meaning of our Saviour Christ. . . . Seeing then that the church is neither the whole congregation nor the pastor alone, it followeth that *by the church here he meaneth the pastor with the ancients or elders. . . .*

That Cartwright was aware, however, of the possibility of even broader interpretations of the word is indicated by his indirect reference to what within a decade was to become the congregationalist view set forth by the two separatists Robert Browne and Robert Harrison: "For to let pass that some and of the ancient writers do expound the place of St. Matthew *of every member of Christ* and of as many as have faith to confess Christ to be the Son of God, and so by that means to have power of excommunication, I say, to let that go."

Oddly enough, even though Cartwright was the first to advocate replacing the episcopacy with his presbyterian elders, he still considered himself a member of the Church of England, which in government was episcopalian, with the Queen as its supreme governor. He and his followers apparently expected in time to convince both the Queen and the Parliament that reformation would never be accomplished while the Church retained the names and offices of the Roman Catholic hierarchy; thus *through peaceful means* the Puritans hoped to effect the adoption of the presbyterian system. Furthermore Cartwright hoped to impress upon the Queen her subordinate position as "nurse" and "servant" to the Church. While protesting that he has no intention that the Church should "either wring the sceptres out of princes' hands" or remove "their crowns from their heads," he holds that the civil magistrate should be liable—indeed, should be privileged—to excommunication by the elders in order that the laws of God, enforced by the presbytery, be properly "excuted and duly observed." Unfortunately, Cartwright was seemingly unaware that the changes in the government of the English Church instituted by the Tudors were intended to be permanent. Consequently, though he preached against its government and liturgy, he never considered separation from it. Moreover, he seemed almost naively blind to the untenable nature of his position.

In addition to condemning this dual form of government by the civil magistrate and the bishops, the nonconformist writers question the authority of the clergy of the Established Church. This third development in antiepiscopalian dialectic was a synthesis of two different complaints made in the first *Admonition* and upheld by Cartwright: first, that the ministry of the Church of England was ignorant and illiterate; second, that as a result of this shortcoming the Church sanctioned the reading of homilies instead of the preaching of original sermons. Concerning the election of ministers, the authors of the first *Admonition* complain that whereas "in the old church a trial was had both of their ability to instruct and of their godly conversation also . . . now by the letters commendatory of some one man, noble or other, tag and rag, learned and unlearned, of the basest sort of the people (to the slander of the gospel in the mouths of the adversaries) are freely received." Criticizing bishops for ordaining men whose "unhonest life" and "lack of learning" scandalized their congregations, the Puritan writers call for the removal of "these ignorant and unable ministers already placed." These complaints are echoed by Cartwright, who reenforces them with numerous biblical illustrations and with similitudes.

In order to emphasize the alleged stupidity of the episcopalian clergy, the Admonitioners particularly attack the homilies approved to be read in the service: "By the Word of God it is an office of preaching; they make it an office of reading." As authority for their objection that the reading of homilies cannot fulfill Christ's instruction to his Apostles, "Feed my sheep," the Admonitioners make numerous marginal reference to scriptural passages, most of which provide the epithets for subsequent Puritan writers to hurl at the episcopalian clergy: "blind guides," "dumb dogs," "unsavoury salt," "sleepy watchmen," "empty feeders," "dark eyes," and so on.

Whitgift, in his *Answere to a certen Libell,* replies that these scriptural passages are directed not at "such ministers as use to read the Scriptures and prayers to the people," but at all "ignorant, foolish, slothful governors and pastors." Unfortunately for his cause, in his eagerness to differentiate between the reading of the Scriptures and of prescribed prayers on the one hand and outright ignorance on the other, Whitgift unwittingly coins an epithet that his Puritan opponents gleefully seize upon and use against him. "If you had said," writes the Vice-Chancellor of Cambridge University, later Archbishop of Canterbury, " 'Against *dumb and unlearned ministers,* view these places,' you had said something."

Thereafter the phrase "dumb ministers" becomes a standard Puritan synonym for all clergymen of the Established Church, whether or not they read homilies. Moreover, since the reading of homilies was liturgically correct, the Puritans assumed, either sincerely or merely for the purpose of propaganda, that ignorance likewise was approved, even fostered, by the episcopacy.

It soon becomes clear, however, that by "ignorance" Cartwright and his followers do not mean lack of education or of learning. In defending the implication in the first *Admonition* that the reading of homilies is intended to "maintain an unlearned and reading ministry," Cartwright states, "Now if a man will say that the homilies do explain and lay open the Scriptures, I answer that the word of God also is plain and easy to be understanded and such as giveth understanding to idiots and to the simple." In other words, he considers an educated reader of homilies to be unlearned when compared with an idiotic or unlettered preacher. Moreover, Cartwright flatly declares that "the Word of God is not so effectual read as preached," for "the ordinary and especial means to work faith by is preaching and not reading"; and again, "the Word read is not so effectual as preached and . . . by bare reading ordinarily there is no salvation and therefore also no faith." [4]

For the Puritan propagandist it was an easy leap to the next step in this semantic war. Since the Puritans thus believed that, as William Haller puts it, "for the understanding of the word, for conversion to the faith . . . nothing was required but the natural capacities of the lowest, most ignorant, and least gifted of men," they took for granted that an "inner light" located either in the man predestined by God to be one of his elect or in the Bible itself, or in both, would enable a man, no matter how uneducated he might be, to understand divine truth. [5] According to Cartwright's biographer, A. F. Scott Pearson, the arch-Puritan from his own reading of the Scriptures, through a process of rationalization, arrived at the conclusion not only that "God has decreed Presbyterianism as the only perfect and perpetual polity of the church" but also that "God is a Presbyterian." [6] Naturally, then, convinced that his inner light, which had revealed to him his system, could not err, he regarded everyone who disagreed with his interpretation of the Scriptures as "ignorant," "blind," or "dumb." And the last and most derisive of these epithets—ironically enough, an unintended gift from Whitgift—was to become a cliché in Puritan dialectic.

But Cartwright himself in the 1570's little foresaw what storms his sermons and his pamphlets would create. His statements made in the heat of argument, frequently ambiguous, were blown up by his zealous followers into dogmas from which in some instances he later was forced to dissociate himself in order to save his own skin. The only noticeable change from his writings to those of his disciples is a sharpening of focus. Whereas Cartwright follows and in most instances expands the attack of the *Admonition* on all "remnaunts of popery" in the Established Church, his followers silently pass over those Catholic ceremonies that the intervening years and the growing strength of Anglicanism had successfully eliminated, and they select whatever might fit in with their own line of attack. In other words, after 1580 the use of the wafer in communion, the place of the service, the function of the congregation, many traditional funeral and wedding customs, the words "Take thou and eat" in the communion service, the injunction "Receive thou the Holy Ghost" at ordination—all of which had been condemned by the authors of the first *Admonition* and by Cartwright—became relatively insignificant and are referred to infrequently, if at all.

Ignoring these dead issues tending only to diffuse the effect of their propaganda, the Puritan writers concentrate on three main lines of attack, each stemming from Cartwright. First, they maintain that since the presbyterian form of church government is ordained by Christ in the New Testament the bishops of the Church of England should be removed; second, they condemn the power of the civil magistrate in the church; third, they elaborate on the ignorance that, in their opinion, characterizes most of the clergy of the Established Church.

Chapter III

The First Signs of Separatism

In the years immediately following 1577, the date of publication of Cartwright's final reply to Whitgift, the author's illogical claim to be a member of a church originally established as episcopalian, while himself demanding the abolition of the episcopacy, was to be vigorously challenged. Not all of his disciples were willing thus to compromise. Literally interpreting Cartwright's condemnation of ecclesiastical government by civil authority and exasperated with ineffectual attempts to introduce the "discipline" against the resistance of an unsympathetic monarch and slow parliamentary action, Robert Browne in 1582 uttered the first stirring appeal for separation from the Established Church. The inflammatory title of his pamphlet *A Treatise of reformation without tarying for anie* expresses his sense of desperation. Opening with the conventional protestation of loyalty to the Queen, which appears in almost every Puritan pamphlet, Browne follows Cartwright's lead in insisting that the civil magistrate should attend to civil, not religious, matters and should be subservient to the church. "Let vs not therefore tarie for the Magistrates," urges Browne, "For if they be christiās thei giue leaue & gladly suffer & submit thē selues to the church gouernemēt."

In another pamphlet, *A Booke Which Sheweth the life and manners of all true Christians,* also published in 1582, Browne sets forth "the pointes and partes of all diuinitie," all of which are imbued with the impatience of separatism. In his eyes, filled with the vision of his utopian primitive church, the civil magistrates "are"—or should be—"persons authorised of God, and receyued by the consent or choyse of the people, whether officers, or subiectes, or by birth & succession also, to make & execute lawes by publike agreement, to rule the common wealth in all outwarde iustice, & to maintaine the right, welfare, & honour thereof, with outwarde power, bodily punishemens [*sic*], and ciuill forcing of men."

In his intense zeal he recklessly expresses such sentiments as the following: "The kingdome of Antichrist, is his gouernmēt, *confirmed by the ciuill Magistrate,* whereby he abuseth the obedience of the people, to keepe his euill lawes and customes to their owne damnation." [1] At first glance this statement might seem innocent enough, but to the Queen's officers, wary of anything savoring of treason, remarks like this were highly suspect. Furthermore, placed in the context of the main body of Puritan literature, in which the epithet "Antichrist" is synonymous with the papacy, they are little less than seditious. Only a decade earlier, indeed, the Admonitioners and Cartwright had described the liturgy of the Church of England as a patchwork of "popish remnaunts" and the Book of Common Prayer as a theft from the "pope's portuis." [2] Hence, Browne is suggesting that the "kingdome of Antichrist"— that is, papal authority—has extended to England and that it has been confirmed by Queen Elizabeth, the "ciuill Magistrate," who is upholding the "euill lawes and customes" of the papacy. In short, with Browne's impatient accusations the velvet glove is removed from the iron hand of the nonconformists.

Following Browne's revolutionary lead, his fellow separatist, Robert Harrison, selecting Joshua and Nehemiah as models for the heads of congregations, strongly recommends the use of force in achieving the desired reforms: "For the Lorde of hostes is with vs, the God of Iacob is our refuge, when we are vnder his Baner, and fighte his battles without vaine fear. For he will teach our handes to warre, and our fingers to fight. He will break the Bowe, and cutte the Speare, and burne the Chariots with fire. But our armes will he strengthen, so that they shall breake euen a bowe of steele." After penning this declaration of war, he unhesitatingly indicates the two enemies to be attacked.

First, like Browne, he directs his fire at the civil government. In his insistence that a minister needs no other justification for his calling than the approval and consent of his flock, he expresses a burning resentment that laymen should have any part whatsoever in church government: "The meanes of our saluation must be kept from vs, vntill a ciuill law send them vnto vs, although there be neuer so long delay: as though they were not sent from heauen, and offred to all that will receyue them. We can defie the Papistes doctrine, for making part of our saluation, to hange vppon oure owne desertes: but wee canne not taste the bitternes of the roote of this doctrine, *that the building of gods kingdome, for the meane and furtherance of our saluation must depend vpon ciuile power, and Christ Iesus with all things pertayning vnto him, are made vnderlings therevnto, and caused to daunce attendaunce vpon it.*" Although Harrison here is specifically defending his personal conviction that a minister needs no other justification for his calling than the approval and consent of his flock, he implicitly is attacking not only the power of Parliament but also that of the Queen as supreme governor of the Established Church.

Next Harrison turns upon Cartwright and his presbyterian followers and berates them for their sloth: "Manie there be in the Realme of Englande, whiche haue bene zealous of Church gouernement, and of the remouing the ceremonies, of mens traditions, and stinted seruice: and because they haue made long tarying, & haue had a colde offeringe, and haue hoped longe of redresse by Parliamentes, wherevnto they haue made sute, and haue bene disappointed of their hope: Therefore as though they hadde done their whole dewtie, they haue set them downe, and waxed colde and carelesse, and haue slept on both eares, and thinke that the Lord must needes nowe holde them excused, vntill the Lord cast it vpon them, & put [it] into their mouthes."

In evident exasperation he turns as a last resort to force: "But they muste knowe, that they are not to ceasse seeking the kingdome of God, and for other thinges they shall be caste vnto them without their carefull thought. The kingdome of God must suffer violence of those, which w^t violent zeale doe drawe it vnto them." And his "little treatise" ends on a note of belligerence: "For what sewe they for vnto the Prince and Parliament? Euen for a lawe to cōpell them to doo that which the Lord haue commaunded them to doo. Why doo they it not in haste, by the vertue of Gods cōmaundement alreadie giuē, so long as they can in peace? *And when they no longer can, why suffer thei not persecution for his sake, whom they must obeye before man?*" [3] Thus Browne and Harrison became the leaders of the movement toward separatism.

The first crisis occurring within the ranks of the Puritans had originally stemmed from a difference in interpreting the word *ecclesiae,* or church, in the passage *Dic ecclesiae* from Matthew XVIII.18. The authors of the first *Admonition* and Cartwright had cited this passage as the scriptural authority for the "discipline," an important part of which was the excommunication of sinners and nonbelievers from the congregation of the saints. To the first *Admonition,* indeed, it is possible to trace the source of the debate which was to rage furiously until it would ultimately lead to separation, namely, whether or not the presence of unexcommunicated sinners in the congregation invalidated the service. In attacking the Book of Common Prayer, the Admonitioners state that in the primitive church "there was then accustomed to be an examination of the communicants which now is neglected."

Though Whitgift denies this statement, Cartwright defends it with the following syllogism: "All things necessary were used in the churches of God in the apostles' times; but examination of those whose knowledge of the mystery of the gospel was not known or doubted of was a necessary thing; therefore it was used in the churches of God which were in the apostles' time." To the Admonitioners' more specific complaint that in the primitive church, according to St. Paul, I Corinthians v.11, "they shut men by reason of their sins from the Lord's supper" whereas "we thrust them in their sin to the Lord's supper," Whitgift replies that St. Paul "doth not particularly touch the secluding of men by reason of their sins from the communion but generally prohibiteth true Christians to have any familiarity or friendship with any such notorious offender." Cartwright in his *Replye to an answere* firmly supports the Admonitioners: "If the place of the v. to the Corinth. do forbid that we should have any familiarity with notorious offenders, it doth much more forbid that they should be received to the communion." [4] But he took no further steps to implement his doctrine.

A few years later he is even less willing to follow up his complaint with action. In a more conciliatory, more conservative, manner in a letter to Harrison (1585) he writes as follows: "If there were but in euery church one truely and vndissemblingly faithfull, al the rest holding the faith of our Lord Iesus christ in wordes onely, yet shoulde all those churches be vnto vs the churches of God." [5] Thus he concedes, as Browne in his *Answere to Master Cartwright* indignantly rephrases it, that since "faith in Christ is the essence, being, or life of the church," whereas the discipline is "but accidental," therefore "the Church of God may haue her being and life, and be named the church of God, without discipline."

Recognizing the self-contradictory position of Cartwright in admitting that the presence of sinners in the congregation would not sully the purity of his ideal church, neither Browne nor Harrison would be satisfied with anything short of complete separation from the Church of England. Though in Browne's scheme the ecclesiastical officers are identical with those of Cartwright—pastors and teachers, elders, deacons, and widows—Browne would restrict their control to each individual congregation, in which "euerie one of the church is made a Kinge, a Priest, and a Prophet vnder Christ" in order to "watch one an other and trie out all wickednes." When, then, each member of the congregation is properly performing this function, the sinner would be prevented from communicating with the saints, each of whom is predestined for happiness with God. Browne also condemns as a refuge for timidity the "odd disti[n]ction of ordinarie ond [*sic*] extraordinarie" ecclesiastical officers, originally made by Cartwright. In Browne's opinion, Christ in his "spirituall kingdome"—that is, his church rightly reformed—has placed "first Apostles, secondlie Prophetes, thirdlie teachers &c.," just as in the primitive church. This perfect church is to be established by a covenant made with God "on God's behalf," "on our behalf," and by baptism which is the "seale." [6]

Harrison, aligning himself with Browne, recognizes the autonomy of the individual congregation and expresses the conviction that "in the Realme of Englande there bee diuers Churches," not parishes of one Church of England. And he asks, "And is it not a dishonour to Christ Iesus the head of euery congregation, which is his bodie: to say that his body together with the heade, is not able to be sustained and preserued in it selfe?" [7]

With specific reference to the discipline, Browne maintains that one man, like the prophets of old, can excommunicate the wicked many, for Christ's words, "whose sins you shall retain," were spoken to every member of the congregation, each of whom is "a king & a priest vnto god." In Browne's opinion, the power to bind and loose belongs "not onely to the preachers but to all the saintes of god." Hence, "any man particularly hath this libertie to admonishe, except for his scornefulnesse and obstinacie he be vnworthie." Once sinners are thus cut off, the righteous members of the congregation "are forbidden to receiue them to house, or to bid them God speede." In defense of this separation of the righteous from the sinner, Browne liberally cites passages from the Old Testament.

Harrison likewise deplores the fact that the Church of England has failed to discriminate between the true believer and the sinner, whose sins—as Leland H. Carlson paraphrases Harrison's ideas—"are more of the spirit than the flesh, more sly, secretive, and diabolical." Harrison then introduces an entirely new element of dissent into the argument between presbyterian and separatist. *He explicitly denies the validity of the sacraments performed in the Church of England.* Sacraments, he contends, are the seals of the promises made by God to the church. Since the Church of England is a false church, it has received no promises; hence its alleged sacraments are no true seals but, instead, merely dead signs.[8] This syllogism was to serve as the fuse for the explosion of separation.

If, then, the nonconformists could not peacefully displace the "dumb ministry" with their own "preaching ministry," it would seem logical that their next move would be to declare the services of the Church of England "idolatrous," as both conformist and nonconformist had earlier termed the Mass, and to pronounce the Anglican sacraments invalid. Since the Queen had been baptized a Catholic, however, no one before Harrison had dared to question either Catholic or Anglican baptism. Instead, as we have seen, most Puritan writers had contented themselves with attacking what seemed to them to be an offensive mingling of episcopalian with Puritan in the congregation, which thereby became polluted.

Faced with an ever-growing resistance against replacing the episcopacy by peaceful means, Cartwright felt called upon to defend his statement that the presence of only one faithful presbyterian would sanctify a congregation otherwise made up of "unbelievers" and "idolaters." For this purpose he uses the metaphor of the branched candlestick representing the Church of England with its various congregations: "If you say the assemblyes, as it were all the branches or armes of the candlesticke haue not lightes set vpon them, the great number of them being dwnped [damped] with dumbe ministerie, notwithstanding by the way you confesse those assemblyes vpon whome the Lord hath set the lampe of a preaching ministery are the churches of God, whiche seemeth to cast downe that hill which standeth in the waye against our reioysing, wherebye you can not afoorde vs the Name of gods churches because we haue not the discipline by him appointed. . . ."

Then interrupting this already too involved sentence, he promises to look further into the matter of the ineffectiveness of the "dumb ministry" and urges the dissenters to conform to the present situation: "Nowe for the other, whether they haue some glimpse of knowledge by the dumb ministerie or no, may afterwardes in another place be considered[.] for the present I answere, that euen in those congregatiōs forasmuch as they both haue and might haue by some former ministrie or means which the Lord hath vsed towards thē receiued faith standing therby in our sauiour christ as in the shaft of a candlesticke they cease not to be a branch in the Lords candlesticke, and being members of the same body they may well receiue some supply of their want from the light that shineth in the next branch vnto them, for if euery assembly being without a lampe of the ministry shuld by & by be holden to be broken from the shaft of the church candlesticke, then at euery vacation of the ministry and whensoeuer by death the Lord shoulde put out one of his lightes, it shoulde followe that that assembly by the fall of their minister into the graue, shoulde from the hyest heauen fall into the graue of hell, but you will say peraduenture, that an assembly that hath a dumbe minister is in worse case than that which hath none at all. if that be graunted, yet followeth it not therefore that the assembly which yesterday being without a dūbe minister was the church of God, shoulde today by hauing such a one set ouer them be the Synagogue of Satan[.]"

He even belittles the concern of the extremists over the danger of the "dumb ministry": "And here me thinkes whilest you go about to make nothing of the dumbe ministerie you ascribe more force to it, then it hath, for you make him not so much as a guide or an head of the church in that those which before in all equall iudgement were to be deemed members of Christ, by hearing them shoulde suddenly become the members of antichrist. . . ."

Moreover, he strongly censures all persons refusing to attend a service conducted by a "dumb minister": "I do not therefore yeeld vnto you, in that you saye they are the chiefe alwayes in the synagogues, our Sauiour Christ in whome those companies do beleeue being the chiefe with whome through faith they growe to be one body, which rather then by hearing the dumbe minister to bee one with him, say therefore that it is a fault in them to heare such a minister thrust vpon them, yet that it is an apostacie from God and an vtter falling away from the Gospell, I see not with what great apparance of trueth it can be spoken."

While thus abandoning his earlier, more radical, position, he also attempts to halt any movement to deny the validity of the sacraments of the Church of England: "The Lorde is in couenaunt with that people to whome he giueth the seales of his couenant; this he doth to our assemblies in England, therefore they are the Lordes confederates. Yf you say that the seals set by the dumb ministery are no seales, (which afterwarde commeth to be examined) yet you thereby confesse that those which are ministred by sufficient ministers, are the true and vncounterfaite sacramentes of the church: whereby it falleth againe, that you seeme to hold that the churches in England are not true churches of Christ, because they haue not his commaunded discipline."

In strong contrast with his former zeal in differentiating between presbyterian and episcopalian, Cartwright now urges conformity: "Although the assemblyes of England had deserued thorough want of discipline, and of a teaching ministerie, to bee cast out from the accompt of the churches of God, yet being holden in by the most voyces of the Churches them selues they ought to haue bene so farre borne withall, as the communicating with them should not make them guiltie of a falling away from the Lorde. . . ."

And he urges his fellow Puritans to accept the will of the majority: "Where therefore there is no ministerie of the worde there it is playne that there are no visible and apparent churches. It is another parte of the discipline of our Lorde, that the rest of the body of the churche shoulde obey those, that are set ouer them in the Lord. Wheresoeuer therefore there is no obedience of the people giuen to the ministers that in the Lordes name preach vnto them, there also can be no churche of Christ, but where these two be, although other points wante, yea although there be some defect in these, that neither the ministers doe in all pointes preach as they ought, nor the assemblyes in all pointes obey vnto the wholesome doctrine of their teachers, yet doe they for the reason abouesaide retaine the right of the churches of God." Thus Cartwright attempted to assume the role of peacemaker.

In conceding that the Church of England, in spite of its "false profession" and "grosse abuses," is still the "Church of Christ," Cartwright perforce has to recognize its courts, its offices, and even the authority of the bishops themselves—in short, everything episcopalian earlier condemned by the Admonitioners and by his own *Replies* to Whitgift—to be "all the Church of God." Not only, indeed, does he now sanction the calling of the "dumb ministers," whom he originally had condemned as "blind leaders of the blind," but he also recognizes the validity of the sacraments administered by them and the prayers read by them. What is even more astounding is to find him now quoting Scripture in defense of the episcopalian suspension of the dissenting ministers—the very action that had incited the nonconformist revolt. Finally, echoing Whitgift's defense for the establishment of the episcopalian hierarchy, Cartwright admits that Christ lived "in the corruptest times of the Churche." Evidently, through the years that had intervened since he wrote his *Replies*, his vision of the "primitive church" had grown dim.

In writing against Whitgift, Cartwright had taken over from the Old Testament the concept of the "chosen people" of God, who must keep themselves undefiled from contact with the "uncircumcised" Philistines. This metaphor captured the imagination of his nonconformist followers, who believed themselves called upon to build the New Jerusalem in England. Now, whereas Cartwright himself was willing to grant that only "one truely and vndissemblingly faithfull" man in a congregation could leaven the loaf, the more extreme among those whom he had educated in dissent were convinced that the faith of a few could not counteract the infidelity of the many. Consequently, Cartwright found himself in the humiliating position of being an outcast among the new zealots trying to carry out the reforms that he himself had advocated.

Very much on the defensive, he writes to a "notable Barrowiste," or separatist, Anne Stubbe, in a letter dated 1590: "And if yo^w shall vnderstand yt [a biblical passage urging the Israelites to separate themselves from the heathens about them] of a dep[ar]ture from the place and companie of ye wicked, yet yo^w haue not proued that we are those *Babilonians*, from whome yo^w (the onely Iewes forsooth of the world) are bidden to dep[ar]t."

As proof that in spite of his willingness to compromise, he is still a "Iewe," he reminds his critics that during the Babylonian Captivity the Jews were willing to practice their religion in the midst of unbelievers: "When the Iewes were in *Babilon*, there was no holy assembly in all the cuntrye of theire captiuity, no not so much as in any priuat howse or secret chamber, wherevnto yf y^e *babilonian* Magistrats would haue thrust themselues, the people of God wuld not haue thrust them from, either in the right of the place wch was the *Babilonians*, or els in might of resistance to them. Do yo^w thincke that in such case Gods people should haue done well, neu[er] in 70. yeares to haue opened theire mouthes in prayre vnto God, neu[er] to haue celebrated the Sacram^ts of

· 33 ·

Circumcision because of their p[re]sence, and offer to cõmunicat wth those holly things."

In fact, with a tolerance quite unlike the fiery T.C. of the days of the Admonition Controversy he defies the separatists: "A X̄rian may heare the word where there are Infidells and vnbeleuers and not onely to cõmunicat wth them in the worde, but to be glad they will so farre cõmunicate wth them therein." [9] Whether Cartwright's willingness to compromise was the result of an illogical tendency already evident in his controversial writings,[10] or whether he feared to jeopardize his living as Master of Warwick Hospital, a position secured for him by his friend Robert Dudley, Earl of Leicester, are questions about which it would be difficult, even presumptuous, to speculate.

In spite of his efforts to reconcile nonconformist with conformist, that in his heart he still despised the episcopacy there is no doubt. For instance, he complains that some people in the Church of England are afraid to confess all of their sins because of some unimportant matter such as "the eating of an egge vpon a Fridaye, so deepelye are the Popishe traditions printed in their tender Consciences, esteeming the breache of them to be a greater offence, thē idolatrye, blasphemye, periurie, theft, slaunder, or any transgression of Gods holy commaundements." And he peevishly attributes their excessive scrupulousness to the "Babilonicall Bishoppes" who should be "ashamed (but y^t they are past all shame already) because they suffer Gods people to be so drowned in ignoraunce, that they can not discern the commaundements of God, frō the dirtye dregs of Papisticall traditions." [11]

Determined to carry out to a logical conclusion Cartwright's original plans for reform and scornful of his spirit of compromise in maintaining that the righteousness of a few could counterbalance the sinfulness of the many, Browne, as Carlson summarizes his convictions, held that "a rightly constituted church was a gathering of regenerate persons whose oral confession and sincere beliefs attested to their salvation" and that "the marks of such a church, in the order of importance, were reformation of life, ministering the sacraments, and preaching the word." One known sinner in this congregation of the saints would corrupt the entire group and cause the breaking of the covenant with God. Indeed, Browne unequivocally states that "to eate the Lordes supper with opon [sic] vnrepentant & wretched persons is not lawfull."

Browne likewise was scandalized that Cartwright would become so lenient as to admit the validity of the reading of prayers by the "dumbe ministers" and of the sacraments administered by them. Defining the "dumbe minister" as one who follows the service book, Browne insists that if these men be "no lawfull ministers" and "Idol mynisters," as Cartwright calls them, then their "action and *deedes of ministration* are vnlawfull and of the deuill." [12] Thus, like Harrison, casting doubt on the validity of the Anglican sacraments, he arrives at the brink of separation.

Chapter IV

Last Attempts at Peaceful Reform

On September 23, 1583, at Lambeth Palace occurred an event destined to hasten the movement toward separation from the Established Church: John Whitgift was consecrated Archbishop of Canterbury. While Vice-Chancellor of Cambridge University in the early 1570's, he had demonstrated his hostility to Puritanism. His accession, therefore, marked the end of all hope, except among the most optimistic nonconformists, for reform through appeals to the Queen, to her Privy Council, or to the Parliament. Even before the month of September had ended, Whitgift had begun strengthening the fortifications of the Establishment.

With the Queen's consent he issued a series of articles designed to restrict the activities of the opposition. First, he set up himself and the Bishop of London as censors of the press. Next, he silenced all preachers and catechists who refused to say the service and to administer the sacraments according to the Book of Common Prayer at least four times a year. He also forbade anyone to preach unless he had subscribed to three special articles, namely, to recognize the Queen as the supreme governor of the Church, to declare that the Book of Common Prayer and the order for consecrating bishops, priests, and deacons contains nothing contrary to the Word of God, and to accept the Thirty-nine Articles of Religion.

In order to enforce these demands Whitgift appealed to the Queen to establish a new Commission for Causes Ecclesiastical, the legal basis for which rested on a clause in the Act of Supremacy (1559) and the main purpose of which, as he himself expressed it, was to enable him more effectively to search out all unlawfully printed books and to deal with those "disordered persons (commonly called Puritans)." [1] In its technique of examination this court, which seems to be an outgrowth of the original Elizabethan High Commission, the function of which had been purely advisory, has been compared to the Inquisition. [2] Under Whitgift's supervision the commissioners devised the oath *ex officio mero*, requiring every prisoner at the outset of his trial, even before he faced his accusers, to swear that he would give a true answer to any question asked him. Thus, determined to defend the Establishment at any cost, Whitgift took the law into his own hands. Thenceforth the oath *ex officio mero* becomes the target of every nonconformist writer.

Although the extremists, like Browne and Harrison, had already declared their unwillingness to compromise in setting up a church "rightly reformed according to the Scriptures," as the Admonitioners had expressed it, the less radical of the Puritan writers continued their efforts to effect a peaceful change by legal means. As might be expected, they all echo Cartwright's illogical claim that he was still a member of the episcopalian church. Nevertheless each writer valiantly strives for an original approach that might prove more devastating than the previous one. The first important Puritan publications evoked by Whitgift's show of episcopalian authority were two anonymous tracts, the *Abstract of Certain Acts of parliament* and *A Briefe and plaine declaration*, otherwise known from its running title as the *Learned Discourse*.

In the *Abstract of Certain Acts of parliament* the author concentrates his attack on the "unlearned ministry" of the Church of England. In his opinion, Henry VIII's "act concerning the submission of the Cleargie," revived by Elizabeth, requires that "al

Canons, constitutions, ordinances, and synodals prouincial made before this act: requiring and commanding a learned Ministerie, prohibiting many benefices to be giuen to one man: prohibiting ciuil iurisdiction to be in Ecclesiastical men, and prohibiting one man to excommunicate . . . are in force, & so by vertue of this act, a learned ministerie commanded." In order to back the Puritan charge that the ministers ordained by the bishops are "altogether vnlearned, vnfit and vnapt to execute," the writer cites passages from canon law which he pretends to interpret as favoring the presbyterian point of view.

Since canon law thus requires a learned ministry, he urges that "these decrees (established first by the enemie of true religion, for the planting of his supersticion but now turned by our pollicie from that vse, and made a law for the gouernment of the Church)" be carried out to the letter in the Church of England. His bitter denunciation of the episcopalian clergy foreshadows Martin Marprelate's exposure of their supposedly scandalous behavior: "Examples in deed they be, but alas such examples, as it rueth, good men to see, howe many by them are drawn to vngodlinesse, and vnhonestye, to Alehouse haunting, to dicing, to tableplaying, to Carding, to bowling, to bearebayting: yea and that on the Lordes day too."

The writer concludes his mock-legal treatise with the following summary of his argument: "Since the statute of 25. Henrie 8. hath authorized all Canons, constitutions, and Synodalles prouniciall, made before that statute, not being contrariant or repugnaunt, to the lawes and customs of the Realme, nor derogatorie to her Maiesties prerogatiue Royall to be nowe in force and executed: and also since these Canons, constitutions, and Synodalles prouinciall before specified, were made before the sayde Statute, and be not contrariaunt nor repugnant to the Laws and customes of the Realme, nor derogatorie to her highnesse prerogatiue: yea, since they are agreeable to the Lawes and vsages of the Realme, and vpholde her prerogatiue Royall: And since by these Canons, and other acts of Parliament, and her highnesse iniunctions, it is euident, that men learned; that men apt and meete to teache, are to be placed ministers in the Churche, and that men vtterly vnlearned, and such as can only read, to say Mattens or Masse, are not to be admitted: That therefore a learned Ministerie is commaunded by the Lawes of England: And if so, then an vnlearned Ministerie forbidden by the same lawes." [3]

What the Puritans really thought of canon law is expressed by John Udall, who in his *Demonstration of Discipline* refers to "that filthie sinck of the Canon law, which was inuented and patched together, for the confirming and increasing of the kingdome of Antichrist." "The Church," writes Udall, "must be gouerned onely by the rules of Gods word . . . by the authoritie of the Eldershipp, to proceed according to the rules of Gods reuealed will, and not by that cursed and monstrous cannon law, which is made manifest vnto vs by these reasons," one of which is that "that which was ordayned to destroy the Churche of God cannot be a good rule to gouerne the same by," namely "the cannon law . . . ordained to strengthen the kingdom of Antichrist." [4] In view of this contempt for canon law, as expressed by one of the most prominent Puritan ministers, the literary efforts of the author of the *Abstract of Certain Acts of parliament* suggest a growing desperation among the nonconformists.

The stratagem of the *Abstract of Certain Acts of parliament* did not escape the eye of the episcopalian Answerer, probably Richard Cosin, who writes that his Puritan opponent cites the laws of Rome "to the intent, and in hope to beat vs with our owne weapons, and not for any loue or liking he beareth vnto them [the laws]." The aim of this legal fiction he declares to be the "obteining their souereigntie of seniors in euerie parish, the want whereof breedeth these threats of hazard to the common-wealth, and which is the onelie thing they meane by Reformation of ecclesiasticall discipline." In a conciliatory tone, however, he concedes that "some Bishops peraduenture inconsideratelie heeretofore haue laid their hands vpon some verie ignorant ministers" but have regretted it. Nevertheless he points out that by condemning "grammarians and poets from Winchester and Eaton, philosophers and rhetoricians of long continuance in the two Vniuersities," the author of the *Abstract of Certain Acts of parliament* requires more "exactnesse in learning and life" than is demanded by canon law. As far as the canons themselves are concerned, the Answerer notes that none of them specify lack of learning as making a man "vnworthie" but rather stress such offences as "infamie by law, bigamie, and diuerse such like there specified," as necessary to disqualify a minister.

The most telling blow dealt in reprisal by the Answerer is his attempt to divide and conquer. Discovering that the Abstractor in his pseudo-legal tract states that the minister should take over the authority of the civil magistrate, the Answerer recalls that in the *Second Admonition* and in Cartwright's *Replies* the establishment of government by elders was declared an essential mark of the Christian church and that the civil magistrate had been denied any place whatsoever; also that one of the nonconformist writers, "no lesse peremptorie than traitorous" (undoubtedly Browne), had gone so far as to write that "if the prince will not establish this gouernment . . . hir subiects need not tarrie for hir but ought t'innouate the gouernment themselues" as did the French Protestants. Furthermore, he adds, the nonconformists cannot even agree upon the same places in Scripture describing their elders, distinguishing between pastor and doctor, or specifying the duties of deacons; and as for the office of widow, Cartwright himself disagrees with the author of the *Ecclesiastical Discipline*, which was an anonymous pamphlet, *Ecclesiasticae Disciplinae,* that Cartwright in 1574 had translated from the Latin and entitled *A full and plaine declaration of Ecclesiasticall Discipline owt off the word off God and off the declininge off England from the same.*

Especially significant of the trend that the controversy was soon to take, the Answerer is the first to point out that a refusal on the part of the nonconformists to recognize episcopalian orders would cast doubt on the validity of the sacraments administered in the Church of England and thus would bring into question all baptisms and marriages in the land. In order to prevent this impossible situation, he himself goes on record as recognizing the validity of "papistical baptism." He even volunteers the observation that some people do not regard the "papists" as heretics as he himself does. Thus the question of the validity of the sacraments in the Churches of Rome and of England, which had been brought up by Browne and Harrison, receives its first episcopalian commentary.[5]

Continuing the Abstract Controversy, the Puritan minister Dudley Fenner undertook to answer the charges made by the Answerer. In his *Counter-poyson* he assures his reader that "the question is not (as the aunswerer would beare the world in hād . . .) about trifles, & things of no waight, as of variable ceremonies & matters of circumstances, which yet are to be squared by the sacred Canons of holy Scripture," but rather about whether or not the "whole Discipline of the Church of Christ" and "a certaine gouernement of the Church" were not set forth "by the infallible Oracles of Gods most holy testimonies," the Scriptures. Even though neither the Answerer nor the Abstractor had given particular attention to these conventional Puritan points of controversy, Fenner thus skillfully returns the debate to its starting point, away from the dangerous issue of the validity or invalidity of the sacraments in the Church of England.

He next reiterates Cartwright's original argument that if Moses had prescribed a government for his church which could not be changed by David and Nehemiah without special revelation, it follows that Christ must have done the same. And he refers his reader to a large number of scriptural passages purportedly supporting the presbyterian system as described by "the admonition & M. Cartwright." Repeating the familiar Puritan complaint that his episcopalian opponent is trying to cast the Puritans into disfavor with the Queen, he seizes the opportunity to attack Whitgift for his alleged efforts to curb the royal power.[6]

In reply to a Latin sermon delivered in 1584 at Paul's Cross by a preacher of Cambridge University, Dr. John Copcot, attacking the *Counter-poyson*, Fenner next wrote his *Defence of the Reasons of the Counter-poyson*. In this pamphlet he expresses the dilemma of the typical Puritan, who, even while making every effort to remove the bishops, still considers himself a member of an episcopalian church: "We holde the Churche for a true Churche of Christ, from which no member may separate him selfe: although he must disallowe the wantes in her." Yet he continues to assail the authority of the episcopacy as "pitche" and to argue for the eldership, who would administer the "true discipline." [7]

Apparently feeling the need for restating the presbyterian platform after this brief foray into the field of the iniquitous canon law, the Puritans in 1584 published the anonymous *Learned Discourse*, probably written by William Fulke some years previously, about 1573. Fenner in his *Defence of the godlie Ministers* gives the following reason for its publication at this late date: "This Treatise was written diuers yeares past, by a learned and deepe Diuine, who hath bin after Master Jewell and M. Nowell, the chiefest Defendor by writings, both in our tongue and in Latin, of the trueth against the papistes: and was nowe only reuised and published by vs. Both because we had it in reuerent regarde for the learning of the man acknowledged of both partes: & because we thought it would appeare to be most voyde of percialitie, whiche was not written vpon the occasion of these late grieuances." [8]

Although the main text of the *Learned Discourse* contains nothing new in its exposition of the presbyterian plan of government (as usual plentifully supplied with scriptural references), its Preface stresses the need for a public disputation, in which for the edification of the bishops the presbyterians hoped "to searche the holie scriptures" in order to ascertain "what order our sauiour Christe our onely housholder hath set foorth in them, by which he woulde haue his house or church to be directed in al things, appertaining to the eternall saluation of vs men." The author also mockingly taunts the bishops with cowardice at their refusal to dispute: "Concerning the maner, they call it to a sudden and tumultuous reasoning, where the readiest wit, the best memorye, the most filed speech, shall carry awaye the truth, at least maruailously moue the vngrounded h[e]arers." [9] This demand for a public disputation was to become one of the weapons in Martin Marprelate's armory.

The outstanding merits of the *Learned Discourse*, as William Pierce points out, are its brevity and its clarity of style. It was, indeed, a sort of compendium of the first *Admonition* and of Cartwright's three *Replies*. Its effectiveness in its own time is proven by the fact that Dr. John Bridges, Dean of Sarum, was appointed first to answer it from the pulpit and then, two years later, to prepare his monumental reply, the *Defence of the Government Established* (1587), 1409 pages in length including the "Preface to the Christian Reader." As a result of Martin's brilliant satirical attacks, as well as of John Penry's scathing denunciation in his addition to the second edition of his *Exhortation*, it is customary for scholars, particularly those with a marked antiepiscopalian bias like Pierce, to minimize the quality of Bridges' volume.

Commenting that the industry producing the *Defence of the Government Established* "would have been commendable had it not been futile," Pierce, on the basis of Martin's exaggerated jibes at the author's "long wearisome periods and his mazy style," terms the work "ponderous" and "ineffectual." [10] Actually the length of the book is due to Bridges' honest effort to set before his reader the exact words of the *Learned Discourse*, line by line, along with his own reply. In fact, he seemingly is attempting what Whitgift had done in his *Defense of the Aunswere*. Bridges himself apologizes for any tedium that might result from his lengthy quotations from his opponent's pamphlet, but the Puritan writers, who were past masters of the devastating technique of quoting out of context, merely laughed at him for giving their ideas the wider circulation. It must be admitted, too, that to Whitgift's earlier statement of the episcopalian position Bridges adds little or nothing new.

Like Whitgift, Bridges is appalled at what seemed to him "too foule a wresting of the Scripture" on the part of his opponent,[11] whom he also chides for a tendency to paraphrase too freely.[12] When, like Cartwright, the author of the *Learned Discourse* resorts to an appeal to "Gods word" as the final authority, Bridges comments, "But can they tell vs in what part of Gods word this ground lyeth: they haue oftentimes told vs, it is grounded on Gods word, but when we come to seeke for the words, wee can neuer find thē, nor any necessary consequence that they haue led vs vnto, in all the word of God, either for any example or commaundement, that wee are charged or bounde to followe." Furthermore, he points out that a passage of Scripture is open to so many different interpretations that the Puritans can hardly call their own the only correct one: "If this be sufficient to make us reckon a thing sufficiently authorized . . . if we must permit this in them, that their collections on the Scripture must goe for authorizings in the Scripture: why must not the same manner of authorizings, where wee proue necessary consequence, bee of as good authority on our parties?"

Again like Whitgift, Bridges recognizes Calvin's skill in scriptural interpretation but does not consider him infallible. Quoting Calvin's conjecture that the primitive church was governed by seniors, or elders—"I suppose (or thinke) that the Gouernors were Seniors chosen out of the common people, which together with the Bishop shold rule the censure (or controulement) of manners, and the Discipline that shoulde bee exercised"—Bridges quite independently adds, "This is but Calvines thinking, who though hee were a most excellent man, yet his supposing and thinking, though it may mooue many to thinke as he did, yet it bindeth none, but that another man may thinke otherwise."

Like Whitgift, too, Bridges tries to define the "primitive

church," in which these seniors ruled and which plays as important a part in the *Learned Discourse* as it did in Cartwright's *Replies*. Regarding the Puritan claim that it was "the time while the Apostles liued," that is to say, the "pure Church," the Dean comments, "Not verye pure I wisse in some pointes, within short while after the Apostles times." "But what time assigne ye to the exercise thereof?" he impatiently repeats, "Date some time!" And Bridges wants to know where the "perpetual office of elder" was hiding before the Puritans discovered it. He also questions the loyalty of the Puritan writers, all of whom appear contemptuous of the Queen in referring to her as "the ciuill magistrate" instead of as "the Supreme Gouernor."

As for a lack of learning among the clergy, Bridges asserts that the course advocated by his opponent might well lead to an unlearned ministry. In this connection, noting that the author of the *Learned Discourse* also indicts the bishops for negligence and bribetaking, Bridges invites the Puritans to document their accusations: "Let the negligence & briberies (with true desire of reformation, as the title of this *learned discourse* pretendeth) be iudicially in forme of law complained vpon, the parties being named, (if aliue) called, accused, heard, considered, & conuicted thereof, before their lawfull magistrate." [13] Perhaps it was this defiant invitation that struck the spark that ignited the Marprelate Controversy, in which this documentation was to be given to the English reading public.

The first two Puritan replies did little more than reiterate the traditional arguments against the episcopalian system. The first of these, Fenner's *Defence of the godlie Ministers,* which must have come out almost immediately after the publication of Bridges' volume, was, according to its title, an "answere to the Preface before the *Discourse of Ecclesiasticall gouernement.* Pierce correctly sums up its significance in his statement that "Fenner's tract for the most part is a plain, sober, scriptural statement, not differing greatly" from the Puritan tracts hitherto written.[14]

The first Puritan reply to Bridges' main text came in the form of a serious pamphlet entitled the *Defence of the Ecclesiastical Discipline,* probably composed by Walter Travers, who unsuccessfully competed with Richard Hooker for the position of Temple preacher sometime before Hooker was employed by Whitgift to write his *Ecclesiastical Polity,* the definitive platform of the Church of England. Travers' work likewise contains most of the arguments for a presbyterian discipline originated by Cartwright—each of them bolstered with numerous marginal references to Scripture —along with the usual charges of episcopalian worldliness and corruption.

Like Cartwright, Fenner, and the other Puritans, Travers is determined to "shewe by the holy Scriptures, what Discipline and order for administration of the Church, Almighty God, who is onely wise, hath appointed." And he builds his entire argument on a foundation consisting of three postulates: first, "that the Church is the house of God," according to I Timothy III; second, that "it ought to be directed in all things according to the order which God the householder hath prescribed"; third, that "the order prescribed by God for the guyding of the same is not to be learned elsewhere but in Gods most holy worde" according to II Timothy III.17. From the analogy that in an earthly kingdom a king will giue instructions regarding the gouernment of his kingdom, Travers concludes that Christ, after his Resurrection and before his Ascension, had instructed his disciples regarding the discipline. Since, according to Matthew XVIII.18–20, Christ had "charged them to preache the worde, then, to minister the Sacramentes (for that is expresslie said of the one, is of like to bee gathered of the other in this respect) and in the end, to teach the Disciples to obserue all things, that he had commaunded," Travers concludes, "Which tenor and course of speache, sheweth that he spake to them, of the Discipline." "For," he asks, "besides the ministerie of the worde, and of the Sacramentes, what other thinges are there belonging to the kingdome of Christ, but the Discipline?"

Like Cartwright, he presumes that every reader of his tract will also have Bridges' book at hand, and accordingly he does not directly quote from it. What he does not care to answer he terms "impertinences & ouersightes, which are too many and too grosse." And over and over again he repeats that the original system of church government established by Christ was presbyterian. More specifically, he takes Bridges to task for inserting occasional sallies of wit, restrained though they may be, into a treatise on religious doctrine. Furthermore, he complains of Bridges' tediousness in writing "a long discourse, not only examining this matters conteyned in it, and speaking to that purpose, but descanting in a maner vpō euery word, tedious for extrauagant matters, & points impertinēt, to the question in hand . . . for tautologies & repetitions, & much idle speache, lengthned out with three or foure of Aesopes fables, and such like conceytes, as serued the pleasant humour he is giuen vnto." [15]

But Bridges was not destined to escape with this fairly moderate criticism of his ambitious volume. The next two replies, both published in 1588, are among the most important nonconformist tracts and succeeded in precipitating a crisis in the dispute between presbyterian and episcopalian that only separatism could resolve. These replies were John Penry's appeal to the Privy Council in his addition to the second edition of his *Exhortation* and the *Epistle* written by the anonymous literary genius who called himself Martin Marprelate. From this point on in any discussion of the evolution of nonconformity it is impossible to mention Penry's name without linking it with Martin's. Moreover, a study of the Martinist pamphlets in conjunction with Penry's acknowledged writings reveals that when Penry eventually abandoned his presbyterian convictions and joined the London separatists his active participation in the Marprelate Controversy had much to do with his conversion.

Chapter V

The Welsh Literary Wizard

While the two advocates of separatism, Browne and Harrison, were laying the ground for congregationalism as a form of church government, a young Welshman, destined to become the most artistically gifted and the most original writer among the Puritan controversialists, was studying at Cambridge University. John Penry was born in 1563 in Breconshire, Wales, the son of a farmer prosperous enough to send his son to Cambridge.

According to the gossip seized upon by the author of the anti-Martinist pamphlet *An Almond for a Parrat*, when Penry entered the university he was "as arrant a Papist as euer came out of Wales." [1] His strongly anti-Catholic biographers question this assertion. Pierce, for example, states that "the Penrys were members of the reformed parish church." Penry's own testimony that he was converted after he went to England, Pierce interprets as "conversion, not from Romanism to the reformed faith, but from nominal Christianity to a living union with Christ." The biographer closes his case by flatly denying Penry's Catholic antecedents: "There is not in all his writings a single allusion to support the fable that he began life as a Romanist. As to his family *we have every reason to believe* that they warmly sympathized with his zeal for the evangelisation of Wales. . . . Not only is the source of the Papist fable utterly worthless, but *for many reasons* it is in itself entirely incredible." The thought of Penry's having been born a Catholic is so repugnant to Pierce that he deems it unnecessary to document the "reasons" against it. Furthermore, his own admission on the opening page of his biography that "the exact place of his [Penry's] birth is a matter of tradition" indicates how little is known of Penry's parentage and childhood.[2]

Similarly, the most recent editor of Penry's pamphlets, David Williams, affirms that the statement that "from being a Catholic, Penry became a separatist while still at Cambridge . . . is demonstrably inaccurate," but Williams never convincingly demonstrates its inaccuracy.[3] Certainly a stumbling block for both Pierce and Williams is the fact that Penry in his writings subsequent to the publication of *An Almond for a Parrat* does not deny this allegation, which in the light of his reiterated attacks on Catholicism would surely have been most offensive to him.

In September, 1580, as a pensioner, he entered Peterhouse College, which was then under the direction of Dr. Andrew Perne, who had won notoriety during the reign of Queen Mary for having changed from Protestantism to Catholicism and then under Elizabeth having reversed the process. Indicative of Perne's "tolerant rule," Pierce records that the college sheltered "all shades of opinion . . . ranging 'from Roman Catholic martyrs like Henry Walpole to the furthest extreme of Puritanism.' " After staying on at the university for a short time following graduation early in 1585, Penry departed for several months, and though he returned, he then for some unexplained reason transferred to Oxford, where he took his M.A. in July, 1586. His removal to Oxford would suggest some source of dissatisfaction with affairs at Cambridge. If, as Pierce maintains, Cambridge had "long been the home of the reformers," [4] Penry's departure certainly was not motivated by religious differences. The real cause may have been his incompatibility with Dr. Andrew Perne, who was to receive unwarrantedly harsh treatment in the Marprelate tracts.

Penry's first biographer, Thomas Nashe, in *An Almond for a*

Parrat paints the following revealing picture of Penry's life at the university:

I am to tel you how laudibly he behaued himselfe in Peterhouse, during the time of his subsistership. . . . I tell you *J. a. P.* in those daies would haue run a false gallop ouer his beades with anie man in England, and helpt the Priest for a shift to saie Masse at high midnight; which, if need were, I doubt not but he would do at this houre. . . . For whiles hee was yet a fresh man in Peterhouse, and had scarce tasted, as we say, of *Setons modalibus,* he began to affect factions in art, & shew himselfe openly a studious disgracer of antiquitie. Who then such an vnnatural enemie to *Aristotle,* or such a new-fāgled friend vnto *Ramus?* This one thing I am sure of, hee neuer went for other then an asse amongst his companions and equalles, yet such a mutinous blockhead was he alwaies accounted that through town and Colledge he was cōmonly called the seditious dunce. For one while he wold be libelling against *Arist.* and all his followers he knew, *another while hee would all to berime Doctour Perne, for his new statutes, & make a by-word of his bald pate,* yea, had the Dean, President or any other officer neuer so litle angerd him, they were sure ere the weeke went about to haue hard of it, in some libell or other. This humor helde him at that time, when, by conversing with French men neare Christes Colledge, of a Papist hee became a Brownist: how afterwards from a Brownist hee fell to bee an Anabaptist, I referre it to those that knewe his after behauiour in Oxford.[5]

Discounting most of Nashe's derogatory personal abuse invented for the purpose of out-Martining Martin in invective, we may infer from the allusion to Penry's ridicule of Dr. Perne that the antagonism between Master and student had become legendary at Peterhouse. In the light of Penry's uncompromising zeal for reform as revealed in his later writings, it is not at all surprising that the young student, newly converted to Puritanism, would be impatient with the old Master, who evidently cared little whether England was Protestant or Catholic.

Sometime after his graduation from Oxford in July, 1586, Penry set to work on his *Aequity*, ostensibly intended to draw the attention of the Queen and the Parliament to religious conditions in his native country, but actually a covert attack on episcopalianism anywhere, especially in the Church of England of which the Church of Wales was a part. On February 28, 1587, it was presented to Parliament by Edward Dunn Lee, "possibly the only puritan among the Welsh members of Parliament in Elizabeth's reign," and Job Throckmorton, the member for Warwickshire, later one of the suspects in the Marprelate Controversy. In presenting the treatise, Lee dwelt upon its principal theme, namely, the prevalence of idolatry and superstition in Wales because of a lack of "learned ministers." It was not long before Penry was summoned before the Court of High Commission for questioning. Particularly offensive to the bishops on the High Commission was Penry's assertion that preaching is the only means to salvation. Surprisingly, however, after only a month's imprisonment for heresy Penry was released from the Gatehouse Prison; evidently he had won support in high places.[6]

Taking Penry's professions of concern for the state of religion in Wales at face value, Pierce sentimentally informs his reader that "we shall learn from Penry's first literary effort how deeply he had brooded over the religious condition of his country"; indeed, it was his "fervid love for Wales," according to Pierce, which "conspired with his austere theology to give a poignant urgency to his *Aequity*."[7] Similarly, Williams refers to Penry's "importunate epistle, written in the white heat of his anxiety for the salvation of the Welsh people."[8]

But Edward Arber more perceptively sees through Penry's patriotic professions—which in themselves doubtless were sincere enough—the real object of his attack, namely, the episcopacy. In fact, Arber expressly states that "the Martin Marprelate Controversy arose out of the following printed words" from the *Aequity*, in which, as he puts it, Penry speaks "on behalf of the Welsh nation":

For what will our children that rise after vs and their children say, when they shal be brought vp in grosse superstitiō, but that it was not Queene Elizabethes will, that we their Parentes should haue that true religion she professed, made knowen vnto vs. Will not the enemies of Gods truth with vncleane mouthes auouch that shee had little regarde vnto true or false religion anie further than it belonged vnto hir profite? I would some of them did not slaunderously cast abroade amongst our people, that she careth not whether the gospel be preached or not preached. If she did wee also shoulde bee most sure to enioy it after twenty eight yeares and vpward of most prosperous raigne. These thinges derogating from her Maiesties honor in a most villanous sort, must be withstoode thorough hir selfe and this whole assembly, by making prouision for vs betimes of the food of our soules. Because I see this most notably detracteth from hir, I cannot in duety but repell and gainsay this slander, and with as loud a voice as ynck and paper can sound, affirme and publish that she would haue the truth made knowen vnto al her people, and wish al of them to be prophets. Which thing I trust in God shall bee manifested vnto the woorld euen at this Parliament, wherein Wales shal be alotted vnto Iesus Christ for his inheritance. And good reason why it should be so, because thereupon standeth the mainteinance of hir credit. Of al the men in the world therfore she may be least beholding to *them that will not deal earnestly in our behalfe.* And we the inhabitantes of Wales may thinke that very straunge that one suite, tending generally to the benefit of vs al, will not bee graunted vnto vs in twenty eight yeares, and that vnder hir Maiestie, whose good will towards vs is no lesse we are assured then to the rest of hir subiects. If wee doubted heereof, behold at this time, opportunity is offered to take away all suspicion.[9]

Analyzing these words as "a fair specimen of Penry's cunning pen," Arber notes that "he [Penry] is herein asserting that which he is ostensibly repudiating" and that though "the words seem innocent enough to us [and, we might interject, also to Pierce and Williams], yet had they never been written, it is probable that Martin Marprelate would never have come into existence."

Exactly what the connection between Penry and Martin was in Arber's mind when he wrote these words is not at all clear. Obviously he was not referring to the content of the passage, for Martin never indicated any particular interest in the Welsh nation. The reference to the "cunning pen" would suggest that Arber senses a stylistic similarity between their writings, and his gloss of the passage in italics, "them that will not deal earnestly in our behalfe," as "i.e., the bishops &c." indicates that he is not misled by Penry's patriotic sentiments. Indeed, to any unbiased reader of the *Aequity* it is clear that everything Penry writes about the Welsh Church is merely an echo of the English Puritan attack on the episcopacy.

In this first pamphlet he repeats the usual nonconformist condemnation of the practices of permitting a nonresident pastor (nonresidence) or a layman (impropriate living) to receive the income derived from tithing or from the yield of church lands. On the whole, however, he follows the post-Cartwrightian trend in concentrating on three main lines of attack: first, that all bishops and ministers of the Established Church are "ungodly"—that is, that they fail to find the presbyterian polity in the Scriptures—in contrast with the "godly" presbyterian preachers; second, that the civil magistrate should willingly yield first position of power to the presbytery; third, that the episcopalian clergy in Wales are ignorant men, "dumme or greedy dogs that delight in sleeping," who read homilies according to the precepts of the Church of England rather than preach according to Puritan doctrine.

Penry's complaint that Wales has no "teaching ministers" to "preach the gospel" must not be taken literally, as it is by Pierce,[10] but must be interpreted in the light of Puritan semantics. "Teaching ministers," of course, were part of the presbyterian polity, which, in addition to elders, deacons, and probably widows, consisted of two classes of ministers—those who teach, or doctors, and those who preach; the "gospel" to be taught and preached was the Bible as interpreted by Calvin, Cartwright, and all other theologians who found a presbyterian system therein. Any clergyman who disagreed with their interpretation was "ungodly" and ignorant. Hence, Penry terms the conforming Welsh pastors, whom he considers responsible for the evil conditions in Wales, as "dumme or greedy dogs that delight in sleeping," who, instead of preaching, read homilies. In Penry's words, however, preaching is "graunted necessary, and the word reade no meanes to saluation." [11]

That Penry, as a typical Puritan, was condemning not lack of learning but rather failure to follow the presbyterian interpretation of the Scriptures is evident in several of his statements. For example, he displays the same blind faith in the "inner light" that frequently led the zealous Puritan to anti-intellectualism [12]: "Priuate men that neuer were of Vniuersity haue well profited in diuinity. These no doubt would proue more vpright in heart, as the Leuits in the like distresse 2 Chr. 29. 34. than many of our learned men." [13]

Without submitting any convincing evidence for a lack of learning among the Welsh clergymen, Pierce expresses his personal approval of Penry's anti-intellectualism: "Penry would employ noncollegiate laymen with a knowledge of divinity; they would probably be an improvement morally upon many of the learned." [14]

Penry himself, however, implies that the failure of the Welsh bishops and clergy to adopt the presbyterian system is equally as important as what might be termed their moral shortcomings. Addressing the Parliament, he writes as follows: "The Lord graunt you of this honorable assembly wise harts before it be to late, to examine aright the cause of these *vngodly* attempts, & to preuent the issues of them. Which shall neuer be done as long as the Parliament wil permitte Non-residences, impropriate liuinges, *swarmes of vngodlie ministers,* the insolent and tyrannical proceedinges of some, ioined with pomp too too vnreasonable, *to keep out a learned and godly ministerie,* by whose means the Lord Iesus would recouer his owne againe." What here is seemingly directed at the Welsh clergy who, in Penry's opinion, obstinately refused to replace their bishops with elders applies equally as well to the English. It is difficult not to suspect that Penry expected his reader to make this application.

His motive, indeed, is only thinly disguised in statements such as the following: "Where by the waie they are intreated with al reuerence to looke better vnto their dealinges, *who vnder the name of conformity, and obedience, stay the course of the ministery in any place,* & desired to acknowledge this vnity to bee nothing else but a consent with Satan to wrest the scepter out of Christ his hand and vndermine his chaire of estate; if they haue done heretofore foolishly, let them now, (following the counsel of the wiseman) lay their hands on their mouthes, and take heede least by defending former practises they ad drunckennes vnto thirst . . . because the preaching of the woorde is thought no better than folly of worldly wisemen, it commeth often to passe that the reiecting of a suite tending thereunto, is made a thing of smal moment."

In other words, whenever Penry's youthful enthusiasm overcomes his discretion, the mask of patriotism slips aside and reveals the Puritan countenance underneath. We can almost see his lip curling with scorn as, knowing full well the attitude of the English bishops toward the Puritans, he sarcastically addresses himself to his Welsh readers on the subject of preaching as essential to salvation: "The diligence beloued which I hope your learned Bishoppes, Doctors and other great Diuines men of famous report haue taken in England, cannot suffer you to be ignorant in these pointes." [15] Indeed, every major fault that he finds in the Church of Wales may also by implication be detected in the Church of England, provided the critic follows the presbyterian interpretation of the Scriptures.

In his references to the Queen he is equally ambiguous. On the surface he is the patriotic and obedient subject. As might be expected, then, Pierce writes of him: "Penry's books always refer reverently to the Queen." [16] But in most of his professions of loyalty may be heard an ironical overtone. For example, assuring his reader that he does not blame the dearth of preachers in Wales upon the Queen but rather upon the Welsh people who have neglected to move the Queen and Parliament in their behalf, he pretends to be so naïve as to believe that Elizabeth is unaware of their situation. Then, conceding that even "a good magistrate may be ignorant of his duty," he holds that she must be "put in mind thereof by an inferior person" like himself: "Onely you are to marcke, that no seruice by piece-meale, but according vnto al the commandementes allowable, and that the Magistrate must practise all that God requireth of him. The wil of God in any particular point of religion being vnknowen vnto him, hee must make diligent search and inquiry for it himselfe (keepe & seeke all the commaundementes saith he). In which wordes the holy ghost noteth, that a good magistrate may be ignorant of his duty, but giuing this caueat withall, that as soone as he is put in mind thereof, though by an inferior person, he must not be borne in hande by any other that all is well (for how can that be well and in good case, which is not according to the Lordes wil?) but see reformation out of hand." What the Queen should do, in Penry's humble opinion, is to provide "teaching ministers"—one of Cartwright's orders—to "preach the gospel" in Wales. In this way she will show that she is on Christ's side rather than on Satan's.

If, however, she fails to "vphold his honour against Sathan," his "Church here vpon earth" will suffer: "For hereby hee [Christ] doth trie their good wils, in that he declareth his honour to be vsually measured in the hart of the people, according vnto the proportion of the magistrates loue towards him: *reseruing alwaies vnto him neuerthelesse the power to beget his loue in the subiects, whose prince may be an Idolater:* and to bridle the furie of his enemies when he will, without the assistance of man: and to reedifie his Church, *though al the kings vnder heauen gainsaie the same.*"

Penry's hint that if Elizabeth is deaf to his appeal she may be guilty of idolatry is here accompanied by the veiled threat of a popular revolt. Hence, his prophetic statement, "The Lord wil not forget Queene Elizabeths kindnesse in this thing towards his house," has a sinister ambiguity. Finally, just perchance the English reader may fail to apply to his own country the lesson Penry is giving to the Welsh, he asks: "Can we euer hope to haue the tidings of saluation proclaimed in Wales, vnlesse this [the presbyterian reformation] be perfourmed in hir days?" [17] Thus, even in Penry's first pamphlet it is evident that he is impatient with compromise and inclines toward Browne's policy of reformation without tarrying.

Much of the effectiveness of this first effort lies in its sprightly style: the short crisp sentences, the irony, the directness of its colloquial vocabulary. Noting that Penry "had the literary instinct" and that "he was sensitive to the magic of fit words," Pierce asks, "Had not a preponderant spiritual interest, ever clamant, exigent, ever clashing against a hard and implacable opposition hustled him through the brief course of his life, how would he, the child of this great century, have responded to the great literature springing into life and beauty all around him, and making his age for ever famous?" [18]

Yet we, in turn, might also ask how any Puritan writer could have better expressed his scorn for the ministers of the Church of England and his conviction that preaching was all-essential to salvation than by the vivid expressiveness of such a passage as the following: "A number of the idle drones now in our ministerie would become fit for that work in one year, if preaching were but here and there scattered among vs, and they weekely driuen to exercise." And how more effectively could he have driven home his lesson that in his opinion England was in as dire straits as Wales in matters of religion than by the following direct appeal to Parliament:

Good my Lords, whose honour in the feare of God I desire, thinke with your selues that the Lord of heauen, being now reiected of most nations of the earth, is thrust into this poore Iland of England, as into the furthest westerne partes (sauadge America, and that continent excepted) but surely his entertainment here, if one handmaid had not better cherished him, had beene very cold. He hath often threatened vs to depart, by taking her with him from such vngrateful subiectes as wee are. Particular men he hath by his seuerall blessing, and the sound of his woord, from the highest to the lowest sollicited vnto his seruice. Al for the most part refused. This one time he wil try whether the whole estate of the land will allowe him anie larger demaines, than hitherto he enioied. And therefore he now knocketh by this our suite, at the doore of the Parliament, to know whether we the people of Wales shall bee graunted him, as his herytage. If it be denied, he protesteth that he will stay no longer. he expecteth an aunswere: Haue a regard what ye doe. A greater matter cannot be consulted vpon. What a shameful thing were it for man to deny his God, that which most concerneth his glory? Alas the day what hinderance wil it be vnto any of you to haue vs poore Welshmen celebrators of the honour of our God? [19]

It is not at all surprising, then, that Archbishop Whitgift and the "Lords of the Convocation House" were disturbed by this master of vivid English prose. Had Penry written nothing but his *Aequity*, his fiery rhetoric, which thus aroused the English hierarchy, would render him a likely candidate for the authorship of the equally fiery Martinist tracts.

Chapter VI

Penry and the Secret Press

The *Aequity* was merely a preliminary effort on Penry's part. After five hundred copies were seized at Whitgift's command, even though publication had been duly approved, and after Penry himself had been arrested, accused before the High Commission, and roughly berated by the Archbishop, the zealous Puritan realized the need for caution.

For his next pamphlet, his *Exhortation*, he did not obtain official sanction but instead sought the aid of Robert Waldegrave, who already had a record of conflict with the Stationers' Company. Perhaps his friend John Udall recommended him to the Puritan printer, who at the same time was printing Udall's antiepiscopalian dialogue *Diotrephes*. It may be, indeed, that Penry became a sort of apprentice to Waldegrave while the first edition of his *Exhortation* was being printed, for sometime between the appearance of the *Aequity*, which had been printed by the experienced printer Joseph Barnes, and the publication of the *Supplication* he seems to have acquired a fair skill at printing. At any rate, the *Exhortation* was printed and safely out of Waldegrave's house when on April 16, 1588, it was raided and the undelivered stock of Udall's *Diotrephes* seized, together with whatever presses and type the officers could lay hands on. Waldegrave himself managed to escape with "a Case of Lettres" hidden under his cloak.[1]

Penry's second pamphlet pointedly ignores Parliament and the

Queen, whose High Commission had made painfully clear its displeasure with his literary efforts, and directs itself "vnto the gouernours and people of hir Maiesties countrie of Wales." It has no date nor any indication of identity of printer or of place printed but is addressed to "The Right Honorable the Earle of Pembroke," to the governors of the Welsh Council, and to the people of Wales of all classes. Although Pierce considers this salutation as evidence that "Penry's faith is still with the civil authorities as the superior source of power," [2] it seems more likely a clever tactical device to bypass Parliament and the Queen, to whom he had appealed in his *Aequity*.

In the main body of the *Exhortation* Penry again hammers away at his earlier thesis that there is "no ordinarie saluation without preaching, and this decree shall neuer be chaunged." He even urges the Lord President of Wales to resign his office if he cannot bring preaching to that country. But now he introduces an invective that greatly intensifies the rhetorical impact of his theme. Condemning all "reading" to hell, he asserts that "our readers be no ministers." If the Welsh people "presume that they may come into heauen, and not submit them selues vnto the voice of the preacher . . . were they the greatest potentates vnder heauen . . . they shal neuer be saued." And he acidly reminds them, "It will not be the losse of a button vnto me, though you should all of you go to hell"; indeed, he adds, even now they "are in hell." "Our reading Baalites, scant able to reade," he compares to "verie Panim, Turke, or Iewe." Turning directly to the bishops, whom he calls "cormorants," [3] with mock piety he protests that he dislikes attacking them lest people will think that he does it just because it is the thing to do.

Taking his apology at face value, Albert Peel asserts that "Penry deplored controversy," but Peel himself immediately associates with the Marprelate Controversy Penry's reference to attacking the episcopacy: "Had Penry already seen a Marprelate manuscript, and is this advance criticism, or has it a more general application? At any rate he now shows himself aware of his own danger, realizing that the bishops will endeavour to construe his attack on them as sedition against the State." [4] If, as Peel surmises, Penry at this point is aware of any danger to himself, he certainly does not hold back on his own verbal ammunition.

On the contrary, in no uncertain terms he accuses the bishops of contempt for the Lord's "holy ordināce" requiring the institution of preaching and threatens them with damnation if they ignore him. Pithily combining the Puritan attacks introduced by Cartwright, he momentarily doffs his patriotism and, including the civil magistrates with the bishops, sets out to prove that "both you our nonresidents, and you our Lorde bishops of Wales, in that you be nonresidents & Lord Bishops, cannot bee warranted by Gods word: yea, or vtterly condēned by the same, and that *all magistrates who tollerate such as you are, to be vnder their gouernement,* are guilty of a fearefull sin before the Lord." Momentarily forgetting that he is supposedly addressing only his fellow countrymen, he includes England with Wales and thereby reveals to the careful reader the true object of his attack: "The great God, the mightie and ferefull Lord, hath a great and a bloudie recconing *with England and Wales,* and *the gouernours of them,* because the ofscouring of all contempt, and derision, are permitted to represēt his place, & parson among vs." In this pamphlet, indeed, he is even less restrained than in his earlier so-called appeal on behalf of the Welsh people; he seems more desperate in his concern for the removal of the episcopacy and the adoption of presbyterianism.

In the concluding pages of the *Exhortation* Penry takes up the question of the validity of the sacraments administered by "reading ministers," in other words, by the clergy of the Church of England, and, undoubtedly quite unaware of the seriousness of his step, starts out on the path to separatism, on which Browne and Harrison had already proceeded a considerable distance. In asserting that "the marks of a true Church, out of our Sauiour Christes owne wordes, are gathered to be three, the worde preached, the right administration of the Sacraments, and the outward forme of gouernement," [5] he is merely rephrasing the words of the first *Admonition*: "The outward marks, whereby a true Christian Church is known, are preaching of the word purely, ministering of the sacraments sincerely, and ecclesiastical discipline." Whitgift's rejoinder to the Admonitioners, that they had no scriptural authority for their complaint that the Word of God is not truly preached in the Church of England, Cartwright had evaded by a quibbling question, "Is it all one to say it is not purely preached and to say it is not truly preached?" [6] Penry, on the contrary, undertakes to defend the Admonitioners' stand. In accordance with his personal conviction expressed before the High Commission, that preaching is the "onely ordinary meanes" to salvation,[7] he explains that "a reading minister, cannot deliuer the Lordes holy seales vnto the people without great sacriledge, nor the people receiue at the hands of such, without dreadful sinnes." This type of minister, continues Penry, may have the outward, but lacks the inward, calling and therefore whoever receives a sacrament from him sins.

Then what of the validity of the sacrament itself? Penry at this point is not prepared to deny that it is a sacrament, his hesitation evidently stemming from the complications involved in a denial of the sacrament of baptism. Always cognizant of the fact that the Queen was baptized a Catholic, he fully realizes that to question the validity of her baptism would be to declare her infidel. Therefore he presents a number of fairly involved reasons as to why "none ought to be rebaptised":

First, wee are already receiued into the boosome of the church, and acknowledged to haue the seale of the couenaunt, in as much as we were once offered and receiued into the nomber of the godly, by the outward element, though corruptly. To what ende then should Baptisme serue vs againe. 2. The absolute necessitie of Baptisme to saluation by this meanes might seeme to bee mainteined. Thirdly, least we should seeme to agree with the hereticall Katabaptistes. Fourthly, other churches haue not publikely decided the cause. Fiftly, that the practise should not inforce them to bee rebaptised, which haue bene alreadie baptised, by such as had commission from the Lord to deale in those mysteries. Lastly, They who (being now in the age of discretion) haue bin baptised by Idoll ministers, are either called or not called to saluation.

Finally, as if his reasoning power is exhausted, he breaks off with a plea to discontinue all discussion of the subject: "Concerning the controuersie then, whether the element administred by an ignorant man, be a Sacrament, being once deliuered, I would wish all men in modestie to abstaine from so vngodly a iarre, because it tendeth not to edification, and it is not the poynt, it is not the question." [8]

In a sort of soliloquy, however, indicative of his own perplexed state of mind, he himself continues this controversy with an analogy to the "private communion" of the sick, already denounced as "popish" by the Admonitioners [9]: "A priuate communion ministred to one alone may be a sacramēt. What then, are men to receiue alone at home being sicke. No for it is a sinfull breach of Gods institution." Then, returning to the subject of baptism, he asks, "In like sort Baptisme, or the Lords supper administred, by a dumb minister, may be a sacrament, is it therfore lawfull to receiue it[?]" Without hesitation he answers his own question: "In no wise, Because it is a sinne, & that is sufficiēt to terrifie any from the action. It hath bene before conuinced for a sinne, and againe is thus proued to be no lesse." More confidently, as he reiterates the familiar Puritan demand for preaching while administering the sacrament, he asserts: "It is a sinne either to receiue the Sacramentes at the handes of priuate men, or to testifie those to be ministers, vnto whome the Lord hath denied that function."

Declaring reading or "dumbe" ministers to be "priuate men," he concludes that to receive the sacraments from them is sinful. With specific reference to baptism he again expresses doubt: "Though the Lorde in mercie make it an authenticall Sacrament, I could be assured of no such thing." Accordingly, he warns the Welsh people not to have their children baptized by "dumbe mynisters." And in a rash moment he assures them that if they cannot get their children baptized by "a true minister of God" they should "leaue them vnbaptised," for "to omitte a sinne is no sinne." Immediately, as if aware that he has gone too far, he concludes with the protest that what he is doing is for his country, and he threatens with God's vengeance anyone who persecutes him. Finally, while conceding that he is writing for the purpose of stirring up his countrymen "to mislike of the *ecclesiasticall gouernement nowe established* among vs," that is, the episcopacy, as "forraine and Antichristian for the most part," he protests his loyalty to the supreme head of that government, the Queen.[10]

Penry's questioning of the validity of the ministry of the Established Church and the sacraments therein administered was not to go unanswered. On May 6, 1588, occurred an event closely associated both with Penry's literary activities and with the Marprelate Controversy; in fact, it furnishes the missing link between the two. Dr. Robert Some, representing the episcopacy, published his *First Godly Treatise*, inspired, as he states in his *Second Godly Treatise*, by the news that certain people in London were denying the validity of baptism by "Popish Priests in the Popish Church" and were even asserting "that the Godly were polluted, which receyued any Sacrament at the hands of vnpreaching ministers." [11] Dr. Some flatly denies that the minister's ignorance can either pervert the sacraments that he administers or can pollute the receiver. Moreover, in answer to the pro-separatist insistence that one sinner in the congregation renders the service null and void, he maintains that "the childe of God is not polluted, though hee bee present at, and partaker of the publique prayers, Sacraments, &c. at such time, as wicked men are present at, and partakers of them." In support of this thesis, he goes to the primitive church of the New Testament, in which "the Apostles receiued the Lords supper with Iudas."

Immediately following this argument, Some advances an opinion destined to throw Penry into the spiritual turmoil from which he emerged a separatist: "They which were baptized in the Popish Church by Popish Priestes, receiued true Baptisme, touching the substance of Baptisme." Some argues that since the Catholic priest baptizes in the name of the "holy Trinitie" he retains "the essential forme of Christes baptisme." Furthermore, though "the Popish priestes haue no lawful calling: yet, they haue a calling, though a faultie one," and "a faultie vocation may hurt him that vsurps an office, but it doth not defile those thinges which are done by that partie." Wherefore, continues Some, "if such as were baptized in the Popish Church, receiued true baptisme," then "they are rightly baptized in the Church of England, which are baptized by vnpreaching ministers." As far as preaching at the administration of the sacraments is concerned, the words used in baptism in the Churches of Rome and of England, "to Baptize in the name of the father, the sonne, and the holy Ghost," and "the summe of Christes Sermon in the Institution and administration of the holy supper by him selfe" are sufficiently edifying to make these two sacraments valid. Thus he arrives at the conclusion that "the godly are not polluted which receiue the Sacrament at the handes of an vnpreaching Minister."

In defense of this last statement Some makes his first reference to Penry. Repeating Penry's three objections to "ignorant" or "vnpreaching ministers," [12] which, he later explains in his *Second Godly Treatise,* had been reported to him by some of Penry's

"faction," [13] he denies them all. After summarizing and condemning Penry's arguments against receiving the sacraments from "vnpreaching ministers," who might have an outward calling but no
"inward graces," Some hastens to hold out the olive branch to
Penry himself: "If any will conclude of these my answeres, that
I mislike M. Penryes desire of a learned Ministerie in Wales, he
takes vp that which I neuer let fall: for I desire with all my heart,
and the Lord for his Christes sake graunt it, that not only Wales
may be furnished with worthy gouernours and pastours, but all
other partes of her Maiesties Dominions, that Gods graces may be
more and more multiplied vpon vs and our posteritie, and his holy
hand watch ouer vs." [14] Containing an implicit challenge delivered with what may have appeared to Penry like episcopalian con-
descension, Some's *First Godly Treatise* seems to have infuriated
the Puritan writer. From this point onward in the pamphlet war-
fare he constantly alludes to his intended reply to "M. Doctor
Some."

The first of these allusions appears in a sort of postscript "To
the Reader" at the end of the second edition of the *Exhortation*,
apparently completed on or about May 6, 1588:

> Master D. Somes booke was published this day, I haue read it.
> The man I reuerence from my heart as a godly and learned
> man. The reasons he vseth against me, in the questions of the
> reading ministrie, and communicating with them, I had aun-
> swered as you may see in this booke before he had written.
> They are faultie, either because they desire that for graunted
> which is the question, or make those things of like nature,
> wherein there is a great dissimilitude, as the arguments drawen
> from the magistracie and the Leuiticall Priesthood. I haue an-
> swered thē. *The cause, & the reuerence I owe vnto the man,
> though the reasons he vseth deserue not to be twise read ouer)
> will enforce me to answere him at large.* There be certaine
> faults escaped in the print, beare with them.

Thus couched in a mixture of compliment and abuse—a distinguishing feature of Penry's style—appears his first announcement of a lengthy answer to Dr. Some to be published at some future date.

This edition of the *Exhortation* has further interest for the student of Penry's writings and of the Marprelate Controversy. As its subtitle impudently advertises, "There is in the ende something *that was not in the former* impression." The phrase "second edition," therefore, is somewhat of a misnomer like Penry's term "impression," for added to the original text of the *Exhortation* are two new sections: first, twenty-four pages containing fifty-three syllogisms presenting the author's reasons for maintaining that the "dumb ministers" are not "ministers indeede," and second, fifty pages, beginning "To the LL. of the Covnsel" and signed "Iohn Penri."

Penry opens the first additional section, attacking the callings of the episcopalian clergy, with the statement that in his second edition he has "set downe the exhortation, word for word, as it was in the former impressiō, without the altering or deminishing of any one thing" except three new "marginall notes" and the correction of "the faults escaped in the printing." [15] A collation of the two editions bears out the accuracy of his statement. Of especial significance in revealing Penry's growing concern over the validity of baptism in the Church of England is the fact that the three new "marginall notes" all are attached to the passage in which he gives his half-hearted reasons why a person should not be rebaptized and then hastens to add that he himself does not deny the baptism administered by those "not preachers" (that is, "dumb ministers" or episcopalian clergymen) to be a sacrament.[16]

The first two notes clearly indicate his doubts of the validity of baptism in the Established Church. In the first note he protects himself by repeating, as in the text, that he does not "deny" the validity of the sacrament there administered, but he admits that he is willing to listen to good reasons against its validity: "As I do not deny that whiche hath bene done to bee a sacramente. *so if any can proue it to be non, I wil not withstand him.*" In the second note he actually invites support for rebaptism: "If these reasons can be answered, I see neither heresie nor error in being rebaptized." But in his third note, while denying "readers" to be ministers and repeating that they "can deliuer no sacrament," he again hedges: "I affirme readers to be no ministers, & for any thing that is raueled in the word, that they can deliuer no sacrament, and yet that which hath bene done by them may be a sacrament, and what contrarietie is there in these assertions."

However, during the interval between the printing of the second and third editions of this pamphlet Penry apparently became aware that he had gone too far; accordingly, in the final edition he blocked out the first syllable in the last word of his second note, "rebaptized," to read "baptized," to which innocuous—and insipid—statement there could be no disagreement.[17] Thus these "marginall notes" would suggest that Penry's original purpose in writing his *Exhortation* was to attack the validity of the sacrament of baptism in the Church of England.

Whereas the first addition in the second edition merely repeats the traditional arguments against a reading ministry, the second addition, to which Penry is directing the attention of his reader by his subtitle "There is in the ende something *that was not in the former* impression," is even more violent than the main text. Addressing himself to the members of the Privy Council, the author interlaces his previous arguments with threats of hell fire and brimstone. He also plainly states that his aim is "the ouerthrowe of these places, callings, and corruptions (L. Bishops, readers, and non-residents I mean) whose continuance standeth with the lords most notable dishonour." [18]

That his concern with religious matters is not confined to Wales alone he makes unmistakably clear: "As for the Church of God: wherevnto I haue bene begotten, through the word preached, *by means of my abode in Englande,* in these peaceable dayes of her highnes, I haue wholye dedicated my selfe to seeke the flowrishing estate thereof. By labouring to beautifie the same, both in the plucking vp of those filthie Italian weeds, wherewith now it is miserablie deformed, and planting therein, whatsoeuer may bee to the cōlines [comeliness] of gods orchard." To seek the "ouerthrowe and confusion" of those "aforenamed callings and corruptions, standing as enemies in the way to hinder my brethren from eternall life," is, he repeats, his goal.[19]

But he cleverly returns to the theme of the *Aequity* and the *Exhortation* proper with the assertion that his supplementary address to the Privy Council is intended to prove "that the most congregations *in Wales* want the verie essential outward marks of a true church, and so the meanes of saluation, and the comfort of faith, by the right administration of the sacraments." After threatening the Councillors with "the Lords wrath" if they do not repent, he turns upon "D. Bridges, who lately in a booke of 7. shillings price, hath vndertaken" to defend—not the Church of Wales, it must be emphasized, but rather—the Church of England, and he promises to "prooue that he [Bridges] hath crammed into this gorge, as plaine poperie for the defence of our prelates: as euer Belarmin, Turrian, Harding, Saunders, or any other the fierbrands, and ensign-bearers of Romishe treason against her Maiesties crowne, haue brought for the title of the popes supremacy."

His attack on Bridges is significant in that it ushers in and tacitly announces the forthcoming publication of the first Martinist pamphlet, *The Epistle*, entitled *Oh read ouer D. Iohn Bridges for it is a worthy worke*, etc.:

Although he [Bridges] hath bene, *and I doubt not shalbe sufficiently answered*, by those, whose bookes hee is not worthie to beare, yet, in asmuch as hee in this booke hath shewed himselfe to bee an Ammonitish, Tobiah, against the building of Ierusalem in Wales, by defending (alasse) reliquias Danaum,

the very breaches and ruines of the Babylonish ouerthrow,
which by the iust iudgement of God vnder poperie, we haue
sustained to be the perfectest building that Syon can be brought
vnto, and so by this slaunder, withstandeth the saluation (which
I doubt not) her Maiestie, and your Hh. wishe vnto my Countrey; I haue so framed my reasons folowing, as they ouerthrowe the verye foundation and whole frame of that wicked
booke. And on the condicion, that his cause maye fall. If I
(*besides that which others wil do*) ouerthrow him, & his cause,
I offer before your Hh. to be in irons, & eat the bread of afflic-
tion, vntill in a twise 7. pennie booke I disprooue by the worde,
make an vtter spoyle, ruine, & ouerthrow of whatsoeuer he hath
brought for the defence of that, whiche in the gouernement, is
oppugned according to the woorde, by the learned in this Lande.

This preamble he closes with a veiled, but ominous, threat: "I
speake not more confidentlye then I should do, for I know the
cause to be a most confident and sure cause, and therefore not
timorouslye to be dealt in, but in the feare of God, with all boldnes
to be stood too and aduouched."

Then, forgetting Wales altogether, he proceeds by syllogism,
as Martin likewise argues in his *Epistle,* to prove that "our dumbe
ministers, non-residents, L. Bb. [the very abbreviation popularized
and punned upon as "but drones" not "bees" by Martin], Archdeacons are nothing els but an increase of sinfull men, risen vppe
instead of their fathers the Idolatrous monks and fryers, stil to
augment the fierce wrath of God against this land, and you our
gouernours, and that this booke of D. Bridges, and whatsoeuer els
hath bene written for their defence, are nothing els but edicts,
traitors against God, and slaunderers to your sacred gouernement,
to defend the sale and exchange of church goods, and the verye
distruction of soules."

Now and then throwing in a reference to Wales, as if to dis-
arm the suspicious reader, he not only castigates the "L. Bb. Arch-

deacons, dumbe-ministers and other ecclesiastical officers there [in Wales—and by implication in England]," but he also calls down "the importable vengeaunce of God vppon such Magistrates as tollerate them." He particularly deplores the power of the civil magistrate, who at pleasure may alter the "external form of gouernment" of the church as established by Christ. In keeping with the Puritan line of argument, this "external form," of course, is presumed to be presbyterian, as prescribed by Cartwright and the Admonitioners. "Or where is it reuealed," asks Penry, "that the apostles gaue the ciuil magistrat, when any should be in the Church, the commission to abollishe the presbyterie established by them, as our aduersaries confesse, (as the word saith by God himselfe, and therefore not to bee abrogated vntill his pleasure in that point be known) because there was no christian magistrate[?]" This rhetorical question he supplements with the following marginal references to the Scriptures: I Corinthians XIII.5, 12; Ephesians IV.4; Romans XII.6; I Peter IV.10; Matthew XXI.25, &c., XII.11.

When Penry reaches that point in Bridges' argument where Bridges defends the authority both of the bishops and of the Queen in governing the Church, Penry pretends that his opponent is trying to undermine the Queen, who certainly would never consent that "som one priest may exercise a lawfull superiour authoritie ouer her Maiestie" or regard herself as not "contained within the vniuersal bodie of the Church," hence, an infidel. Thereby apparently hoping to separate the Queen from the bishops, Penry adds that Bridges' entire argument for the supremacy of one man over the Church is merely a repetition of "Bellarmines own reason" for papal supremacy. Thus, argues Penry, Bridges would move the papal seat from Rome to Canterbury or Lambeth.[20]

He concludes his attack on "the vitall parts of this popish warehouse of Doctor bridges" with a vitriolic challenge to anyone who questions his reasons taken "out of the infallible trueth of Gods eternall word": "And let me see who will dare to replie vpon them?" This shout of defiance he rounds out with one last insult directed at Bridges himself:

As for D. bridges himselfe, his vnsauery and vnlearned stile, his popishe reasons, long since bannished out of the schooles of all sound deuines, hys translation of other mens writings, throughout hys whole booke, his vngodly and abhominable praier that the preaching of the word may neuer bee had generally throughout the land, his scripture being the subscription of the second epistle to Timothie, his alleadging of writers, as cleare against himselfe, as black is to white, as of Augustine, Caluin, Aretius, &c, *his imperfect periodes without sence or sauour* [which Martin likewise ridicules], his Bishop Iames, Archbishops, Tim. and Titus, his translations of vos autem nolite vocari rabbi, into will not you be called rabbi, with thousand other monumen[t]s of his prophane impiety, sottish ignorance, and want of learning, euidently conuince, that he was neuer as yet, in Platonis Politia, where any good learning grewe, but hath wallowed him selfe all his life in Romuli fece, whence learning hath ben long since bannished, & godlines neuer shone. And therfore he of al others can disproue nothing: vnlesse the question before hand be granted of his side. For to omit, that in 160. sheets of paper, he hath don nothing, but ouerthrown him selfe, vtterly shamed his whoorishe cause, by shewing the nakednes thereof, translated other men's writings [an echo of Cartwright's taunt at Whitgift's scholarly references [21]], taught the reader howe to vnderstand the learned discourse, and added marginall notes, so that if other men had neuer written, he would haue said nothing, this shalbe vndoubtedly true throughout the whole booke, that he hath made a couchant before hand, not to dispute, vnless you graunt conclusion, & all, and rather flatlie to be non plus then prooue any thing.

· 73 ·

A similar antipathy to Bridges' book, which, as has been mentioned, is both a learned and a well-written, though lengthy, defense of the Church of England, appears in the Martinist tracts published shortly afterward.

With Bridges thus disposed of, Penry launches a threat of imminent destruction at the members of the Privy Council:

> My Ll. be not deceiued, the Lord of heauen is angrie wyth you, and his whole hoast for the Babilonish garments of these Achans. Retaine them no longer, if you would not fall before the enemie; When the Lorde shall plead with you, your wiues, children, families, and the whole land, with pestilence, or with blood, as he is likely to do, for these wadges of execrable gold, it is not, the pontificall Lordships of byshops, at whose commaundement, the lordes sword will returne againe into his sheath, when your gasping soules, shall cry for mercy at the Lords hands, it is not the proud, & popelike Lordships of bishops, their vsurped iurisdictions, their prophane excommunications, their railing slaunders against Gods truth and his seruants, their blasphemous breathing of the holye ghost vppon their Idol priests, that will driue the Lord to giue any cōfort.[22]

In a country facing invasion by a foreign power—a Catholic power at that—it is scarcely surprising that Penry's threats of bloodshed, combined with his attacks on "popery," would strike terror into the hearts of English statesmen. But more pertinent to the subject at hand, the vehemence and facility of Penry's expression in such passages as this quite refute the claim that Penry's style is completely different from Martin's.[23]

Proceeding on the assumption—whether he believed it or not—that the Queen is misinformed of the "ungodliness" of the bishops in Wales (and, by implication, in England), Penry urges the Councillors to move her "again, & againe, and neuer leaue vntill" she listens. Repeating the conviction first expressed in his *A equity* that "Hir Maiestie knoweth not . . . the exacting necessitie that lieth vpon her shoulders, of redeeming the Churche," Penry re-iterates that the members of the Privy Council must "put her in minde hereof, and in submission intreat her, yea, and neuer leaue entreating, vntill she yeeld, to turne away the wrath of God from her selfe and her kingdome, by abolishing vngodly ordinances, and restoring beutie vnto Siō."

In a passage aimed at the episcopacy in general—obviously not just the Welsh bishops—he stresses the danger in suffering "the people brought by her Maiestie, out of Egypt, to remaine still in the wildernes, on this side Iordan, euen vnder those men, the dumbe ministers, nonresidents, *L. Bb. I mean,* who are fit for nothing, but to be captaines, (whensoeuer opportunitie shall serue) to bring them again into Egypt." Accordingly, he promises that if the Councillors "wilbe ruled by the canon of the word," as he intends to interpret it to them, of course, then they may be deliv-ered "from the heauie wrath of God." On the contrary, if they follow the word as interpreted by "L. bish. and other corruptions of the Ecclesiasticall state"—here he carefully excludes the "ciuill gouernement"—they will become "an astonishmēt and an hissing vnto all the nations vnder heauen."

The Word, according to Penry, requires that the Privy Council remove all "dumb ministers, non-residēts, the L. bb." from Wales and in their places install "as many godly learned, as can be found, to call the people, and see them prouided for"—in other words, the presbyterian ministers. Of the ministers now holding livings in Wales, the small number who "haue gifts for the ministery" should be retained and "compelled to bee faithfull," but "the most of them are vnsauerie salt" and should be dismissed with "some part of that which now they possesse with sacriledge, bestowed vpon them." If there are not enough "good ministers" to conduct "the publike meetings on the Sabboth" and to administer the sac-raments, the people should meet just the same and appoint "some discreet man from among themselues . . . to read the word, and vse some forme of praiers as shalbe thought meetest by the aduise of the godly learned." Since the only sacrament requiring the office of a preaching minister is baptism, Penry urges his Welsh brethren not to "keepe their children vnbaptized any longer than they must of necessitie." However, he does not specify what this limitation of time should be.

With another urgent call to action he reproaches the Privy Council for treating a recently illegally published Welsh book favoring Rome with greater kindness than they accorded his own *Aequity*, "pleading the causeof Sion, coming forth priuileged by publike authority, & alowāce." Then he winds up his supplement with an appeal larded with threats of vengeance (especially from the impending Spanish invasion), decorated with numerous scriptural references, and sugar-coated with protests of his own sincerity in that he is willing to give his life for his cause:

> If I haue spoken any vntruth, beare witnesse thereof, if a truth I dare by the lords assistance stand to it, and demand what he is, that wil presume to obiect, and throw himselfe vnto the vengeance of God, by punishing me an innocent? The Lord may for my other sinnes, bring mine head vnto the graue with bloud: but in this cause, what haue I offended and therfore vndoubted woe wil betide him that shall molest me for this worke, Howsoeuer it be, thus I have performed a dutye towardes the Lorde, and his church, my countrey and your Hh. which I would doe if it were to be done againe, though I were sure to endanger my life for it. And be it known, that I am not afraid of earth in this cause. And if I perish, I perishe, my comfort is that I know whether to go, and in that day, wherein the secreats of all hearts shabe manifested, the sinceritie of my cause also shall appeare.[24]

Unquestionably these words, burning with fanatical zeal, come from the pen of a man utterly fearless in the conviction of the righteousness of his cause. His pious expression, however, only half conceals the threat of retaliation, which he delivers with a touch of daredevil impudence. Certainly Penry would never shrink from becoming embroiled in a controversy with the hierarchy, no matter how hazardous it might prove. What further insults could he invent except possibly to deride individual bishops, even Archbishop Whitgift himself, with as satirical a pen as he here uses on the unfortunate Dean Bridges?

The change in the opening words in the note "To the Reader," from "Master D. Somes booke was published this day" in the second edition to "I haue read Master D. Somes Booke" in the third, suggests that the latter edition followed the former by only a few weeks. In this final edition Penry retains his section of syllogisms against the "dumbe ministers," which follows the conventional Puritan pattern. But as has been pointed out, the "re" in "rebaptism" in the second "marginall note" in the main text of the *Exhortation* is blocked out.

A more extensive alteration is the omission of the lengthy address to the "Ll. of the Covnsell." Apparently becoming convinced of the futility of appealing to the Queen and her Privy Council, Penry decided to revise and expand it to a *Supplication* to the Parliament instead, as which it was published a few months later. The revised note "To the Reader" in the last edition in part echoes the earlier one: "I haue read Master D. Somes booke, the reasons he vseth in the questions of the dumbe ministerie, and communicating with them, I had answered (as you may see in this booke) before he had written. The man I reuerence, as a godly & learned man. The weaknes of his reasons, shalbe shewed at large Godwilling." [25]

This odd blending of flattery and disparagement—quite typical, we repeat, of Penry's rhetorical style—is followed by three corrections: "Page 42. line 24. read made and full, page 52. line 22. read axiom." Two of these corrections puzzle Williams, who writes as follows: "Also it [the third edition] has the startling *erratum:* 'Page 42 line 24. read made and full,' that is, for 'mad Deacons or foule Priestes' should be read 'made Deacons or full Priestes,' an error apparently noticed only after the third impression had been printed off." [26]

The more plausible explanation for this "startling *erratum*," it seems to me, is that at this point Martin, Penry's *alter ego*, is making his preliminary bow. With a justifiable pride in the rapidly growing power of invective that, as Martin, he is developing in his *Epistle*, Penry is calling the attention of his readers to these comically derisive epithets for fear that they may be overlooked. The pretended misprint and the misstatement for comic effect are, indeed, stylistic characteristics of the Martinist pamphlets. For example, on the title pages of both the *Epistle* and the *Epitome* Martin refers to the English clergy as "Parsons, Fyckers, and Currats." Without commenting on Martin's use of *f* for *v*, which, incidentally, is the conventional English way of expressing Welsh dialect, Pierce changes the obviously satirical "Fyckers" to "Vicars" and "Currats" (a combination of *cur* and *rat*) to "Curates." [27] Perhaps in order to avoid such bowdlerism as this, Penry ostentatiously invites the reader to share in his appreciation of his own satire.

Chapter VII

Penry's First Reply to Some

In the notes directed "To the Reader" at the end of the second and third editions of the *Exhortation* Penry promises a reply "at large" to Some's *First Godly Treatise*. While the last edition of the *Exhortation* was being printed, Penry was working on what he apparently considered a brief *"ad interim* statement," [1] his *Defence of that which hath bin written in the questions of the ignorant ministerie*. Here as elsewhere in his writing, the phrase "the ignorant ministerie" is synonymous with the episcopalian ministry. Although he pays lip service to scholarship in his admission that "the Lord doth not ordinarily bestowe vpon any in these our dayes" the proper "fitnes to teach" demanded in the Scriptures "without the knowledge of the artes, especially the two hand-maydes of all learninge, Rhethoricke and Logick, and the two originall tongues wherein the worde was written," yet like Cart-wright he ridicules "our absurd doctors . . . who can bring nothing into the pulpit, but that which other men haue written." [2] In other words, even though the minister might be a university scholar of Greek and Hebrew, if he does not find presbyterianism in the Scriptures, he is still an "ignorant minister."

The *Defence of that which hath bin written in the questions of the ignorant ministerie* seems to be a desperate effort on Penry's part to escape the trap set for him by Some's exposure of his doubts concerning baptism. In his opening paragraph he pays

Some a typically dubious compliment as he ironically registers surprise that the *First Godly Treatise* "might seem to proceed rather from any, then frō a man whose giftes and learning seemed to promise the affordinge, of greater and more waightie matters, then any set downe in that treatise." Then he accuses Some not only of touching but two of his reasons but also of "a manifest going from the controuersie," in other words, changing the subject. The "question" discussed in the first two editions of his *Exhortation*, he insists, is "whether ignorant men, not ordained of God for the gatheringe together of the Saints, be ministers or no," from which, in his opinion, Some has digressed in introducing the question whether "the Sacraments administred by them, viz. by popishe priests, and our dumbe ministers in the daies of blindnes and ignorance" are really sacraments. Some's question, according to Penry, "is no part of the matter in controuersie, but another point to be discussed (if men will be gotten at all to enter therevnto) when the former is determined and decided." Like the "three marginall notes" in the second edition of his *Exhortation*, his parenthesis indicates a burning desire to bring the validity of Catholic and Anglican baptism into question.

His full awareness of the danger of opening a controversy on this subject appears in his statement that in order to "prooue the lawfulnes of communicatinge with dum ministers," Some has handled "two needles[s] points." The first of these is "that they which were baptized by popish priests, haue receiued true bapti[s]m as touching the substance"; the second is "that they are the sacramentes of baptisme and the holy supper of the Lorde, which are deliuered in the Church of England by vnpreching ministers." "In these two pointes, M. Some," he goes on, "you haue prooued nothing that my writinges haue denied; but *you haue quickened a dead controuersie, not vnlikely to giue the wrangling spirits of this age, cause to breed greater sturres in the Church.*"

His rebuke to Some for introducing a subject, which he himself first mentioned, suggests his acute discomfort, not at all eased by such awkward disclaimers as the following: "Of this I am assured, that neyther popish priests, nor any other ignoraunt guides are ministers. whether the element administr̄ed by thē, be a sacrament or no, looke you to that, which haue in your treatise debated that, *which my writings neuer called into question.*"

Yet the fascination that the subject has for him is revealed in his inability to steer away from it. He continues: "Now I coulde well ouerpass these two pointes, because of themselues they containe nothing that I haue withstoode: But in as muche as you haue not onely grounded them vpō false principles, and such as in no wise can be warraunted by the canon of the word, but also inferre vpon their grant, that our readers are ministers, and consequently, that it is no sinne to communicate with them, I am first to set downe the state of the question, which in deed is and ought to be decided betweene you and me concerninge the elemente administred, both by popish priests, and other vnpreaching ministers: and secondly to examine the groundes whereby you prooue the element alreadie deliuered by them to be a sacrament, *which you know I do not denie to be so.*"

Nevertheless, immediately after stating that he does not deny "the elemente administered, both by popish priests, and other vnpreaching ministers" to be a sacrament, he resorts to a sophism several times repeated throughout the *Defence of that which hath bin written in the questions of the ignorant ministerie,* namely, that whether or not the sacraments in the Catholic and Anglican churches are valid, if the recipient is not *assured* of their validity, they are invalid to him: "The question therefore is not whether the one or the other of them haue deliuered a sacrament in respect of the action done; but whether a christian going vnto them for those holy seales, may be assured, that hee can receiue the same at their handes."

In spite of his ambiguity, which may be deliberately planned to confuse his opponent, Penry's use of the syllogism continues to bring him back to the fateful subject. His denial that a Christian can be *assured* of receiving a sacrament at the hands of "popish priests and other vnpreaching ministers" leads him to conclude "that the question is now growne to this issue, whether popish priestes and our vnpreachinge ministers, bee ministers or no." Taking the more remote of these two orders, he states that since "euery minister must be at the least by profession, a member of the true Church" and since "no popish priest is by profession a member of the true Church," therefore "no popish priest is a minister"; furthermore, "the popish religion is such a religion as whosoeuer liueth and dyeth in the profession thereof: he liueth & dieth out of the Church, where saluation is not possibly to be had, for any thing that is made knowen vnto man." This outburst of intolerance brings him back into dangerous territory.

In opposition to Some, who defends the validity of Catholic baptism, Penry declares: "I see no shew of probabilitie wherevpon my fayth, or the faith of any can be assured to receiue true baptisme at their hands. . . . Therefore men can not be *assured* to haue the substance of baptisme in the popish Church." Only a few lines further on, as if caught in the vortex of a whirlpool, he repeats, "But popery is out of the Churche, and so are all popish priests. Therefore no man can *assure* himself to haue the substance of baptism in popery by any popish priest."

In spite of this forthright denial he continues his struggle to avoid the dangerous issue of the invalidity of Catholic baptism: "Nowe to the examination of your reason brought to prooue that they which were baptized in popery, haue receiued true baptisme. *Your conclusion you must remember, I do not deny,* though your reason prooueth not the same, which is thus framed." [3]

Nevertheless, on the basis of some distinction that he professes to discern between, on the one hand, "substantiall baptisme," which in his opinion is "true baptisme" and must be accompanied by preaching, and, on the other hand, the act of baptizing "in the name of the trinitie," he flatly denies Some's arguments that, first,

An exhortation vnto the gouer-
nours, and people of hir Maiesties
countrie of Wales, to labour earnestly,
to haue the preaching of
the Gospell planted a-
mong them.

There is in the ende something
that was not in the former
impression.

PSAL: 137. 5,6.

If I shall forget thee, O Ierusalem, let my right hande forget her selfe, if I do not remember, thee, let my toong cleaue vnto the roofe of my mouth : yea, if I prefer not Ierusalem vnto my cheefe ioye.

2. COR. 1. 13.

For wee write no other thing vnto you, than that you reade, or that you acknowledge, and I trust you shal acknowledge vnto the ende.

1 COR 5. 13,14.

For, whether we be out of our wit, we are it vnto God, or whether wee be in our right mind, wee are it vnto you For, that loue of Christ doth constraine vs.

1588.

Oh read ouer D. Iohn Bridges / for it is a worthy worke:

Or an epitome of the

fyrste Booke / of that right worshipfull volume / written against the Puritanes / in the defence of
the noble cleargie / by as worshipfull a prieste / Iohn Bridges /
Presbyter / Priest or elder / doctor of Diuillitie / and Deane of
Sarum. Wherein the arguments of the puritans are
wisely preuented / that when they come to answere M. Doctor / they must needes
say something that hath
bene spoken.

Compiled for the behoofe and ouerthrow of
the Parsous / Fyckers / and Currats / that haue lernt
their Catechismes / and are past grace: By the reuerend
and worthie Martin Marprelate gentleman / and
dedicated to the Confocationhouse.

The Epitome is not yet published / but it shall be when
the Bishops are at conuenient leysure to view the same.
In the meane time / let them be content with
this learned Epistle.

Printed ouersea / in Europe / within two fur-
longs of a Bounsing Priest / at the cost and charges
of M. Marprelate / gentleman.

"whosoeuer deliver Gods baptism, they deliuer true baptisme," and second, that since "popish priestes deliuer Gods baptisme" they therefore deliver "true baptisme." [4] He terminates his discussion of Catholic sacraments with the sweeping assertion, "For as I haue shewed, popish priestes haue no calling at all in the Church."

From this attack on Catholic baptism, which would find ready acceptance from an anti-Catholic English reading public, he then directs his fire at his real target, the episcopalian hierarchy, and sets out to prove that "vnpreaching ministers are no ministers." Summarizing his arguments as set forth at large in the first addition to the second edition of his *Exhortation,* to which he directs his reader, he inevitably returns to his favorite theme of the questionable validity of the Anglican sacraments: "Nowe to the conclusion, If vnpreaching ministers be no ministers, and if I cannot be *assured* to receiue a sacrament, but onely at the hands of a minister . . . then cannot I *assure* my selfe, that an vnpreaching minister can deliuer a sacrament vnto me: and therefore it is vnlawfull for me or any christian to go vnto an vnpreaching minister for the sacraments; if vnlawfull, then a sinne, if a sin, thē the godly are polluted which goe vnto them for the sacramentes." Thus his spiritual dilemma is evident in his inability to avoid the subject of baptism.

Arriving at his conclusion that he cannot be any more "assured" of receiving a true sacrament from "vnpreaching ministers" than from "popish priests," he hastily draws back from the next step which would be to deny the validity of both Catholic and Anglican sacraments: "Your conclusion, page 22. that they which were baptized by vnpreching ministers, are rightly baptized as touching the substaunce of baptisme; I do not gainsay. Your reasons are weake. For how coulde wee proue your conclusion, if men should denie popish baptism to be true baptism, *as I do not you know & he shuld do me great iniurie, which would lay that to my charge.*" Yet, by comparing persons "which denie popishe baptisme" and remain unbaptized to the Jews who "were vncircumcised in the wildernesse fortie yeres almost," he continues to cast doubt on non-presbyterian baptism.

Finally, after repeating his denial that the mere pronunciation of the "wordes of institution with the deliuerie of the element" would validate the sacrament being administered, he declares that "the godly do sinne, which do communicate with vnpreaching ministers"—the battle cry of separatism. Thus he all but declares the Anglican sacraments invalid. Although his use of the word "communicate" might imply that he was referring only to the sacrament of communion, he slyly slips in a reference to baptism. One of the reasons why the godly thus sin is that "they eyther make the element to bee a sacrament naturally in it selfe, and not by the ordinance of God, or els think the ordinance of God in the institution of the sacrament onely to consist in the recitall of the words; *I baptize thee,* &c or take eate, &c, whereas a minister is a most principall part of the ordinance."

Throughout his pamphlet he employs a mixture of flattery and ridicule, far more biting than open abuse, much like that in his original references to Some in the notes appended to the second and third editions of the *Exhortation* in which he protests that he reverences Some as a "godly and learned man," but nevertheless deplores his inability to reason. Similarly, Penry here questions Some's honesty: "Not that I wold any way disgrace, you whō I reuerence, for that is no part of mine intent, the Lorde is my witnes. Nay, I would be loth to let that syllable escape me, that might giue you or any els the least occasion in the world, to thinke that I carrye any other heart towards you, then I ought to beare towards a reuerend learned man fearing God. And howsoeuer, vnles you alter your iudgment, I can neuer agre with you in these pointes; because I am assured you swarue frō the truth." [5]

Nevertheless, in the *Defence of that which hath bin written in the questions of the ignorant ministerie* Penry is at his least effective. As he moves in circles around the forbidden subject of baptism, he either denies his own statements previously made or, contradicting Some's refutation of these statements, merely repeats them without adding anything new. These defects seem to indicate his consciousness of the danger pointed out by Some, namely, that in denying the validity of "popish baptism" he is denying that the Queen and many other important persons have truly been baptized.

A longer reply to Some might never have been written if on September 19, 1588, Some had not issued a second edition of his *Godly Treatise,* with an extensive addition under the following subtitle: *A Defence of Such Points in R. Some's Last Treatise, as M. Penry hath dealt against* (which we have entitled the *Second Godly Treatise*). Penry's implication, in the conclusion of his *Defence of that which hath bin written in the questions of the ignorant ministerie,* that difficulties have overtaken him which have prevented him from writing a full answer to Dr. Some, is taken by Pierce to indicate trouble "no doubt in Waldegrave's department, and most likely the requisition of the services of the printer by the arrival of a batch of Marprelate 'copy.' " [6] In fact, if Penry had been personally engaged in the composition of this "copy"—as I believe he was—he might very well have been willing to forego further perilous controversy with Some.

In Some's *Second Godly Treatise* he quotes directly from the *Defence of that which hath bin written in the questions of the ignorant ministerie* and then gives his own rebuttal in a style almost as pungent as Penry's. Referring to his opponent's condescending compliments, Some wryly comments: "It is gently done of you: when you haue broken my head, you giue me a plaister: but I refuse your surgerie. You wil not, you say, disgrace me: You reuerēce me: Good words. A foule hooke vnder a faire bait. If you reuerēce your friends on this fashion, what shal your enemies looke for?" Like Penry, Some uses a prose style enlivened by colloquialisms, epithets, and plain terms bordering on the abusive. He does not feel it beneath his dignity to jeer at Penry's syllogisms, of which the Puritan writer was enormously proud: "Many Carre-men in London can make better arguments than these."

Moreover, Some's analytical mind enables him to go directly to the weaknesses in his opponent's argument, particularly Penry's Puritan semantics and his indecision regarding the validity of baptism performed by Catholic or Anglican clergy. The Puritan distinction between "godly learned" and "ungodly ignorant" or "dumb" ministers, for example, does not in the least confuse him: "The question between him and me, is not whether ignorant men may either enter into, or continue in the holy ministerie: for, my resolution is negatiue, that is, that they ought not: but the question is, whether such as were and are baptized by Popish priests and ignorant ministers, haue and doe receiue a Sacrament: and whether the godly communicant is polluted by receiuing the Sacrament at the hands of vnpreaching ministers. The most famous men and Churches, are peremptorie for me, and against him." [7] Not only does Some resent Penry's habit of quoting him out of context—a Puritan weapon of retaliation, if we may cite Cartwright as typical [8]—but he also tries to correct his opponent's misstatements.

For example, in the *Defence of that which hath bin written in the questions of the ignorant ministerie* Penry accuses him of neglecting to reply to the arguments of the first two *Exhortations:* "Al men may easily see, that there was a great ouersight committed by M. Some, in deeming that the oppugning of a cause countenanced by most of the godly learned, would be taken in hand by any, who could not answere the reasons which he might be sure would be obiected by al. And who could bee ignorant, that the odious controuersie, cōcerning the profanation of baptisme, both by popish priests, & our dumb ministers, would offer it selfe in the forefront to withstand the trueth?" [9]

In reply Some reiterates what he has already stated in his *First Godly Treatise,* finished before he had seen Penry's complete book: "Certaine in *London* gaue out in my hearing: first, that such as were baptized by Popish Priests in the Popish Church, and

PENRY'S FIRST REPLY TO SOME

by vnpreaching ministers in our Church, receiued no baptisme: Secondly, that the Godly were polluted, which receyued any Sacrament at the hands of vnpreaching ministers." Since, therefore, he has already answered these two objections given him by hearsay, he is indignant at being accused of intentionally neglecting to reply to the treatise as a whole. After thus defending himself from the implication of cowardice, he scores Penry's confused remarks on the subject of baptism: "No maruaile though you dissent from me. . . . You are at warre with your selfe. Your wordes agree like harpe and harrowe. One while, you denie not that popish priestes and vnpreaching ministers haue deliuered a sacrament: An other while you knowe not what they can deliuer: for, they are, as you say, no ministers." [10]

Then Some delivers the blow that Penry is desperately trying to dodge, namely, that if Penry proves, as he maintains that he can prove, that "popish priests" are no ministers and that therefore no one can be assured of receiving a valid sacrament from them, he also proves that the Queen and many other persons are unbaptized. In maintaining that "popish priests" are no ministers, Penry in his *Defence of that which hath bin written in the questions of the ignorant ministerie* had made a feeble attempt to forestall this fairly obvious deduction: "You must remember that I speake not of that which hath bene done yesterday, but of the assurance that may be had of that which to morow is to be done." [11] This evasion Some triumphantly counters: "You graunt it to be baptisme which was administred yesterday in the Popish church: but, you doubt of that which is deliuered to morow. Then yesterday a Sacrament, and to morow none. You dare not for your eares, say in flat termes, that it was no baptisme which was deliuered heretofore in the Popish church." [12] Reminiscent of Whitgift's comment to Cartwright,[13] Some holds that "the Popish church is a church though an vnsound Church" and that "Popish priestes haue a calling though a faultie one"; consequently, he stands by his statement in his earlier *Treatise,* that "there was & is true baptisme in the Popish church." He even makes a concession hitherto expressed only by Whitgift among the Protestant controversialists: "I doubt not, but that many which liued and died in the time of popish darkenesse, died Gods seruants." [14]

Thus Some's *Second Godly Treatise*, coming as it did in the midst of the preparation of the first Martinist tract, left Penry with a sense of uneasiness and frustration that, as we shall see, is glimpsed here and there in the depositions of the various suspects. But for the next few months he was to be too preoccupied with his Martinist activity to do anything about it.

Chapter VIII

The Formation of the
Martinist Conspiracy

The only *external* evidence bearing on the Marprelate Controversy, and particularly on the identity of Martin Marprelate, is to
be found in the depositions made by the suspects. These were
collected and edited by Arber in his *Introductory Sketch to the
Martin Marprelate Controversy*.[1] Although he intended the *Introductory Sketch* to be "the first scientific attempt . . . to unravel
this Controversy," Arber includes with the depositions numerous
items of "miscellaneous information, some of a later date." Ever
since 1875, when Arber's collection appeared, his interpretation of
one of these items has had the curious effect of obscuring the problem of Martin's identity for all succeeding investigators of the controversy.

This item is an excerpt from a pamphlet published in 1595, some
five or six years after the Controversy had ended, and two
years after Penry's execution, Matthew Sutcliffe's *Answere unto
Iob Throkmortons Letter*. In this pamphlet Sutcliffe accuses Job
Throckmorton of being "the man that principally deserveth the
name of Martin." Arber, in presenting his own "belief on this
subject," accepts Sutcliffe's belated emotional attack and thus
implies distrust of the testimony of everyone immediately connected
with the publication of the Martinist tracts. In fact, Arber terms

Sutcliffe's accusations "a most important testimony as to the Authorship, by one who had seen all the impounded documents, many of which are now lost." [2]

Pierce, however, questions a full acceptance of Sutcliffe's account on the ground that, as he puts it, "Sutcliffe is neither so free from violent partisan prejudice, nor from error in matters of fact, that we can unhesitatingly accept his conclusion." Instead of accepting Sutcliffe's biased statements Pierce declares that the deposition of Henry Sharpe, the bookbinder of Northampton, which Arber reports in full in all of its startling frankness, is "our chief source of information *on several points*." Pierce's qualifying phrase "on several points" typifies the subjective approach of most students of the Controversy, who refer to the depositions given before the High Commissioners in 1588 and 1589 only when a sentence or two happens to fit in with their own hypotheses. Indeed, after conceding the importance of Sharpe's testimony, Pierce describes the bookbinder as "a very inquisitive man" and "an inveterate gossip," who "appears to have been drawn to the business by mercenary motives, rather than by any strong and impelling religious convictions." [3]

The most startling example of this type of bias may be found in the biography of Penry by John Waddington, the Congregationalist historian, in which he denies that his "pilgrim martyr," as he calls Penry, had anything whatever to do with the Martinist publications. In order to clear Penry's name, Waddington maintains that the confessions of the Martinist suspects, which all but name Penry as Martin, were "extorted by fear" with "no validity as evidence." [4] Considering Elizabethan punitive procedures of hanging, drawing, and quartering and of torturing with thumbscrews and the rack, indeed, we have no reason to doubt that these unfortunate prisoners were harshly treated by the government officials. Furthermore, the master printer, John Hodgkins, in his testimony as quoted by Pierce, protests that the confessions of his two assistants Valentine Symmes and Arthur Tomlyn "had bene violent[ly] extorted from them" and that "by his one [own] confession he was forced thereunto by rackinge and great torments." [5] Accordingly, since torture can force a man to distort the truth merely to placate his torturers, the testimony of these men has to be carefully weighed.

A comparison of their confessions with Sharpe's deposition makes it immediately clear that neither of the assistant printers was taken into the confidence of the Martinists as was Sharpe,[6] for they knew Penry only as Mr. Harrison (the anglicized form of his name), and it was not until after their arrest that they learned the name of Job Throckmorton. With considerable admiration for their courage, however, we remark how carefully they concealed what they did know. As we read Symmes's statements that he "thinketh" the remaining sheets of *Martin Junior* were brought to the press by Throckmorton, or that he "thinketh that m^r Throckmort[on] was the author" of *Martin Senior*, or that he "doth think that 'more work for the Coop[er]' was likewise of Mr Throckmorton's penninge: for that it was the same hand that 'm^{r}tins senior' and 'martin Junior' was," [7] we can almost feel the agony caused by a twist of the thumbscrews. Nevertheless, while regarding any information extracted from them as possibly distorted, we can test its accuracy by correlating it with that in the other depositions.

As for Sharpe, however, his good reputation seems to have limited his harsh treatment to imprisonment only. No sooner was he liberated, according to Sutcliffe, than he notified Penry of his confession.[8] Evidently Penry bore him no ill will, for in his *Appellation*, published while he was a refugee in Scotland, he deplores a second attempt on the part of the High Commission to arrest Sharpe, "wel known to be a dutiful subiect, and for the loue he beareth vnto Gods truth to haue bene heeretofore so cruelly dealt with at some of their hands, by long imprisonment." [9] Hence, though the confessions of Hodgkins and his assistants may have been colored by fear of torture, there is no indication either in

Sharpe's words or in anything said about him that he was subjected to any violence beyond imprisonment.

A reconsideration of the story of Martin Marprelate, as extracted from the records of the depositions of all persons suspected of having been associated with the secret press, should begin with the final paragraph of Sharpe's sworn statement, in which he sums up all that he knows of the affair:

> Being further demanded, whether he had no reasons, than are above mentioned, whereby he was induced to thinke, that Penry was the Author of all the said Books of *Martin*. He answereth negatively: saying that he neuer saw or knew any other Man to deale in suche sorte as Penry did about them. The Press wherein they were all printed was Penrys, he was the Dealer with Men to print them, he had Books with the first, he could talk of them before they were printed, and of the tymes of their coming forth, he diuided stakes (as this Examinate hath heard) with Wal[de]grave for the Second, third, and fourth *Martin,* and afterwards he allowing of Hoskins [Hodgkins], after seven shilling a Reame for the printing (as the said Hoskins told this Examinate) had the Commodity of the Sale of *Martin Junior* and *Senior* as he thinketh.[10]

No confession could be more forthright. Of its significance Mc-Kerrow writes that "from the beginning of 1589 Sharpe seems to have had much to do with the publication of the Marprelate books, and his testimony with regard to them has every appearance of being accurate." [11] And though Wilson passes by Penry in favor, first of Job Throckmorton [12] and then of Sir Roger Williams,[13] in his original essay on the Controversy he makes the following admission: "This man Sharpe, it may be mentioned in passing, is not the least interesting among those who were brought into contact with the Martinist circle. *Personally, I believe that he was one of the very few who knew the secret of 'Martin's' iden-*

tity." As might be expected, then, in this same essay Wilson unequivocally calls Sharpe's confession "the most important testimony we possess as to the movements of the Marprelate press and very reliable upon all matters of which the deposer had first-hand knowledge." [14]

From the depositions of Sharpe and, in spite of occasionally conflicting testimony, of the other suspects it is possible to piece together a mosaic of the tragedy of Martin Marprelate—the time, the place, and the dramatis personae. Since the press was rapidly moved about the countryside, always just a jump or two ahead of the pursuivants of the High Commission, the scholarly detective, working on this baffling conspiracy against the Church of England, must carefully follow the chronology of events. Yet only infrequently do allusions to time appear as specific dates. Usually, as might be expected from persons depending on their memories, these allusions appear as approximations such as "after Midsommer," "Allhallowtide," "shortly after," "about two years since," "about three months," "about the moneth of September last," "about a fortnight before Michaellmasse." The locations of the press, however, are more definite.

The witnesses, in order of their appearance before the authorities, are the following: Nicholas Kydwell, William Stanghton, Cutbert Cook, John Good—all residents of Kingston-on-Thames who gave their testimony on November 14, 1588; Walter Rogers of Richmond, who gave his on November 29, 1588; Nicholas Tomkins, who first appeared on February 15, 1589, and then again on November 29 of that year; Henry Sharpe on October 15, 1589; Stephen Chatfield, probably the same autumn; and John Udall on January 13 and July 13, 1590. In addition, in the brief held by the Attorney General Sir John Puckering are to be found summarized reports of the testimony of the following persons who complete the cast of characters in this confusing drama: Mistress Elizabeth Crane, Robert Waldegrave, John Penry, Sir Richard Knightley, Lawrence Jackson, Jeffs of Upton,

Humphrey Newman, Stephen Gyfford, John Hales, Esq., Roger Weekston [Wigston] and his wife, Job Throckmorton, and finally John Hoskins [Hodgkins], Valentine Symmes, and Arthur Tomlyn. As the plot unfolds, the identities of these individuals and their part in the Martinist activities will become clear.

Although Arber pinpoints a specific passage in Penry's *Aequity* as the source of the Controversy, he passes by the man whom he has thus designated as the prime mover and sets off in pursuit of other quarry. In his unwillingness to implicate Penry he is followed by Pierce, Wilson, Peel, and Williams. Eschewing the advantage to the present argument in accepting Arber's unsupported statement, which would seem like begging the question, I prefer to begin with the death in February, 1588, of John Field, minister of Aldermanbury, joint author with Thomas Wilcox of the first *Admonition,* published in 1572.

Embittered by the fact that this biting antiepiscopalian tract had had no appreciable effect on either Parliament or the Queen, Field had vaguely decided on another course, foreshadowed in some of the scurrilous passages in the first *Admonition.* He would deal in personalities; he would name names. To this end, therefore, he had for years been assembling notes detrimental to the reputations of important people in the hierarchy of the English Church and anecdotes of what he believed were abuses of ecclesiastical authority. Before he died, however, he repented that he had collected them and willed that they be burned.[15] But his friends disobeyed his dying request, for after all they had contributed some of the material. And these slanderous documents fell into the hands of three disgruntled men of strong Puritan sympathies: John Udall, his friend John Penry, whose company because of his scholarship, his honesty, and their common interest in religion, Udall particularly enjoyed, and the Puritan printer Robert Waldegrave.

After obtaining his B.A. from Cambridge in 1580–81, Udall had continued for his M.A. and holy orders. He then had become minister at Kingston-on-Thames, where his preaching of Puritan doctrine had aroused so much antagonism among his flock that he had been summoned before the High Commission at Lambeth. Through the intervention of powerful friends among the nobility he was temporarily restored to his ministry, but on June 10, 1588, he was finally suspended and deprived of his living. In his resentment at episcopal tyranny he had already written the dialogue *Diotrephes*, which was printed in the early spring of 1588 by Waldegrave, and he was working on his second Puritan tract, the *Demonstration of Discipline*. Penry, too, had recently had his own troubles with the episcopacy. After the publication of his *Aequity* in March, 1587, he had been summoned before the High Commission, where he had been forced to endure a humiliating trial, later reported in detail in Martin's *Epistle*,[16] and had been imprisoned for a month. It was almost inevitable that Udall and Penry should get together and talk over a course of action aimed at the overthrow of the bishops, ardently desired by both men.

Casting about for a weapon, Udall recalled the notes that Field had been collecting, some of which Udall himself had contributed. About a year before his silencing he had been so indiscreet as to show them to the vicar of Kingston-on-Thames, Stephen Chatfield, perhaps in order to test their effect. After reading a few of them, Chatfield had been so horrified that, as he himself testifies, he "clapt them vp together agayne" and refused to read any more. When he asked Udall whence they came, Udall evasively replied that "they were sent him from a frend of his." Whereupon Chatfield warned him that "if he Loued his owne quietnesse, he should retourne them where he had them [from]," for "they did importe suche matter" as Chatfield was later to read in that "scandalouse Libell," the *Epistle*.

Despite Chatfield's warning Udall had treasured Field's antiepiscopalian artillery. In the next suspicious conversation between Chatfield and Udall, occurring about a year later, in the middle of September, 1588, Udall expressed his resentment at being silenced and boasted that if they stopped his mouth "he would then sett himself to writing and geue the Bishoppes suche a blowe as they neuer had the lyke in their lyues." He was probably alluding not so much to his own *Demonstration of Discipline,* then on the press, as to something far more ambitious in this war of religious ideas, namely, the Martinist attacks on individual bishops —what today would be termed character-assassination—for the preparation of which he had contributed much deadly ammunition.

From the four earliest deponents—Kydwell, Stanghton, Cook, and Good—we learn that Udall, as Kydwell vaguely phrased it, "did kepe one in writing for the space of three weekes in Richemond," but at whose house they either could not or would not say. To this information Walter Rogers, vicar of Richmond, was able to add that "one William Parkes dwelling in Ritchmond" had volunteered the gossip that the anonymous individual, thus kept "writinge of a booke . . . for and in the behalf of Master Udall of Kingston," was living at the "Howse" of a certain man "addicted unto Puritanisme" by the name of [Thomas] Horton. This mysterious writer undoubtedly was Penry, for after Udall's silencing on June 10, 1588, he and Penry had met apparently for the purpose of sizing up the situation and of plotting their campaign.[17] Penry at once set to work organizing Field's notes, which during the summer were to become the first Martinist tract, the *Epistle.*

Waldegrave had had an even longer record of Puritan activity than the other two men. For the past ten years he had been known as a printer of Puritan tracts, and as a result had been in continual trouble with the authorities. In 1584, for printing unauthorized pamphlets attacking the Church of England, the Wardens of the Stationers' Company had authorized his arrest and that of his assistants along with the seizure of his press. In 1585, for a similar offense he had spent twenty weeks in prison.

During the early part of 1588 he had printed the first edition of Penry's *Exhortation* and Udall's *Diotrephes.*[18] On April 16,

1588, his shop was again raided and the undelivered stock of *Diotrephes* seized along with the presses and all fonts of type except at least two concealed by Waldegrave under his cloak, one of which was the famous "Dutch letters," later to be used to print the first four Martinist tracts, and the other already used to print *Diotrephes* and the first edition of Penry's *Exhortation,* and soon to be used for printing his *Defence of that which hath bin written in the questions of the ignorant ministerie,* and eventually the "Epistle to the Reader" in *Martin Junior* and Martin's entire *Protestation.*[19] Shortly afterward,[20] with the type that had been concealed, Waldegrave and his wife appeared at the London residence of Mistress Elizabeth Crane, a wealthy widow of Puritan persuasion. According to Mrs. Crane's servant Nicholas Tomkins, the Waldegraves "layd" the salvaged type "upon the boorde [table] in the Howse," and he removed it to a suitable hiding place where it remained for "about 3. Months," that is, until early July, when Mrs. Waldegrave came and took it away with her to Mrs. Crane's other house at East Molesey.[21]

There at about the same time Penry was given permission by Mrs. Crane to leave a "lode of stuff," in which, testifies Tomkins, "he beleveth the Press and Lettres were." [22] He did not know— or at least he did not admit [23]—that Penry had his own press and the font of Long Primer type which had already been used in the second edition of his *Exhortation,* published shortly after May 6, 1588.[24] Penry immediately got to work on the publication of the third edition of his *Exhortation,* mainly a reprint of the second minus its second addition, and also on the composition of his *ad interim* reply to Dr. Some, his *Defence of that which hath bin written in the questions of the ignorant ministerie.*

It seems fairly apparent that Udall, Penry, and Waldegrave did not set up residence at their base of operations at Mrs. Crane's. If, as we conjecture, Penry was the mysterious occupant of Horton's house in Richmond, where he was frequently visited by Udall, he probably commuted between this place and East

Molesey, three miles away, where Waldegrave was printing the third edition of his *Exhortation* and his *Defence of that which hath bin written in the questions of the ignorant ministerie*. While Udall was visiting the unnamed writer at Richmond, he also, according to Tomkins, "resorted *sundrie times* to Mistress Cranes Howse at Mowlsley, whilst Penry and Wal[de]grave were there." More specifically, Tomkins states that Waldegrave and Penry were at Mrs. Crane's house "about 3. weeks" after midsummer and again at Michaelmas (September 29); in other words, none of the three was in continuous residence at Mrs. Crane's during that momentous summer. Udall's purpose for conferring with Waldegrave was doubtless to discuss the printing of the *Demonstration of Discipline*, which Tomkins believed took place at his mistress' house [25] and of which Udall admitted himself the author. And—more important to this study—as a service both to Udall and to Penry, Waldegrave was to print the first Martinist tract, which was published during the latter part of October.[26]

Even while work was progressing on the secret presses at Mrs. Crane's house in East Molesey, Mrs. Crane herself was becoming more and more uneasy, and she eventually prevailed upon Penry to seek another hiding place.[27] Sometime in September he approached Sir Richard Knightley, several times member of Parliament,[28] about obtaining a room in his house at Fawsley in Northamptonshire, where he might print a book similar to the *Aequity*. Though Sir Richard did not immediately consent, he eventually gave permission. About the first of November Penry employed Jeffs, a tenant of Sir Richard's, to carry the presses from Mrs. Crane's to Fawsley. When on the first of November Mrs. Crane visited her house at Molesey, she found it vacated.[29]

Indicative of Penry's close connection with the itinerant secret presses is Jeffs's deposition that "the load of Stuffe which *by Penries appointment* he received at Mistress Cranes Howse in Mowseley he carried *by the said Penries* direction to Fawsley and left it with one Jackson Ke[e]per of Sir Richard Knightleys Howse at Fawlsley." [30] Furthermore, "about a fortnight or three weeks after Hallowmas," it was Penry himself, who, by "one Houre or two" preceded Jeffs and his "load of Stuffe" and presented their credentials to Jackson, namely, a "Ring of three Gymawes" or "gimmal-ring" given Penry by Sir Richard, with whom, as Sharpe testifies, Penry was "very familiar." And when Jackson deposited the "Stuffe" in the "Nursery," he gave the key to Penry.[31]

A couple of days later a stranger who called himself "Sheme," "Shamuel," "Shamne," or "such like name" appeared with his servant and told Jackson that he had come to look over and sort Sir Richard's "evidences," or title-deeds.[32] This newcomer turned out to be Waldegrave, who began printing the second Martinist tract, the *Epitome*. Sir Richard confessed that this tract was printed in his house. "Touching the Author of the Booke," he also told the High Commissioners that "he knoweth not, unless yt were Penry." But without hesitation he added that he knew Waldegrave to be the printer. Not only did Sir Richard himself admit that the *Epitome* was printed in his house, but the local minister at Fawsley, Edward Sharp, coming to Fawsley to visit Waldegrave's ailing servant, found "new printed" copies of this tract, one of which he immediately delivered to Sir Richard with a stern warning of its dangerous contents.[33] From Jackson's testimony it is evident that the *Epitome* appeared about the end of November.[34]

Sometime in December, after the *Demonstration of Discipline* was printed, Udall disappears from the action. At the request of friends in Newcastle-on-Tyne the Earl of Huntingdon invited him to that city, where he remained for a year, until December 29, 1589, when he was summoned to London, tried on January 13, 1590, and sentenced to death. After a brief reprieve he died in the Marshalsea Prison about the end of 1592. Since no one has ever doubted that the two tracts following the *Epitome* and printed in the same type—the *Minerall Conclusions* and *Hay any worke for Cooper*—were written by the same pen that wrote the *Epistle* and the *Epitome*, Udall's withdrawal effectively removes him from suspicion of authorship.

Perhaps as a result of the disapproval of members of the family, particularly of his son Master Valentine, on or about January 8, 1589, Sir Richard called an end to the printing and ordered his trusted servant Gyfford to remove the presses from Fawsley to his farmhouse at Norton, where they remained idle for a fortnight or so. Then about January 23 Sir Richard ordered Gyfford to take cart and horses and to convey the presses to the home of his nephew by marriage, Master John Hales, in Coventry, who in his own deposition says that shortly after Christmas, 1588, Sir Richard had written a letter, brought by Waldegrave, asking permission for a room for the printer until another place could be found.[35] At Coventry was to be played the next scene in this dangerous drama.

Chapter IX

The Role Played by Henry Sharpe

With Udall's departure Penry apparently felt the need for another assistant, perhaps only for moral support. At this point enters the man whose deposition is generally considered the most authoritative and revealing, Henry Sharpe, bookbinder of Northampton. That Penry did not immediately take Sharpe into his complete confidence, however, is evident from the disparity between Sharpe's chronology and what has subsequently become recognized as accurate.

For example, according to Sharpe, the *Epistle* "came out in ye beginning of December, 1588"; [1] on the contrary, the first pamphlet must have been in print before November 14, 1588, when the Lord Chancellor and Lord Treasurer wrote Archbishop Whitgift a letter directing him to search out the "Authors and abettors" of the *Epistle*.[2] Sharpe also conjectures that the *Epitome* "came out and was published in February [1589]" [3] instead of "at the end of November," as correctly dated by Pierce.[4] Furthermore, Sharpe gathered "by Master Penry's words" that the *Epistle* was printed at Kingston; [5] hence, he knew nothing of Mrs. Crane's establishment at East Molesey. Regarding all these discrepancies, McKerrow writes as follows: "From the beginning of 1589 Sharpe seems to have had much to do with the publication of the

Marprelate books, and his testimony with regard to them has every appearance of being accurate, but at this date he perhaps knew less of what was going on and must, I think, have been mistaken." [6]

About the first of December, when Penry learned that Udall was leaving, what he apparently did was to show Sharpe a copy of the *Epistle* in order to test his reaction; in other words, Penry's implication to Sharpe that this pamphlet was then in the process of being printed was merely a subterfuge for the purpose of self-protection. His conversation was so vague, indeed, that Sharpe supposed that the *Epistle* had been "Master Feilds doing." [7] Sharpe also inferred that Udall had been the "Corrector of this first Booke in ye printing of it"—that is, the proofreader—because his *Demonstration of Discipline*, which Penry said "was of Udalls makeing," was, as Sharpe gathered, "about the same tyme printed there at Kingstone also with the first Martin." [8] Yet Mrs. Crane's servant Tomkins, at this juncture far more intimately connected than Sharpe with the Martinist activities, believed that Udall's tract was printed at East Molesey "because the printing Press was there."

In early January, 1589, when Penry again approached Sharpe, he intimated that "the fetching of the Press from Kingston" (actually from East Molesey) to Sir Richard Knightley's house in Fawsley was only then under way. But according to Lawrence Jackson, Knightley's housekeeper, it was "about a fortnight or three weeks after Hollomas," or mid-November, when he received Penry, followed "within one houre or two" by "one Jeffs of Upton, Tenant to Master Valentyne Knightley," Sir Richard's son, carrying in baskets "a Load of Stuff," ostensibly the press and other printing equipment. In order to make the story more convincing, Penry specified the exact amount, fifty shillings, paid Jeffs, "who did fetch yt with his Carte." Obviously for the purpose of throwing Sharpe off the scent, Penry gave him the impression that "at a Muster in Northampton" Waldegrave had made the initial arrangements with Sir Richard for sheltering the press at Fawsley. Mistakenly inferring that the press had arrived at Fawsley "about the latter end of Christmas Holydays," Sharpe made two false assumptions: first, that Waldegrave's conference with Sir Richard had taken place shortly before his own conversation with Penry in January, and second, that "shortly after" Jeffs carried the press to Fawsley. Sir Richard himself, however, later confessed that "a little before Michaelmas [15]88" (the end of September) Penry had requested "a Ro[o]me in his Howse" in order to print a "Booke" similar to the *Aequity*.

Although Sharpe admits that he never actually saw the press at Fawsley House, he deduces that it was in operation there, first, because he had "h[e]arde it reported" that "a Mayde that had dwelt with the Keper of the House there at that tyme, gave yt out . . . that there had bene Bookes printed lately at Fawsley"; second, because Humphrey Newman, the cobbler, who later was discovered to be the chief distributor of the tracts, had told him that the *Epitome* was printed there; third, because Stephen Gyfford, Sir Richard's most trusted servant, "one whome he used secretly in these matters," also admitted carrying the press away from Fawsley; fourth, because "the voyce of the Country was, that this Booke was printed at Fawsley, and that there was a Press there"; finally, because in Sharpe's presence Master Valentine Knightley had deplored his father's action in befriending the Martinists.

As Penry became more and more assured of Sharpe's honesty, he let him little by little into the secret. Since Sharpe deposes that the *Epitome* "came out and was published in February [1589], *as he thinketh*," he must at that time have had his first glimpse of it. According to his deposition, indeed, in early February, 1589, a month after the press was moved from Fawsley to Norton, where it remained for a fortnight and then was conveyed to Coventry, Penry took him to a spot "within a mile of Fawsley," where Sharpe was left "bayting his Horse," while Penry went to Sir Richard's house and returned with a "Cloke Bag with Bookes behinde him." Next day someone delivered at Sharpe's home some copies of the *Epitome,* which Sharpe presumed had just been freshly printed on the press that he supposed was then hidden at Fawsley. Presuming, therefore, that they came from Penry, he paid Penry for them. Three or four days later Newman stopped by, picked up the pamphlets, and took them off—as Sharpe surmised—to London. Speaking professionally, Sharpe noted that the pamphlets had been bound by Waldegrave. Penry's mysterious behavior would lead us to believe that he was using the copy of the *Epitome* that he first showed Sharpe, just as he had earlier used the *Epistle,* as a means of testing Sharpe's feeling about this method of attacking the bishops.

Gradually Sharpe became suspicious that Penry was the author at least of the *Epitome.* With the same frankness that permeates his entire deposition, from which most of these facts are taken, he voiced his suspicion directly to Penry: "Surely . . . I thinke this booke (the *Epitome*) to be of your making, because there are two or three Phrases in ye *Epistle* of it, which are yours certainly." Penry merely laughed. Then it began to dawn on Sharpe that something was faulty with Penry's earlier implication that Master Field was the author of the first pamphlet, which had foretold the writing of the second. When the *Epitome* eventually did appear—in other words, when Sharpe first saw it—Field had been dead a year. Sharpe then discovered that all of Penry's intimates likewise suspected him of being Martin; indeed, Newman told Sharpe that "Penry was thought generally at London to be the Author of these Bookes." Finally convinced of Penry's dissimulation, Sharpe decided to ask him whether "this were a lawfull Course, that Martyn had taken in the two said Bookes to jest in such sort, and to detect to the world such mens Infirmities." Without any hesitation Penry "answered that godly men had taken heretofore the like Course" and backed up his statement with the names of Theodore de Beza and others.

Even yet Sharpe had not been taken into Penry's full confidence. Some time after the removal of the press from Fawsley in January, 1589, Sharpe, seemingly unaware that the press was gone, asked Sir Richard how he would explain the printing of the *Epitome* and whether or not he feared having his house searched. To these questions Sir Richard angrily replied: "Let me alone ye Knaves durst not search my House, yf they had, I wo[u]lde have courst [chased] them, they know well inough, but now yt ys gone, and that danger is past." Though Sharpe thus learned of the departure of the printers from Fawsley, he apparently was unaware of the concealment of the presses for an interval of "about a fortnight" at Sir Richard's farmhouse in Norton, for he does not allude to it. And of their arrival in Coventry he first heard shortly after mid-February, while he was traveling in Stephen Gyfford's company to visit his father-in-law at Wolston. As the pair were "riding together over a gutter," Gyfford accidentally let slip the comment that "he was never so affraid as he was least his Carte should haue stuck fast in ye same gutter as he was dryving it to Coventry," presumably with the secret presses.[9]

At Coventry, then, infers Sharpe, was printed the third Martinist tract, *Certaine Minerall and Metaphysicall Schoolpoints*, usually referred to as the *Minerall Conclusions*, which Penry about February 20 showed him in manuscript form. Reading the broadside to Sharpe, Penry praised it "as a pretty thing to be set out before the other Bookes" and evasively remarked that "yt was sent him from London."[10] Sharpe accordingly states that on or about February 20[11] the broadside was printed by Waldegrave and immediately sent to Sharpe's home at Northampton. Reading the text for himself, Sharpe was struck by "some taunts against Doctor Some" which he had not heard in the copy that Penry had previously read to him. In the *Second Godly Treatise*, published on September 19, 1588, Some had specifically attacked

Penry's theological doctrines. In December, when Penry first showed Sharpe a copy of the *Epistle*, he had said that Waldegrave had printed it instead of Penry's "Boke agaynst Doctor Some," which he would have preferred printed first. Knowing, therefore, that a reply to Some was on Penry's mind, Sharpe "began then to suspect" the *Minerall Conclusions* "to be of Penrys makeing." Next day Newman stopped by and, picking up all but about fifty copies, set off for London.[12] Thus, even though Sharpe was not in possession of all of the facts, he was being used as a middleman —a sort of fence.

The next pamphlet to be printed on the secret presses was Penry's *A viewe of some part of such publike wants & disorders*, commonly known as the *Supplication*. It was printed in Penry's own type earlier used for the second and third editions of his *Exhortation* [13] and was published during the first week in March, 1589. Two weeks before it appeared, while Sharpe was visiting at his father-in-law's home in Wolston, he met Penry, who may have been in the vicinity making arrangements for transferring his press from Coventry to Mrs. Wigston's at Wolston Priory. At any rate, he had occasion to ride with Penry to Coventry, and on the way, as if to sound out Penry as to Waldegrave's whereabouts, he suggested that they both visit Waldegrave. Penry, however, refused on the ground that his visits to Fawsley had aroused so much suspicion that Waldegrave had forbidden him to come. In other words, even though Sharpe suspected that Waldegrave was in Coventry, Penry himself was not yet ready to admit him to the inner sanctum.

Upon arriving in Coventry, the two men stopped "at Master Pigots in that city." For a brief interval Penry managed to detach himself from Sharpe, but Sharpe, looking around for him, discovered him with Master John Hales going toward Hales's residence, White Friars. As they saw him following them, they waved him back. Obediently he withdrew to Wolston, four miles away. When two weeks later the *Supplication* appeared, Newman called on Sharpe, still or again in Wolston, and asked him to bind a thousand copies which were at the Wigston residence. Probably not wishing to incriminate his relatives, Sharpe refused to work at Wolston but agreed to help Newman carry the unbound pamphlets to Northampton, where he bound them. Leaving a hundred copies with Sharpe, *for which Sharpe admitted that he paid Penry,*[14] Newman took the remainder to London.

The next book to be printed was the Martinist pamphlet *Hay any worke for Cooper,* a reply to Bishop Cooper's *Admonition to the People of England,* probably published January 10, 1589.[15] On or about Palm Sunday, March 23, 1589, after Sharpe had returned home to Northampton from visiting Sir Richard Knightley at Fawsley and his father-in-law at Wolston, Newman brought him about seven hundred copies of the latest Martinist pamphlet to be bound. Thus at long last Sharpe was actively initiated into the secret circle of the Martinists. From this point on, then, what he has to say in his deposition is no longer based on rumor or on personal guesswork. When, therefore, he attributes *Hay any worke for Cooper* to Master Penry on the ground that he found in it the same defense for "lawfullness in iesting" that Penry himself had made when Sharpe questioned him about its propriety in the first two tracts, he seems to be speaking with greater conviction and assurance than he did in his conjectures on the times and places of the printing of the earlier Martinist pamphlets. After Sharpe had bound the books, Newman took all except a hundred, which he left in Mrs. Sharpe's care. Later he relieved her of most of this remnant. Indicative that Sharpe was not working entirely for the "cause" is his dour comment that on this occasion he chid Newman "for that he was loth to haue any to gayne but himself." [16]

And now the second member of the original triumvirate of Udall, Waldegrave, and Penry found himself at the parting of the ways. Unlike Udall, whose need for a livelihood forced him to leave Kingston-on-Thames for Newcastle, Waldegrave offered excuses, partly doctrinal, partly economic. After dining during Easter Week (March 30–April 6) with Sharpe at his father-in-law's in Wolston, Waldegrave, while walking through the fields with Sharpe, told him that, first, "he wolde no longer meddle or be a dealer in this Course, partly because," as he had put it, " 'All the Preachers that I have conferred withall do mislike yt,' " and second, that "he had now gotten the thing he had long desired and wo[u]lde go [and] print yt in Devonshire." This "thing," Sharpe inferred from a later remark of Penry, was "Master Cartwrights *Testament* against the Jesuits." And when Sharpe casually asked him "how it chanced that he looked so palely," he replied that "one of Master Hales men kept him so closely at worke, that for that tyme, he had lyved as in a Prison, and could not haue oftentymes warme meate." In short, Sharpe's reflection of the Puritan printer's state of mind reveals Waldegrave's relief at withdrawing from his hazardous occupation. Indeed, "matters" had become so "very hot" that, according to Sharpe, Stephen Gyfford was forced into hiding.[17]

Chapter X

Exit Sharpe, Enter
Throckmorton

The news of Sharpe's active participation in the illegal enterprise had swiftly reached the ears of the authorities in London.
Upon learning "how he was layd [sought] for by the High Commissioners" and "how the Lord Chancellor [Sir Christopher
Hatton] was offended with him," Sharpe, terror-stricken, decided
to cast himself on their mercy. But Sir Richard Knightley warned
him that if he turned himself in now they were "so moved, as
surely they wo[u]lde hang him" and advised him to "withdraw
himselfe, untill they were better pacifyed." [1] Obviously, in giving
this advice, Sir Richard was speaking at least one word for himself: the bookbinder already knew too much of the whereabouts
of the secret presses. Accordingly Sharpe decided to await developments.

For a month or so nothing of importance happened. Around
the first of May, however, Sharpe met Penry and asked him two
questions: first, "what became of Wal[de]grave"; second,
"whether they sho[u]lde haue any more new Bookes." Penry
replied that "Wal[de]grave was surely in hand in some corner
with the printing of Master Cartwrights *Testament* and that he
[Waldegrave] looked daily for his [Penry's] *Appellation* from
him [Penry] and that then he [Penry] sho[u]lde goe in hand

with [that is, get to work on] *More worke for Cooper*." Penry added that Waldegrave had taken with him the "Dutch letters," in which the first four Martinist tracts had been printed.[2]

A week or two later, "a little before Whitsontide" (May 18, 1589), Penry asked Sharpe "if he co[u]lde not worke about the Press." As an excuse for his request, he implied that he had heard that Waldegrave had gone to La Rochelle, supposedly for a temporary visit. Sharpe cautiously answered "that he could in some sorte, but that he wo[u]lde not so doe, except the Lord Chancellor refused to remit him." And he dispatched his wife with a supplication to Sir Christopher Hatton in London.

Toward the end of May, Penry came to Sharpe and told him that he had given up hope of Waldegrave's return and had therefore procured "one Hoskins" (John Hodgkins) in his place. Shortly before midsummer (June 24) Mrs. Sharpe returned from London with word that Sir Christopher had stated "that there wolde be no remission obteyned." Penry again besought Sharpe to assist Hodgkins. Since Mrs. Sharpe had told her husband of the indignation at Court over the illicit publications, Sharpe again "utterly refused to have any dealing therein." A few days later Hodgkins, obviously sent by Penry, came to Sharpe with the intentionally vague tale that "he had sent a Press into the North to printe some such new Books, as Master Penry sholde sett him on worke withall." To Hodgkins' request for assistance Sharpe hesitantly replied that before he committed himself he must first see what he was to print.

Sometime after Waldegrave's departure in early April, Hales had informed Penry that the printing at White Friars must cease. Whereupon Penry had persuaded Mrs. Wigston of Wolston Priory, with whom he was staying, to send a wagon to White Friars in order to convey the press to her home. The exact date of the removal of Penry's press from Coventry to Wolston Priory is not stated in any of the depositions; indeed, Sharpe specifically comments that he did not know "how long this Press remayned

at Coventry before yt was fetcht to Wolston." [3] Yet, as McKerrow points out, it was at Wolston when Hodgkins and his men
arrived and must have been removed from Coventry before the
end of May. [4] At any rate, in early July, when Sharpe, "being
drawn by necessity to leave Northampton, went to dwell at
Wolston with his wives Mother," the printing press was in operation at the Priory.

Although Sharpe had believed Hodgkins' story about the removal of the press to some place in "the North," the bookbinder
found him in a "low Parlour" at Mrs. Wigston's residence, under
pretense of being an embroiderer, hard at work on the fifth Martinist tract, *Martin Junior*. Noting that it was being printed with
the same type as that used for Penry's *Supplication*, Sharpe warned
Penry that the similarity in type would "descry him to be Martin."
But Penry carelessly brushed aside Sharpe's warning. When, on
July 22, *Martin Junior* was completed, Sharpe abandoned his own
scruples and bound up the sheets. The ubiquitous Newman, for
his own personal protection now wearing Sir Richard's livery and
cognizance, at once set off for London with "700 or 800" copies.
About a week later appeared *Martin Senior*, set in the same type
as *Martin Junior* and, of course, Penry's *Supplication*. These, too,
Sharpe bound and gave to the "Carrier of Warwick" to be taken
to London. The package, Sharpe noted, was directed for deliver-
ance to "one Lawrence Wood a Taylor dwelling at the end of
Fish Street, to convey them to Newman."

With both pamphlets out of the way, Hodgkins ostensibly refused to print a third manuscript, *More worke for Cooper*, on the
grounds, first, that he had promised his wife to be at home three
weeks before that time and, second, that he "misliked *Master
Penrys press*." The real reason for the printer's sudden departure
from Wolston Priory undoubtedly was Master Wigston's discovery of the activities in the "low Parlour," of which, as Mrs. Wigston told Sharpe, her husband at her request had deliberately remained ignorant. Moreover, instead of going home, Hodgkins

and his two assistants, Symmes and Tomlyn, set out northward
to Newton Lane near Manchester, where on August 14, 1589,
they were arrested as they were beginning work on *More worke
for Cooper*.

Hearing of their arrest, Sharpe asked Penry "what Bookes they
were then in printing." Penry replied that "he thought, they were
printing the *Epistle* to *More Worke for the Cooper*." Then when
Sharpe with trepidation inquired "what Lettre [type] they had,"
Penry audaciously told him that "they had his own Letter, that
Martin Junior and *Martin Senior* were printed withall." [5] Sharpe
earlier had been disturbed by the use of the same type in the two
Martinist tracts and in Penry's *Supplication*.[6] Now, appalled at the
thought of discovery, Sharpe again warned Penry "that both he
and this place [Wolston] would be more notoriously descryed."
As before, Penry brushed aside Sharpe's fears, this time by telling
him that the captive printers would confess that they had likewise
printed the last two published tracts in the same place, that is,
Newton Lane.[7] After Hodgkins was captured, Sharpe himself was
arrested and questioned. His deposition before his examiners ends
with the eloquent paragraph already quoted, in which he frankly
designates Penry as the author of "all the said books of Martin."

But the final curtain had not yet fallen on this drama. As might
be gathered from Sharpe's increasing uncertainty concerning
Hodgkins' whereabouts, Hodgkins and his men were aware of
much activity of which Sharpe knew nothing. It almost seems as
if Sharpe's concern for the good opinion of Sir Christopher Hatton
had lessened Penry's confidence in him and had removed him to
the outer circle where he had been hovering prior to the appearance of *Hay any worke for Cooper*. In his place as Penry's con-
fidant now appears Job Throckmorton, lord of Haseley Manor,
member of Parliament, and staunch Puritan, whom Pierce designates "the chief known person in connection with the Marprelate
tracts." [8] In spite of the fact that his name nowhere appears in
Sharpe's testimony, he is accused by Sutcliffe after Penry's execu-

tion: "Next to Penry that was hanged for libelling against the State, Master Throkmorton deserveth the first place." [9] Since Sutcliffe's distortion of the facts has elsewhere been pointed out,[10] I shall, for the present, pass over later arguments stemming from Sutcliffe's stinging indictment of Throckmorton's denial of guilt and shall return as before to the depositions dated between 1588 and 1590, when the excitement was at its height.

According to Hodgkins, when Newman employed him to leave London and to go into the country to print, Newman gave him a letter for Penry, "then lying at Master Throckmortons Howse." Arriving there, where he stayed overnight and until noon the next day, he received a second letter *from Penry himself* introducing him to Mrs. Wigston, at whose house he was to work.[11] At the same time Penry told him that the manuscript to be printed would "come to his hands." Coincidentally, *"in the company of Penry, walking with him* on the way from Master Throckmortons toward Warwick . . . about one birdebowe shot from the said Master Throckmortons House" he "saw lying before him in ye way a Roll of paper wrapped up together" and, as he inferred, "layd there of purpose by some other . . . against" the printer "should come that way," which "Roll" turned out to be nothing else but the manuscript of *Martin Junior.*[12] The manuscript of *Martin Senior* he received *"at Penrys hands,* in the Howse of Master Weekston." [13] Both tracts were printed with the press and letters that Hodgkins found waiting for him at Mrs. Wigston's, identified by Sharpe as Penry's. Furthermore, Sharpe testifies that "the Corrector of these two Bookes," he thinks, "to be Master Penry who was there diuerse tymes by starts [*at intervals*], at Master Wigstons." [14]

As has been explained, Hodgkins' two assistants, Tomlyn and Symmes, were almost completely in the dark as to what was going on. They knew Penry only as "Harrison" and never discovered Throckmorton's identity until after everything was over. Yet Symmes's deposition, wrung from him with torture, is considered most important by those scholars who identify Throckmorton as Martin. Symmes hesitantly admits that he "thinketh" Throckmorton delivered to the printers all except one or two sheets of *Martin Junior*. To this self-admitted conjecture he adds that when Hodgkins handed him the manuscript of *Martin Senior*, he perceived that "this copy was of the same hand writinge wth the former [*Martin Junior*]." Putting together these two unrelated facts—the delivery of the first manuscript by someone that might have been Throckmorton and the similarity in handwriting—he confesses that he "thinketh that m^r Throckmort[on] was the author of it [*Martin Senior*]." From this inference he proceeds to a second, equally illogical. Having observed the same handwriting in *More worke for Cooper* as in *Martins Junior* and *Senior*, he concludes that Throckmorton was the author of all three manuscripts.[15]

While the printing was proceeding at Mrs. Wigston's, an episode occurred that Sutcliffe and his disciples have advanced as certain proof of Throckmorton's authorship of the Martinist tracts. "Coming to the place where the books were printed," writes Sutcliffe, "he [Throckmorton] corrected certain faults: and shewed Simmes how he should read certain places interlined." [16] Actually, according to the depositions edited by Arber and Pierce, Symmes deposed that "Master Throckmorton coming *with Penry* to the Printers in Master Weekstons Howse, and looking upon the written Copy, which was interlined in diverse places, he asked Symmes, if he could read the same places, pointing him unto them, among which [there] being two wherein Symmes doubted, the said Master Throckmorton did presently read them distinctly and plainly, and found fault with the orthography." Symmes also "ouerh[e]ard Master Throckmorton askinge Hodgkins softly in the eare, whether the same Symmes and Tomlyn were good workemen and able to serve the tourne." [17]

In Symmes's statement are two facts obviously incompatible with Sutcliffe's interpretation. In the first place, Throckmorton's ability to read the interlined passages may be interpreted in either of two ways. On the one hand, he may have felt that he was so familiar with Penry's handwriting that he could read it for the printers, or on the other, he may have been reading additions or revisions that he himself had interpolated. Neither possibility points toward his authorship of the two pamphlets in their entirety. Second, the statement that Throckmorton criticized the spelling definitely indicates that he was not the original author. A writer may apologize for, but hardly "find fault with," his own spelling. The logical interpretation, it seems to me, would be that Throckmorton, like Udall and perhaps, to some extent, Waldegrave, was merely acting as a "corrector," or proof reader, for Penry. Moreover, Symmes' statement that he overheard Throckmorton inquiring about the skill of Hodgkins' assistants suggests not authorship but rather Throckmorton's capacity as co-manager of the enterprise.

Justifying this interpretation of Throckmorton's behavior is Hodgkins' testimony that the handwriting of *Martins Junior* and *Senior* and *More worke for Cooper* was "the same or very like to the hande *where with Penry corrected the print* [i.e., the proofs]," and that furthermore, when Symmes questioned the logic of a passage Penry crossed it out and inserted a correction.[18] And in the deposition discovered by Pierce, Symmes himself testifies that "when 'martin Senior' was in printinge," he, "p[er]using the copy found falt wth somethings in it towards the end as being written wthout sense"; whereupon Hodgkins took it to Penry, who "strooke owt certayne lines and interlined that wch should be supplied."[19]

As for the manuscript on which Hodgkins and his men were working when they were captured, *More worke for Cooper*, Hodgkins states that Penry and Newman planned it so that the manuscript would "by agreement" be "let fall in a voyd [empty] Chamber in Master Weekstons Howse *by the said Penry* and Newman," where Hodgkins would find it.[20] According to the "summary of the information in the hands of the Queen's Government as to the Martinists on the 22nd September 1589," as reprinted by Arber, the handwriting in this manuscript seemed to be that of two different writers. Consequently the authorities assumed that one was "Penryes, and the other his mans hande [writing]; as by a collation of such their writinges (as haue bene heretofore taken) may appeare." [21] Oddly enough, Peel observes that Penry in his Notebook uses three distinctly different styles of handwriting. Though Peel does not overlook the possibility that one of these might be that of "Penry's man" or "Penry's scribe," he inclines toward the opinion of those "experts" who, he writes, "rule that Penry may have used all three forms." [22] The "rule" of these "experts" certainly may likewise apply to the different styles of handwriting in the manuscript of *More worke for Cooper.*

Finally, it was Penry, not Throckmorton, who paid Hodgkins his wages and assured Symmes and Tomlyn that they would be properly paid on condition that "they would be faythfull unto Hodgkins." After Hodgkins and his men left Wolston Priory for Newton Lane, they had printed only "about a Six Quires of one side" when they were arrested by the officers of the Earl of Derby.[23] Thus ends that section of the plot provided by the sworn testimony given by the unfortunate suspects in the Marprelate affair.

After the capture and imprisonment of Hodgkins and his assistants on August 14, 1589, the final Martinist pamphlet, the *Protestation,* appeared. Indicative of McKerrow's opinion as to the identity of Martin, the editor of Nashe writes that "Penry managed to get one more book printed, the *Protestation of Martin Marprelate.*" [24] In spite of Sutcliffe's statement, as quoted by Arber, that it "was printed with ink sent by James Meddows to Throkmorton's house, and that not without his privity," [25] McKerrow believes that since "we hear nothing, however, of the press being transferred thither," it is "at least equally likely that it was printed at Wolston," along with *Martins Junior* and *Senior.*[26]

Further strengthening the likelihood of Penry's authorship of the *Protestation* is the fact that it is printed with the same type as that used in the two previous Martinist tracts and also in Penry's *Appellation* and *M. Some laid open in his coulers,* almost certainly by Penry, both of which will be discussed in later chapters.

Only by discarding this impressive body of evidence in favor of the "lost documents" that Arber imagines were seen by Sutcliffe [27] can we even pretend that Job Throckmorton or anyone except Penry could have remained concealed from everyone connected in any way with the Martinist activity from the spring of 1588 to the end of 1589, when Throckmorton's name first appears in the depositions. And in view of the glaring inconsistencies in the accusations of Sutcliffe, it seems unwise to substitute this latecomer into the Marprelate Controversy for Henry Sharpe, who was on hand almost from the start. Indeed, even Pierce, while accepting Sutcliffe's conclusions, nevertheless questions his reliability as a witness: "Sutcliffe is not beyond making assertions for which he possesses no evidence, and which we know from other sources to be erroneous." [28] On the contrary, while criticizing Sharpe as a busybody, a gossip, and an informer, Pierce never seems to doubt the validity of his testimony. Accordingly, when all the events in the confused plot are arranged in proper chronological sequence, it becomes evident that the only man whose name consistently appears throughout is John Penry.

Chapter XI

Penry's Hand in the Martinist Tracts

Not only does all the external evidence presented by the various suspects questioned by the Government point toward Penry as the author of the seven Martinist tracts, but the content of the tracts also reflects the spiritual turmoil, either expressed or implied, on almost every page of his signed writings during this period. In spite of his intense dissatisfaction with the slowness of the Puritans to effect their desired reforms, all seven tracts are still Puritan in doctrine. After delivering the opening blast in the *Epistle*, Martin, in his *Epitome*, aligns himself with his "brethren the puritans" rather than with the extreme nonconformists advocating separatism. The theological content of these tracts is of little importance. What there is merely restates Cartwright's doctrines. But in their outspoken belligerence they are separatist in spirit; this paradox weights their significance, not only in Penry's career but also in the history of Protestant controversy in England.

In the second and more serious of the two opening pamphlets, the *Epitome*, Martin reiterates the fundamental difference between his own presbyterian stand and that of the episcopalians, that is, "whether the externall gouernement of the Church of Christ be a thing so prescribed by the Lorde in the new testament as it is not lawfull for any man to alter the same any more then it was lawfull to alter ye form of regiment prescribed under the law in the old testamēt" [1]—that form, of course, being understood to be presbyterian. Martin likewise accepts the two Puritan corollaries to this postulate regarding church government: the prince has no right to change the offices and officers thus ordained, and contrariwise, a church governor cannot wield civil power. In demanding the presbyterian officers—elder, minister, doctor, and deacon—Martin, like Cartwright, cites scriptural authority for each. Repeating his charge made in the *Epistle,* that all bishops are "pettie popes & pettie Antichristes," [2] he maintains that they have no scriptural counterparts. [3] In his subsequent pamphlets he merely repeats these charges and in typically Puritan phrases condemns the traditional episcopalian practices of permitting the income from some parishes to go to nonresident clergymen or to laymen.

In his manner of presenting his religious doctrines, however, Martin moves away from the conventional style of the Puritan pamphleteer and aligns himself with the separatists, like Browne and Harrison, who had given up the idea of effecting reformation through peaceful means. His first pamphlet mainly consists of satirical anecdotes intended to show the worldliness and venality of the bishops. These anecdotes are filled with puns and epithets, the like of which had never before appeared in religious controversy. With skillful use of alliteration he adds to the rhetorical effect of his style: "right poysond [puissant] persecuting & terrible priests," "proud popish, presumptuous, profane, paultrie, pestilent, and pernicious prelates." Especially noteworthy in his style is his playful mispronunciation of words for comic effect: "conspiration house" for convocation house, "his grace Doctor turnecoats (Perne I shoulde saye) scholler," "Mas Deane," "Mas Doctor," and "masse D." for Master Dean or Doctor Bridges, whom he twits of "popery," "his gracelesnes of Cant." for his grace the Archbishop of Canterbury.

In the *Epistle,* in a pattern recognized by his contemporaries to be a successful imitation of the patter of the noted clown Dick

Tarleton, Martin in rapid succession tells one shocking story after another, each denigrating a member of the episcopalian hierarchy. First come a series of allusions to Richard Cosin's allegedly unlearned *Answer to the Abstract* and to his negligence in failing to respond to Fenner's *Counter-poyson,* then to Bishop Elmer's letter to the Archdeacon of Essex forbidding public fasts, then to Dr. Copcot's silence after the Puritan confutation of his sermon, which, in turn, reminds him that Whitgift, too, is playing the coward in not answering Cartwright's last two *Replies.* Next he quotes a favorite oath of "John of London," Bishop Elmer. Whereupon he interrupts his raillery with a serious bit of Puritan propaganda regarding the equality of ministers.

In order not to lose for a moment the interest of his reader, Martin immediately resumes with a scandalous story of some thieves who had been caught robbing cloth from the dyers in Thames Street and had been brought before Elmer, who claimed the cloth as having been stolen in his diocese, even though one of the thieves confessed whose cloth it really was. This story concludes with a reference to Mistress Margaret Lawson, the "shrew at Pauls gate," who told Elmer to throw himself at the Queen's feet and admit that he was "unsaury salt," a typical Puritan epithet for any clergyman of the Church of England. Mentioning Mrs. Lawson's name recalls to Martin that Whitgift had threatened to send her to Bridewell for showing "the good father D. Perne a way how to get his name out of the booke of Martyrs where the turnecoat is canonized for burning Bucers bones." From this first reference onward Perne's name frequently recurs in the Martinist tracts, occasionally, as here, accompanied with a taunt at his recantation under Queen Mary. Throughout the pamphlet, too, Martin constantly returns to Elmer, "Dumbe John of London," who, he asserts, made a "dumb minister" out of "the porter of his gate," forced his ministers to subscribe against their will, bribed a minister to wear a surplice at Easter, cut down the elms at Fulham (for which he was supposed to have earned for himself the title of "marelme"), bowled on Sunday, refused to pay a debt of nineteen pounds owed the estate of a dead grocer, and fought with his son-in-law, who gave him a bloody nose.[4]

Not these scurrilous tales, which have been paraphrased in every account of the Controversy,[5] but rather the striking similarities between the seven tracts and Penry's acknowledged writings are our chief concern in this study. For example, the principal target of Martin's satirical pen, especially in the first two pamphlets, is Bridges, whose *Defence of the Government Established* was particularly offensive to Penry. The title of the *Epistle* begins with what amounts to a comic dedication to the Dean: "Oh read ouer D. Iohn Bridges for it is a worthy worke." Martin's references to Bridges himself are little short of insulting: "I haue heard som cleargie men say that M. Bridges was a verie patch and a duns when he was in Cambridg"; in addition, he is a papist, a traitor, a nonresident, a card player, and a blasphemer. His "bookes seeme to proceede from the braynes of a woodcocke as hauing neyther wit nor learning." Like Penry in his distaste for Bridges' literary style, Martin ridicules the long involved sentences in the *Defence of the Government Established* and accuses its author of accepting "other mens helpes." Perhaps, suggests Martin, Dr. Perne may have collaborated with the good Dean.

Another resemblance between the *Epistle* and Penry's *Exhortation* is the frequent occurrence of the syllogism. In Penry's set of fifty-three syllogisms in his addition to the second edition of the *Exhortation* he was deadly serious, but Martin deftly adds an absurd conclusion to each of his in order to cast ridicule on his opponents. Again like Penry, he repeatedly refers to the bishops as the "Bb." as though suggesting certain derogatory epithets beginning with that letter. Also like Penry—and no other contemporary—he pretends to believe that the Queen is unaware of the bishops' perfidy.[6]

Just as Penry expresses resentment at Whitgift's harsh treatment of his *Aequity* while at the same time the Archbishop was favoring the publication of a Catholic treatise in Welsh, so Martin accuses Whitgift of favoring "knaue Thackwell the printer which printed popishe and trayterous welshe bookes in Wales." [7] Who in England except Penry, we may parenthetically ask, would be aware of, or could read, Welsh Catholic treatises? Martin, too, recounts the explicit details of Penry's trial before Whitgift and the High Commission, even to the very names that the archbishop hurled at him: "boy, knaue, varlet, slanderer, libeller, lewde boy, lewd slaunderer, &c." Immediately after this list of epithets, as if aware that his accurate reporting of a secret trial might give him away, he inserts in a parenthesis a somewhat unconvincing explanation for his omniscience: "This is true for I haue seene the notes of their conference."

In the light of these resemblances between the *Epistle* and Penry's *Exhortation* we can understand the numerous slighting remarks directed by Martin at Penry's legendary foe, Dr. Perne, Master of Peterhouse College while Penry was in Cambridge [8]; otherwise, it would be incomprehensible why Perne, who had never written against the Puritans and who held no position of unusual prominence in the Church, should even be mentioned in this context.

Like the *Epistle*, the *Epitome* is dedicated to Bridges with the same title, "Oh read ouer D. Iohn Bridges for it is worthy worke: Or an epitome of the fyrste Booke of that right worshipfull volume written against the Puritanes in the defence of the noble cleargie by as worshipfull a prieste Iohn Bridges, Presbyter, Priest, or elder, doctor of Diuilitie and Deane of Sarum." As might be anticipated, then, he continues to scoff at the size and style of Bridges' *Defence of the Government Established*. He complains about its roughness: "There be not 3. whole periods for euery page in the book that is not graced with a verie faire and visible solacism." He ridicules its long translated passages of equally long quotations from Latin authorities. With mock affection he protests, "Thou knowest not how I loue thee for thy wit & learning sake, brother Iohn," and then parenthetically, as if *sotto voce*, "(as for thy godlines I might cary it in mine eye and see neuer a whit the worse)."

In this second pamphlet, while spicy anecdotes and personal abuse continue to be intermingled with the Puritan criticism of the episcopacy, a new note may be heard. Martin has discovered that his attacks on the bishops have offended some leading Puritans because, as they complain, he is "to open." His rejoinder to his critics provides a clue as to why neither John Penry nor John Udall nor any other Puritan would consider it perjury to deny that he was Martin, whether he was or not. The author of the Martinist tracts impersonally considers himself the mouthpiece of Puritan dissent when he urges everyone of his fellow Puritans to admit the responsibility for the authorship of the tracts: "Let them say that the hottest of you hath made Martin and that the rest of you were consenting there vnto and so go to our magistrates and say, lo, such and such of our puritans haue vnder the name of Martin written against your lawes: and so call you in and put you to your othes whether you made Martin or no." The result will be, continues Martin, that the bishops will identify as Martin anyone who "will refuse to take an othe against the lawe of the land," even though he is actually protesting against the oath rather than tacitly admitting himself to be Martin.

Further evidence of Penry's increasing doubt as to the validity of the sacraments of the Church of England appears in Martin's insistence that salvation depends on justifying faith, rather than on the sacraments.[9] It is as though Penry's indecision, expressed in the various editions of the *Exhortation* and in his *Defence of that which hath bin written in the questions of the ignorant ministerie,* all written during 1588 along with the first two Martinist tracts, is here being further rationalized. Finally, it may be recalled that Penry in his *Supplication,* published two or three months after the *Epitome,* changed the direction of his appeal from the Queen's Privy Council, as it had originally appeared in the second edition of the *Exhortation,* to the Parliament. Similarly, Martin, employing Penry's trick, as described by Peel, of "putting into the mouths of others opinions with which he had some sympathy," [10] quotes Bishop Elmer as his authority for defying the Queen: "Prechers must not be afraid to rebuke the proudest, yea kings and Queenes." [11] Martin even advises Parliament, if necessary, to overrule the Queen.

The third Martinist publication, the broadside *Minerall Conclusions,* presents a satirical outline, or parody, of the episcopalian defense. First stating the argument, Martin then names the particular bishop or minister who supposedly advanced it. For example, the thirtieth statement "that it is the general disease of Englishmen to haue in admiration the persons & states of other countries and to loath their owne," he attributes to "father Thomas [Bishop Cooper] of Eastmeane, *alias* profane T.C." This is only one argument, ridiculous because it is taken out of context, of the many attributed in this publication to Bishop Cooper, whose *Admonition to the People of England,* published a few days earlier, in January, 1589, was to be the butt of Martin's next pamphlet *Hay any worke for Cooper.* Perhaps, indeed, the reason for bringing out only a single sheet was that Martin was already working on his extended reply to Cooper. External evidence linking the *Minerall Conclusions* with Penry is his conversation with Sharpe, earlier mentioned in reference to the depositions, in which Penry had referred to a forthcoming "Boke against Doctor Some." Thus aware that a reply to Some was on Penry's mind, Sharpe deposed that upon reading the printed broadside he began to suspect Penry's hand in it because of certain "taunts against Doctor Some," which were not in the manuscript as originally read to him by Penry.[12]

The next Martinist tract also contains a possible allusion to Penry's reply to Some. After the publication of the *Epitome* the main body of Puritans, including Cartwright, loudly (whether sincerely or not remains a moot point) expressed their disapproval of Martin. Fortunately for Bridges and, at least temporarily, for Some, the publication of Bishop Cooper's *Admonition to the People of England,* intended as a rebuke and silencer for Martin, took the heat off the two Doctors and put it instead on the Bishop. Little did Cooper dream how many details of his private life were in the Puritan files. Not only does Martin twit him for playing cards and gambling, but in commenting on Cooper's criticism of the outspoken Puritan Mrs. Lawson he even levels at the bishop the more cruel charge of cuckoldry: "Concerning Mistresse Lawson, profane T.C., is it not lawfull for her to go to Lambeth by water to accompanie a preachers wife going also (as commonly godly matrons in London do) with her man: No, saith T.C., I doe not like this in women. Tushe, man, Thomas Lawson is not Thomas Cooper, he has no such cause to doubt of Dame Lawsons going without her husbande *as the bishop of Winchester hath had of dame Coopers gadding.*" This bit of sarcasm he concludes with a promise that is more like a threat: "But more worke for Cooper will say more for Mistresse Lawson." [18] The important fact in Martin's closing remark in its relationship to Penry is not the insinuation of Mrs. Cooper's infidelity but rather Martin's foreknowledge of the contents of the pamphlet *More worke for Cooper,* as yet unpublished and perhaps even uncomposed, which, according to government records was written by Penry [14] and apparently was to be his first reply "at length" to Dr. Some.

Another trace of Penry's hand in this fourth publication is Martin's defense of his use of invective as a means of accelerating the presbyterian reform:

I am not disposed to iest in this serious matter. I am called Martin Marprelat. There be many that greatly dislike of my doinges. I may haue my wants I know. For I am a man. But my course I knowe to be orderly and lawfull. I sawe the cause of Christs gouernment and of the Bishops Antichristian dealing to be hidden. The most part of men could not be gotten to read any thing written in the defence of the on and against the other. *I bethought mee therefore of a way whereby men might be drawne to do both perceiuing the humors of men in these times (especially of those that are in any place) to be giuen to mirth. I tooke that course. I might lawfully do it. I for iesting is lawful by circumstances euen in the greatest matters.* The circumstances of time, place, and persons urged me thereunto. I neuer profaned the word in any iest. Other mirth I used as a couert wherein I would bring the truth into light. The Lord being the authour both of mirth and grauitie, is it not lawful in it selfe for the trueth to use eyther of these wayes when the circumstances do make it lawful? My purpose was and is to do good.[15]

Aimed at disarming Puritan criticism, these words also express the disillusionment of a man who in all sincerity has attempted to advance the cause of reformation and now finds himself repudiated by the men whom he most admires—even the great "T.C.," whose doctrines he is promulgating.

But without wasting any more compassion on a zealot whose conviction of the righteousness of his cause could easily surmount personal unpopularity, we submit the italicized passage in his apology as the most important evidence for Penry's authorship of this pamphlet—and since it is generally agreed that all the Martinist tracts were the product of the same pen, of the other six as well. This undoubtedly is the passage to which Sharpe referred when he stated that while binding the copies of *Hay any worke for Cooper* he had come across the "same reason" for the propriety of jesting in religious matters that Penry himself had earlier given when Sharpe, accusing him of being Martin, questioned him on the subject. As a result, Sharpe, whose observations always deserve consideration since he was at the scene, concluded that this fourth tract was "of Master Penrys makeing." [16]

After defending his "course," Martin admits his unpopularity among his fellow Puritans, but he warns the authorities, "The day that you hange Martin assure yourselues there wil 20. Martins spring in my place." Then, with a reckless daring in decided contrast with the moderation of Puritans like Cartwright, Travers, or Fenner, but quite in keeping with the impassioned statements of Penry, who had already suggested that Parliament might overrule a Tudor monarch, Martin actually takes the responsibility for all four pamphlets on himself and even names Penry among the suspects: "I am alone. No man vnder heauen is priuy or hath bin priuie vnto my writings against you, I vsed the aduise of non therein. You haue and do suspect diuers, as master Pagett, master Wiggington, master Udall, & master Penri, &c. to make Martin. If they cannot cleare their selues their sillinesse is pitifull and they are worthy to beare Martins punishment." [17] What he considers as pusillanimity in the Puritan leaders is evidently rankling in his heart and adding to his disapproval of their willingness to tarry for the magistrate.

Indicative of a common printer—and certainly not ruling out the possibility of common authorship—the remaining three Martinist tracts are set up from the same type as that used in Penry's *Exhortation* (second and third editions), his *Supplication*, his *Appellation*, and the two anonymous tracts *M. Some laid open in his coulers* and *A Dialogue wherein is plainly laide open*, both of which in style and content closely resemble the Martinist tracts.[18] The fifth Martinist publication, the *Theses Martinianae* or *Martin Junior*, is introduced by a short prologue and concludes with an epilogue supposedly written by Martin's son after the disappearance of his father, whose "vnperfect papers" have been assembled into this tract as his "*cygneam cantionem* viz. his farewell to bookemaking." In Martin's own "preface" he admits his uncertainty as to the wisdom of his "course," though he believes that "those whom foolishly men call Puritanes" approve of the "matter" in his writings but not of their "forme." In the "epilogue" Martin Junior defends his father's "course" by pointing out that in attack-

ing the bishops his father is merely following such eminent reformers as "M. Tindall, M. Frith, M. Barnes, M. Hooper, M.
Knox, M. Lampert, &c. which were the first planters of the Gospell amongst vs," all of whose writings were in their own time
sanctioned by royal permission.

In addition to the author's sense of personal injury because of
Puritan disapproval—an attitude of mind to be anticipated in a
man already inclining toward separatism—these last three tracts
exhibit several specific marks of Penry's hand. First, Martin Junior
mimics Dr. Some's manner of writing, "my reason is" [19]—an indication of the author's hostility toward Penry's enemy. He also
promises to publish *More worke for Cooper*, the half-printed manuscript, which, when shortly thereafter captured by the Queen's
officers, was found to contain many slurs on Some's character and
on the basis of handwriting was attributed to Penry.[20]

The most convincing evidence for Penry's authorship of *Martin
Junior*, however, is Martin's foreknowledge of how Penry was
to convey the manuscript of this tract into the printer's hands.
Martin Junior writes that it was "taken vp (together with certaine
other papers) besides a bush, where it had dropped from some
body passing by that way." [21] It is as though while composing the
tract he had had a premonition—call it inspiration, if you will—
as to how it would be delivered *by Penry* to the printer. For it was
John Hodgkins, as we have recounted, who testified that while
he was walking toward Warwick *with Penry* he "saw lying before him in ye way a Roll of paper wrapped up together, and layd
there of purpose by some other . . . against" his coming that
way, "which Roll" turned out to be "the Copie [*manuscript*] of
Theses Martinianae, otherwise called *Martin Junior*." [22]

The next Martinist tract, the *Just Censure* or *Martin Senior*,
was purportedly written by Martin Junior's elder brother, Martin
Senior, "sonne and heire vnto the renowmed Martin Marprelate
the Great," who desires to rebuke "the rash and vndiscreete headines of the foolish youth." With a desperate courage equaled only

by that displayed in Penry's advice, accompanied by thinly veiled threats, first to the Privy Council in his *Exhortation* and then to the Parliament in his *Supplication,* Martin Senior feigns a speech supposedly made by Whitgift to the pursuivants ordered to search for Martin, in which he daringly designates Penry as Martin: "Or, haue you diligently soght mee out Waldegraue the Printer, Newman the Cobler, Sharpe the booke binder of Northampton, and *that seditious Welch man Penry, who you shall see will prooue the Author of* all these libelles." Then, after taking this terrific gamble that naming these men, all of whom later were proved beyond question of a doubt to be the ringleaders in the conspiracy, would put the pursuivants off the trail, Martin Senior adds another statement, deliberately misleading *and likewise false:* "Marke whether those poore men before named, to wit, Penry, Sharpe, Walde graue, Newman, &c. with many other good men, *who I dare sware for them, did neuer medle nor make at anie time, with the metropoliticall writings of our renowmed father,* shal not be now as hotlie pursued after, as euer they were."

If, in spite of the fiction of Martin's two sons, the style of this pamphlet were not enough to indicate its common authorship with Martin's earlier writings, several other parallels may be noted; for example, another reference to *More worke for Cooper,* which Martin intends to write *but which Penry eventually wrote,* the attack on Whitgift as "the Canturburie Caiphas" and "no Minister at all in the church of God," the mock address supposedly delivered by the archbishop to the pursuivants, the bitter condemnation of old Dr. Perne as "a persecutour, an atheist, an hypocrite, and a dissembler" merely for being Whitgift's friend, and the suggestion that Dr. Some become Bridges' successor "to reade the *starue-vs* [*sic*] booke" in the archbishop's "Chappel at Lambeth." All of these resemblances point directly at the man who wrote the first four Martinist tracts—namely, John Penry—as author.

Finally, Martin Senior bitterly blames the ministers for not being "more forward in casting off these oure popes." He urges them to petition the Queen for a learned ministry, for removing "al vnlawful and sinful callings" from the church, for placing in the church only those offices and officers "which the Lorde Christ Iesus hath set downe in his worde," and for a "quiet meeting" concerning the government and ceremonies of the church "betweene our Prelates, and those learned men, which are contrary minded vnto them" [23]—in short, the entire presbyterian platform for reforming the Church of England.

A few days after the publication of *Martin Senior* Penry found himself in great trouble. His printer Hodgkins and Hodgkins' two assistants were caught in the act of printing *More worke for Cooper,* which was identified as Penry's because of the similarity in handwriting between it and Penry's known writings and also because "the stile of it and the spiritt of the man (*where he is out of his scoffinge veyne*) doth alltogether resemble such his writinges, as he hath published with his name to them." This half-printed manuscript apparently was Penry's first long answer to Some, for it is described by those who seized it as "very longe and most bitter and virulent against him [Some] and his bookes." On the way to prison, however, Hodgkins told his two helpers that there still remained "another parte of *More Worke for the Cowper,* which should serve them to print . . . and the other parte was almoste as big again." [24]

Not in the least disheartened by his ill fortune Penry succeeded in publishing the final Martinist tract, *The Protestation,*[25] in which was announced the capture of the printers and their press, along with a warning to the High Commission that torturing these unfortunate men would not settle their differences. After offering to appear in public disputation with the bishops, Martin alludes to "M. Fenners, & *M. Penries syllogismes,* whereby Doctor Bridges his booke is confuted, and the cause of reformation vnanswerably prooued." [26] In a vain attempt to interpret this allusion to "M. Penries syllogismes," Pierce writes, "Of the works ascribed to Penry, none seem to answer Martin's description." Then he is struck by an alarming possibility that would entirely destroy his theory that Throckmorton was Martin: "Of course, it is just conceivable that Martin hints that Penry contributed the Syllogisms which appeared in the earlier Marprelate tracts!" But with a flat denial, "It is a suggestion which I dismiss," he refuses to examine the possibility that he has conjured up; nor does he give any reason for his denial.[27] If, however, he had examined the second edition of the *Exhortation* at the University of Wales and the third edition at the British Museum, he would have found in them Penry's fifty-three syllogisms against the "dumb ministers," to which Martin undoubtedly refers.

Of course, it is not entirely impossible that Penry, realizing that he is about to be reported to the authorities, in the *Protestation* is boldly taking unto himself credit for writing Martin's *Epistle* and *Epitome,* both expressly directed at Bridges and filled with syllogisms which Martin boasts are his own.[28] If this conjecture were correct, then when Martin distinguishes between "M. Penries syllogismes" and "Master Martin Marprelates writings," he may be giving another clue as to the attitude of the Martinists toward their hoax. The syllogisms in the tracts were indeed Penry's, whereas the anecdotes came from the files that Field had ordered destroyed at his death but that instead were preserved by John Udall.[29] In the eyes of the Martinists, therefore, Martin would be not a man but rather the personification of nonconformist zeal; hence, his statement that "Martin had neyther wife nor childe in all his life," which he admits "may seeme strange vnto many," and has indeed perplexed Pierce and Penry's other biographers, would no longer appear inconsistent with the rest of the evidence sustaining Penry's authorship.

To this literary fiction, as if as an afterthought to his anticipation of his own capture, he adds the following ominous prediction: "It may be . . . I may be maried, & that ere it be long. . . . But whensoeuer I am maried, it would do me good at the heart, to see a dozen of good and honest L. bishops daunce at my wedding.[30] Other remarks in this tract made clear in the light of Penry's probable authorship are Martin's protest that he writes in his "pleasant vein" only in order to deliver the church of God from episcopalian bondage—an echo of Penry's defense of Martin's jesting when questioned by Sharpe,[31] also his account of the contents of *More worke for Cooper,* but most important of all, his tacit admission that he has about decided to abandon Puritanism. Martinism, he explains, acknowledges no sect and defies all enemies of God and the Queen: "To be a right Martiniste indeede, is to bee neither Browniste, Cooperist, Lambethist, Schismatike, Papist, atheist, traytor, nor yet L. byshop; but one that is at defyaunce with all men; whether he bee French, Ducth [*sic*], Spanish, Catercap, pope or popeling, so far forth as he is an enimy to God and her Maiestie."

With a final taunt at those Puritans who have criticized his writings and *with a last scornful blast at "Chaplain Some,"* [32] Martin winds up the most cleverly written series of pamphlets in the dispute between the nonconformists and the Church of England.

Chapter XII

Penry's Supplication

During the summer of 1588, while Penry was guiding through Waldegrave's press his *Defence of that which hath bin written in the questions of the ignorant ministerie*, his *ad interim* reply to Dr. Some, he also was engaged in the preparation of the first Martinist pamphlet, the *Epistle*. For the next several months his itinerant presses were being moved, always one jump ahead of the pursuivants, from Mrs. Crane's house at East Molesey to Sir Richard Knightley's at Fawsley, from there for hiding at Sir Richard's farmhouse at Norton, thence to the residence of Master Hales at White Friars, and finally to Mrs. Wigston's at Wolston Priory. Hence, he was unable to prepare his answer "at length" to Some. Unwilling, however, to abandon his self-appointed position as champion of religion in Wales—an excellent smoke screen behind which he could attack the episcopacy of the Church of England—he therefore decided to revise the second addition to his second edition of the *Exhortation.* This revision, which he entitled *A view of some part of such publike wants & disorders,* came to be known from its running title, *A Supplication vnto the High Covrt of Parliament,* as the *Supplication.*

Stating that "it is no other than the lengthy appendix to the second edition of the *Exhortation,* with slight alterations and amplifications" and that "for the most part both documents agree word for word," Pierce does not undertake the tedious task of collation. Indeed, he points out only the most obvious difference, namely, that the addition to the *Exhortation* is addressed to "your Hh. my Lordes of her maiesties priuy Counsel," whereas the *Supplication* is addressed to "this High Covrt of Parliament." [1] Even this change, however, is significant in that it suggests that Penry is coming to realize that the only hope for the Puritan cause is—to reiterate the phraseology of the leading separatist—"reformation without tarying" or, at least, without "tarying" for the magistrate.

Actually the differences between the two pamphlets are more relevant to an understanding of the Marprelate Controversy than Pierce seems willing to admit. In the first place, as Williams explains, "in the *Supplication* the address is amplified to twice its length, and is prefaced by a long 'Epistle to the Reader.'" [2] This "Epistle" Penry opens as follows: "To all those that faythfully loue the lord Iesus, and vnfainedly desire the flowrishing estate of Sion, together with the vtter razing of whatsoeuer obscureth the perfect beutie therof: & namely, to such of my brethren and countrimen, as the Lord hath enlightened with a true knowledge, the ioy of an vpright and comfortable profession, with the encrease of all other the Lords good graces, be multiplyed in Iesus Christe our Lord." Aware that the previous rejection of his cause by Parliament might generally be considered a deterrent, he nevertheless is making a second attempt "to try whether men will not acknowledge the Gospell." Undecided whether to publish this *Supplication* or to compose "an answere to M. D. Some," who has charged him "of late . . . to be not onely a defender of many blasphemous errors, but also an vnderminer of the ciuill State," Penry has decided upon publication, first, because he fears prevention "of the means to publish it in any due time," and second, because Some in his "booke . . . hath freely graunted . . . the contro[ver]sie" between them, that is, "that vnpreaching ministers are no ministers, and consequently, not to be communicated with." Since Some "so far beyond christian modesty" has charged

Penry "for defending nothing els in these points, but that which his owne writings do publikely witnes against him to be Gods truth," Penry vows that "by the grace of God he shalbe answered, and that very shortly."

Proceeding to his present intention to publish his *Supplication,* he leaves no doubt that he is attacking the Church of England as well as that of Wales. Although his enemies may not desire the knowledge of God's ways "any further then it may stand with the vpholding of the corruptions receaued and mayntained in our Church, by the consent of the State," Penry in strong terms, obviously directed at the episcopacy, rebukes his adversaries: "It is not a matter of dalliance, to withstand the powerfull ordinance of God, *in the gouerment of his Church,* especially when in the steede thereof, the marchandize of shamelesse Babylon is maintayned. It is but folly to fight against the lambe, in the defence of her pleasant things; For the lamb shall ouercome, because he is the king of kings, and the Lord of Lords, and they that are of his side, chosen, and called, and faythfull."

Then with biting insult he attacks the Church of England itself as the "daughter" of the Church of Rome: "Great Babylon the mother, that mighty harlot, being in her ful strength in this land, was not able to stand against him [the Lamb]; what then shall it boote the weake daughter to striue? And let them feare and take heede, who defend the daughters fornication, least they be made partakers of the punishment denounced against them, who committed adultery with the mother."

As if recalling his own painful grilling by the High Commission, he urges Parliament not to fear "many of high place and authoritye" but to remove the episcopacy and in its place to institute the presbyterian system: "All those whosoeuer they be, I do from the bottome of mine heart earnestly beseech, that they would consider, that in dealing for the putting downe of the dumbe ministery, for the abolishing of Nonresidency, and the rooting out of Lord Archb. [certainly not a Welsh ecclesiastical office] and Lord

Bishops, and whatsoeuer els the right hand of the Lord hath not planted: and in seeing that the worde preached, may freely sound thorowout this kingdome, they do thereby nothing els, but desire that the God of heauen and earth may be acknoledged, and accounted worthy alone to rule in his Church within this land."

If Parliament will cast aside fear and work for the "free passage of the Gospell in this land, together with the speedie remoouing of all that hindereth the same," God, "*who hath controlled kings and great Monarches, yea quite ouerthrowne them & their kingdomes,* for denying the free use of his seruice within their dominions," will come to their aid. This veiled threat to the Queen, Penry supplements with scriptural examples of monarchs who have opposed "the cause of God"—"Pharaoh, Achitophel, Senacherib, Haman." [3]

Anyone accepting Pierce's unsupported assertion, "that Penry was not Marprelate is obvious enough to those who are familiar with their respective writings," [4] must reckon with such flaming passages as his indictment of the episcopacy, in which he ceases to plead and commences to threaten:

> The practices of the aduersaries, I mean of our bishops, shew manifestly, that these reliques of cursed Babylon, which they maintayne among vs, must needs go away with a noyse, as the rest was ouerthrowne. They will not yeelde to the trueth, howsoeuer it hath gotten the vpper hande of them. The Lord must vse violence to throw them out, as he did against the caterpillers their forefathers. Reuel. 18.19. [5]

Though until now the bishops have refused "to yeelde a quiet and a brotherly conference or disputation, with those who are contrary minded vnto them" (one of Martin's demands), Penry hopes to obtain one "with our BB. [another "martinizing" device] in Wales," whom he has vowed to overthrow. Thus bringing back his discourse to religion in Wales—the professed target of his displeasure—he closes the "Epistle" to his *Supplication*, written while he was actively engaged in publishing the Martinist tracts and revealing, like them, an increasing impatience with a peaceful reformation of the Church of England.

In addition to the many changes in the main body of the *Supplication* necessitated by Penry's turning to Parliament from the Privy Council are the following pertinent revisions, reported as they appear in the text. First must be listed the innumerable rephrasings for rhetorical effect, all of which reveal a remarkable sensitivity to the subtle nuances of English idiom that one would expect from the master satirist who composed the Martinist tracts.

The second important change appears in the writer's attempt, whether intentional or not, to insert a wedge between Parliament and the Queen, to whom he was apparently directing his earlier version when he addressed it to her Privy Councillors. Although he retains the fiction expressed in the *Exhortation*, namely, that he is "perswaded" that she is being misled "by the vngodly perswasions of some godlesse and irreligious men of the Ecclesiastical state," [6] his address to the Parliament contains the following warning evidently intended for the supreme governor: "I haue by his [the Lord's] grace taken a bonde of my selfe, to seeke the promoting of his honor by al means possible: and in the seeking thereof, to vtter the truth as far as my calling wil permit, without respect of person, time, place, estate, or conditiō of life whatsoeuer; and so to become an vtter enemie vnto all these corruptions [here he tactfully deletes from the original text in the *Exhortation* the parenthesis specifying these "corruptions," "L. Bishops, readers and non-residents I mean," [7] and in its place inserts another parenthesis hinting at criticism of the Queen] (*by what authoritie or person soeuer they be maintained*) whereby his holy seruice is hindered."

Penry also expresses doubt regarding the validity of placing ecclesiastical power in the hands of the civil magistrate: "If you

think it vnlawful for a minister, to ioine the office of a ciuil Magistrate with his ministerie, *and to beare rule and dominion ouer his*
brethren either as a spiritual or temporal Lord . . . thē there is
no question to be made, but that either you wil vtterly raze the
memorie of this wicked and vngodly generation out of the
Churche of Wales, or openly manifest, vnto men and angels,
that you will to the contumelious dishonor of your God, and the
vndoing of his church, countenance and maintaine L. Bishops,
Archdeacons, dumbe ministers, with the rest of that vngodly race,
whose corruptions in youre owne consciences you cannot but
detest." Thus, while slightly tempering the bitterness of his invective in the earlier version, he is none the less clear in expressing
his disapproval of combining civil with ecclesiastical offices as in
the Established Church.

Moreover, maintains Penry, any book or books, such as "this
booke of D. Bridges with al other books of this grieste"—for example, Cooper's *Admonition to the People of England*, which
had just been published in January, 1589—that defend the existing government of the Church of England, which may be altered
"at the pleasure of man" (or "the magistrate's pleasure" as in
the second edition of the *Exhortation*), are "vngodly and pestelent
bookes." For "where is it reuealed," asks Penry, "that the Apostles gaue the ciuill magistrate, when any should be in the Churche,
the commission to abolishe the Presbytery by them established; because there was no christian magistrate in the Churche, as our
aduersaries themselues confesse: but as the worde sayth, established
by the Lorde; and therefore not to be abrogated *by the magistrate*
[this pointed phrase in italics represents an addition to the earlier
address], vntill his pleasure in that poynte be farther knowne[?]" [8]

In spite of this bold attack on the supreme governor, Penry
tones down some of his vivid imagery in his polemics against
Bridges, which to a suspicious ear might resemble Martin's style.
For example, "al other excrements of the Romishe vomit, as non-

residents, &c, remaining in Wales" [9] becomes "al other remnants
of the sacriledge brought into the Churche by that Romishe
strumpet and now remaining in Wales" [10]—the use of the epithet
"Whore of Babylon" for the Roman Church being acceptable
to both sides in this controversy. As might be expected, then,
instead of a long diatribe against Bridges, who by now in the
Epistle and the *Epitome* has been sufficiently belabored, Penry is
content with a few passing references. Since the size of Bridges'
Defence of the Government Established was one of Martin's principal targets, Penry changes his earlier phrase "a booke of 7. shillings price" [11] to the less specific "a large volume." [12] Of even
greater significance as far as authorship is concerned is Penry's
elimination of all references in the original text to an imminent
answer to Bridges soon to appear in print. Finally, instead of including the long rebuttal of Bridges' argument in favor of inequal-
ity of rank among ministers, labeled in the *Exhortation* as a defense
of the power of the papacy,[13] Penry dismisses the Dean with a
marginal note: "If you read D. Bridges pag. 448, line 3 you shall
finde him not far from auouching this point."

In place of Bridges he attacks the four bishops of Wales. It is
as though from his experience in "martinizing" he has learned the
effectiveness of specific reference. In other words, instead of be-
rating bishops in general, he uses the syllogism to prove that "the
Pope of Rome, whose superioritie all sounde hearted christians
doe acknowledge to be intollerable and accursed, hath altogether
as good warrant from the worde for his ecclesiasticall hierarchie"
as the "L. bishops in Wales," whose claim to possess superior
power over other ministers by the consent of the civil magistrate
is no different from that of the Pope himself. Furthermore, Penry
denies that the Queen and Parliament, according to the Word of
God, have the power to appoint bishops.

Completely new is a ten-page attack on the Convocation House,
beginning "In deed if the conuocation house were such as it

ought to be, vz. a sinod of sincere, and godly learned ministers.
. . ." If this condition were to exist, Penry goes on to explain,
then it would be unlawful either for Parliament or the Queen
to interfere with the dictates of this synod, who would be ruling
"according to the word." As he reminds the members of Parliament of their duty, he again seems to forget that he is supposedly
appealing only for his Welsh country men: "You of the honorable
court of parliament are to vnderstand, that the conuocation house
condemneth this cause of christ now in hand, before it be hard:
and that their onely endeuours who are there mett, is howe to
preuent him from bearing rule in the Church by his owne lawes.
For it is well knowne, that all of them haue banded and linked
them selues together, to maintaine the corruptions of our Church,
whereof I haue before spoken: *as the vngodly and popish hierarchie of bishops, the ignorant ministery,* &c."

In marked contrast to the "godly learned ministers" that
would be found in his ideal synod Penry describes two "sorts" of
men now being "admitted vnto the consultation & meeting in the
Convocation House": "First, these whoe by reasō of the superiority
they vsurp over their brethrē, must needs be the chief doers in
that house, how ignorant, vnconscionable, and vnfit for the
gouernment of the Church soeuer they be. *Of which number, are
our Archbb. and L. bishops,* &c. The second sort is of these, who
hauing no interest to be there, in respect of anye superioritie they
beare in the Churche, are therefore elected and chosen to be there
as the clarks of the Convocation house, &c. Thus, contradicting
the sentimental interpretation of Penry's patriotism, the passages
in italics indicate that Penry himself was concerned, not with
religion in Wales alone, but with the Established Church as a
whole.

Lest his readers, like some of his modern apologists, have any
doubt as to the extent of reformation desired, he explicitly includes the entire episcopacy in his attack: "I haue alreadye

shewed, that you ought to be so far from permitting vnto L. Bb. the disposition of any thing behofull vnto the Church of God, as the very names and places should be razed from vnder your gouernment. And wofull experience these 30. full yeares, hath taught vs what a lamentable reformation these men now bring to passe, if they may haue their owne wils." Indeed, in place of the bishops —all bishops, not just the Welsh—Penry hopes that "the Cōuocation house will see, that no calling be henceforth tollerated in the ministerie, but such as the Lord in his worde warranteth to be lawfull," namely, "the officers which he in his word hath appointed may rule in his church" [14]—in other words, the presbyterian orders recognized by all Puritan theologians. Penry then enumerates the crimes of which he insists the Convocation House is guilty, the main one being its support of the episcopalian form of government. His hostility therein parallels Martin's attack in the *Epistle* on the "fickers" of the "confocation house," [15] written while the *Supplication* was being revised for publication.

His attack on the Convocation House ends with a bold warning to the Queen of the dangers ahead for her if she remains obdurate:

Concerning her Maiestie, who (as it is thought) can neuer be induced to aulter the established gouernment, I answere, that if it be made known vnto her, and proued out of the word, that the established regiment of the church, is traiterous against the Maiestie of Iesus Christ, that it confirmeth the popes supremacie. O therfore it is dangerous vnto her crown, that it is besides the commission giuen by our Sauiour Christ vnto his apostles; and therefore accursed, that it sheweth them to be void of all care of religion, who wittingly countenance the same, that *it calleth for the judgments of God against her, and her kingdom,* and then if shee yield not vnto the razing of all sinful callings, out of the church, I will not desire to liue, if this

be thought a matter worthy of death, for a man to be dutyfully
perswaded of his soueraigne.[16]

The threatening note concluding this somewhat incoherent series
of "answers," along with Penry's final reference to his own death,
would suggest that by this time he was fully aware of the dangerous game that he was playing in presuming to dictate to a Tudor
monarch.

Another less important change in the *Supplication* appears in
the addition of a long passage expatiating on the moral lessons
that the English people should have learned from the defeat of
the Spanish Armada, to which in the *Exhortation*, published only
a few weeks before the invasion, he had referred as "the whole
hoast of the Spanyardes (that intend our ouerthrow)." [17] In his
revision he seizes upon the "late deliueraunce" as a judgment
of God and a reminder that the English, like the Israelites of
old, must mend their ways. This self-correction, Penry insists,
must come through the removal of "the corruptions" of the Lord's
service, in other words, the episcopalian liturgy.

Just before ending the *Supplication*, Penry inserts a threat
doubtless intended to be a rhetorical figure in the manner of the
prophets of the Old Testament but, in the light of the recent
national emergency, particularly ominous to the authorities:

I admonish you, in the name of God, to looke vnto your selues,
and thorowly to waigh, what the Lorde by the mouth of
Ezekiel, threatneth against you, if you stil refuse his waies
and mainteine these bypaths of mans inventions in his Church.
You haue feared the sworde, sayth the prophet, and I will bring
a sworde vpon you sayth the Lord Iehouah, and I will bring
you out of the middest of this land, and deliuer you into the
hands of strangers, and execute judgements among you. You
shall fall by the sworde.

Whereupon, craving immunity from legal prosecution, he reminds Parliament of the injury that he had sustained after a similar appeal and concludes with the closing lines of the *Exhortation*, containing another allusion to his possible martyrdom and, finally, prayers for "poore Wales," "her Maiestie," and the members of Parliament.[18]

Chapter XIII

Penry's Appellation *and*
His Answer to Some

Penry with his literary flair was doubtless well aware of the insipid quality of the *Defence of that which hath bin written in the questions of the ignorant ministerie,* his *ad interim* reply to Dr. Some, marred as it was by his own indecision. His next signed writing, the *Supplication,* was certainly not his promised answer "at large" to Some; indeed, his revision of the original addition to the *Exhortation* merely changed the direction of his appeal for presbyterian reform from the narrow circle of the Queen and her Privy Council to the wider audience of the Parliament and the people therein represented. His first long reply to Some was probably the manuscript *More worke for Cooper,* part of which was captured near Manchester by the pursuivants in August, 1589, while it was being printed by the Martinist printers, Hodgkins and his two assistants. Since, as Symmes testifies,[1] Hodgkins admitted concealing almost half of the manuscript before the raid, Penry doubtless still intended to print it. But the last of the seven Martinist tracts, the *Protestation,* demanded priority.

Sufficient internal evidence in the *Protestation* of its close relationship with *More worke for Cooper* appears in Martin's summary of the contents of the captured pamphlet.[2] Still another link between Penry's abortive reply to Some and the Martinist tracts is typographical. From Arber's reprint of the "Summary of the information in the hands of the Queen's Government as to the Martinists on the 22nd September 1589," under the heading "Towchinge the printinge of the two last libells [*Martin Junior* and *Martin Senior*] in a litle Romaine and Italian [italic] letter [type]," appears the following statement: "When his [Waldegrave's] other letters [type] and presse were defaced about Easter was twelve moneth . . . he saved these lettres . . . in a box under his Clo[a]ke, and brought them to Mistris Cranes howse in London, as is allso confessed; *and they are knowen by printers to be Waldegraves letters. . . . And it is the same letter that was taken with Hodgkys.*"

Apparently Penry either had purchased or had been given this type. In a conversation with an apprehensive Sharpe after the capture of the Martinist printers and their half-printed manuscript he frankly admitted that *More worke for Cooper* was being printed with the same type as that used for *Martins Junior* and *Senior*, namely, "his own Letter." [3] Then, after printing the *Protestation*, he learned of Sharpe's arrest. When, on October 15, 1589, the bookbinder of Northampton gave the Lord Chancellor his detailed account of the activities of the Martinist press, in which he specifically named Penry as Martin, Penry himself was well on his way to Scotland with the remainder of the type that had not been turned over to Hodgkins. [4]

In spite of Penry's confident assurance that the captured printers would be able to put the pursuivants off the trail of the Martinist tracts, modern bibliographers vindicate the bookbinder's anxiety that the use of the same type to print *More worke for Cooper* and the two Martinist tracts might well lead to discovery. The typographical similarities, indeed, extend much farther and include not only these three tracts but also the second and third editions of Penry's *Exhortation*, his *Supplication*, his *Appellation*, Martin's *Protestation*, and the so-called "auxiliary" Martinist tract *M. Some laid open in his coulers*. Both Pierce and McKerrow agree that all of these pamphlets were printed from the same type —not always, however, in the same size. Without reservation Pierce states that " a careful examination of the style of the type employed [in "Penry's *Exhortation* (2nd and 3rd editions); *Supplication* (*A Viewe*); *Th'Appellation;* . . . M. Some in his Coulers;* Marprelate's *Theses Martinianae* and *Just Censure;* and Udall's *Demonstration* (main text)"], made with the assistance of an expert at the British Museum, conclusively shows that they were all printed *from one and the same fount of types* . . . known to the printers of the time as Waldegrave's 'letter.' " [5] Adding Martin's *Protestation* to this impressive list, Pierce elsewhere declares that "the type they employed [in the *Protestation*] was that used in the 'Epistle to the Reader' in *Theses*." [6]

Similarly, McKerrow, whose knowledge of Elizabethan typography is unparalleled among modern scholars, maintains that Penry's type, previously "used by Waldegrave at his press in London," consisted of "a Roman letter in four sizes, the two middle sizes being used for text, and being provided with italics, the largest size appearing in titles alone, and the smallest serving generally for marginal notes." This type, according to McKerrow, was used in *Martins Junior* and *Senior*, in the *Supplication*, in *M. Some laid open in his coulers*, in the *Appellation*, and in the *Protestation* (in the last of which he recognizes *only two sizes*). More specifically pointing out that, instead of the customary *i* for *j* as in most Elizabethan printing, "in the *Just Censure* [*Martin Senior*] the lower-case letter *j* is used as at present," McKerrow notes that this peculiarity reappears in several pamphlets either signed by Penry or else attributed to him: "We find the same thing in the *View of public wants* [the *Supplication*], *Some in his colours*, and the *Appellation*, a fact which is not very easy to explain, as it seems to point to their being set up by the same compositor, and this is apparently contradicted by the rest of the evidence." [7] This contradictory "evidence," to which McKerrow refers, which might rule out the possibility of all these pamphlets being set up by the same compositor, concerns the whereabouts of the printer Waldegrave after he left Penry in early April, 1589.

During Easter Week, 1589 (March 30–April 5), Waldegrave told Sharpe that he "wolde no longer meddle or be a dealer" in the Martinist affair. A month later, "about May day," Sharpe asked Penry what had become of the printer and whether they could expect "any more new Bookes" from him. Penry replied "that Wal[de]grave was surely in hand in some corner with the printing of Master Cartwrights *Testament,* that he looked daily for his *Appellation* from him, and that then he sho[u]lde goe in hand with *More worke for Cooper.*"[8] The very vagueness of Penry's answer would suggest that at that time Waldegrave was no longer with him. And in this seemingly evasive, rather than informative, comment, Penry also mentions two of his own pamphlets, not yet published.

From this ambiguous statement, as reported by Sharpe in his deposition, Wilson extracts the meaning that Penry daily looked for his own *Appellation* from Waldegrave—in other words, that this tract had already been written.[9] But since Sharpe's inquiry concerned the whereabouts of Waldegrave and since Penry had replied that Waldegrave was at work on "Master Cartwrights *Testament,*" it would appear that the pronoun "he," immediately following, logically refers to Waldegrave rather than to Penry. Hence, the passage, as earlier construed, should read as follows: "That he [Waldegrave] looked daily for his [Penry's] *Appellation* from him [Penry] and then he [Penry] shoulde goe in hand with [that is, get to work on] *More worke for Cooper.*"

In support of this interpretation, we may first quote Arber's bewildered annotation: "Note, that Waldegrave never *did* print T. Cartwright's *Annotations* on the Rhemish *Testament,* and that Penry's *Appellation* is dated 7th March, 1589," which Arber glosses as March 7, 1590. To Arber's reservation may be added the fact that it was not Waldegrave but Hodgkins, who eventually was captured with the partly printed manuscript of *More worke for Cooper.* Therefore, in the light of Penry's incomplete confidence in Sharpe, who had asked him point-blank about Waldegrave, Penry's vagueness seems intended to conceal, rather than to reveal, what was going on in the inner circle. Again, "not long after, that is a little before Whitsontide [18 May 1589]," while urging Sharpe to "worke about the Press," Penry, without apparently making any direct statement, cleverly conveyed to Sharpe *the impression* of having heard that Waldegrave "was gone to Rochell[e]." [10]

Compounding this confusion concerning Waldegrave, Sutcliffe, in his effort to identify Throckmorton as Martin, makes the following assertion: "The book called *Some in his coulours* was likewise made by J. Throckmorton. That is proved first, by the deposition of Waldegrave that upon his oath testified so much, and at Rochelle where he printed it, spake it openly." [11] From this assertion, for which Sutcliffe offers no proof, Wilson concludes that it is "morally certain" that the *Appellation* was printed by Waldegrave at La Rochelle in the summer of 1589 because of "its typographical likeness in every particular to 'M. Some laid open in his coulers,' which the Marprelate printer *affirmed, under solemn oath,* to have been printed by him at Rochelle." [12] A rereading of Sutcliffe's words, however, shows that in his eagerness to implicate Throckmorton, Sutcliffe declares that Waldegrave testified *not that he printed the pamphlet at La Rochelle* but rather that Throckmorton "made" (that is, composed) it. Enlarging upon Wilson's faulty interpretation, Pierce, in his biography of Penry, also cites Sutcliffe as the authority for the assertion that Waldegrave returned from La Rochelle in September "along with the two books which he had printed" there, the *Appellation* and *M. Some laid open in his coulers.* [13]

Yet, in his *Historical Introduction,* written prior to the biography of Penry, Pierce absolves Waldegrave from any connection with Penry and the Martinist tracts after the publication in the spring of 1589 of *Hay any worke for Cooper.* As reasons for

Waldegrave's departure, Pierce points out that "the work was no doubt laborious and dangerous" and "besides, his health was suffering." To these excuses, however, he adds this contradictory statement: "He is reported by Penry, about the middle of May 1589, to be at the Huguenot city of Rochelle. *If we may trust the story of Matthew Sutcliffe,* he remained till late autumn at Rochelle, and there printed *M. Some laid open in his Coulers,* and Penry's *Appellation.*" [14]

Fifteen years later, in his life of Penry, Pierce still seems to doubt Sutcliffe's story. After a somewhat self-conscious protest that "there was nothing incredible in the statement of Penry that Waldegrave, still bent on printing antiepiscopal and Puritan books, was at Rochelle," Pierce frankly acknowledges that "an examination of such works of reference as are available at the British Museum shows no trace of English works, or of works by English authors, during the period to 1590," printed at La Rochelle.[15] In accepting with reservation Sutcliffe's garbled account, Pierce, like Wilson, never once considers the possibility that the La Rochelle story might be merely a trick, thought up by Penry on the spur of the moment, to put the overinquisitive Sharpe off the scent.

From the "important document," the deposition of Symmes and Tomlyn, that Pierce adds to Arber's "valuable collection," he might well have derived evidence in support of his original conviction that Waldegrave's departure from Coventry in the spring of 1589 had ended his close association with the Martinists. In this deposition Symmes reports the bitter reply of his master Hodgkins to a query as to Waldegrave's whereabouts: "Hodgkins answered that he [Waldegrave] *had played the knave notably wth the brethren* in that having gotten the copy of Cartwrights book agaynst the Rhemish Testament he was gone to print that for his comoditye and *had given the brethren over.*" [16]

The most perplexing problem connected with Penry's *Appellation* has to do, not with its typography, but rather with its date of publication. On its title page appears the date 1589, and the short dedication on page one is dated March 7. But since the legal year began on the Feast of the Annunciation, March 25, and ended on the following March 24, Elizabethan writers, referring to dates between January 1 and March 24, arbitrarily used either the date of the legal year or the date of the calendar year or both: for example (in this instance), March 7, 1589, for the legal year; March 7, 1590, for the calendar year; or March 7, 1589–90. Presuming that Penry was using the date of the legal year, Arber [17] and initially McKerrow [18] date the *Appellation* 1590. Moreover, in Penry's earlier writings internal evidence reveals his preference for the legal year. Perhaps, since he was directing his appeals to the Privy Council and to Parliament, he may have considered the reference to the legal year more suitable than to the calendar year.

For instance, instead of dating his *Supplication* 1588–89, he dates it 1588, but evidence in the several depositions definitely proves that it was published in March, 1589.[19] In fact, Pierce specifies March 9, 1589, as its date of printing.[20] Furthermore, in the text of the *Supplication* Penry clearly indicates that he was writing in that year, for he addresses the members of "this highe court of parlament," who are "now to be assembled togither"— in other words, Elizabeth's seventh Parliament, which opened on February 4, 1589.

In the *Supplication,* too, Penry's references to the regnal year, which is dated from the day when the monarch ascends the throne, are always explicit. In his introductory epistle to this pamphlet, which was not part of the earlier *Exhortation,* he writes "now *in the 31. yeare* of the raign of Queen Elizabeth." Similarly, in the main text he refers to the Welsh people, who "for the space nowe of *30. yeares complete*" have wanted the preaching of the Word, and to the free profession of the gospel in England "for the space of 30. yeares." [21] In these last two references he is alluding to the length of the reign of Queen Elizabeth (following that of the Catholic Queen Mary), which began on November 18, 1558, thirty years of which had been completed by November 18, 1588.

In the original text of the addition to the second edition of the *Exhortation*, which formed the basis of the *Supplication* and which was composed in the spring of 1588, Penry writes, "It is now *ful 29. yeares and vpward*, since Babilon hath bin ouerthrown in Wales, rather by the voice of hir Maiesties good lawes . . . then by the sound of anye trumpet"; [22] that is, it is well over twenty-nine years since the Queen's accession on November 18, 1588. In revising this same passage for the *Supplication* in 1589 he changes the date to "it is now *full 30. yeares and vpward*," etc.[23]

Finally, in his *Reformation No Enemie*, dated by Pierce "probably during the month of April 1590," [24] Penry refers to the regnal year as follows: "The Lord by the mouthes of his seruantes, and by his fore-named blessings, hath *these 31. yeares* besought and earnestly intreated . . . ," "although *within these 31. yeres*, there haue bin many seditious and treasonable attempts, vndertaken against her Majestie and the state . . . ," "for let it once be sene that popery hath gotten such strength among vs, that *after 31. yeares* banishment. . . ." [25]

In the light of these accurate references to the regnal year, when Penry in his *Appellation* writes "nowe after 31. yeares of the gospell enjoyed," he is implicitly dating this pamphlet *after November 17, 1589*. Hence the date of the short opening dedication, March 7, becomes March 7, 1590; likewise the date on the title page, 1589, should be interpreted as 1590. This conclusion is further supported in the same pamphlet by two direct references to the *Supplication* (dated by Pierce, as has been mentioned, March 9, 1589) as already in print.

Two additional internal clues to the date of composition appear in the text of the *Appellation*. The first of these is Penry's reference to the ransacking during his absence of his home at Northampton "on the 29. of January last":

This furye of theirs, at diuers times shewed by many of their instruments, did especially manifest it selfe on the 29. of Ianuary last. At which time one Richard Walton hauing a commission from the Archb. and others, wherein all her maiesties officers were chardged and commaunded in her name, to assist the sayd Walton to make entry into all houses, shops, &c: to apprehend all those whome he should any waies suspect, and to commit them at his discretion vnto the next Gaol or prison, vntil farther order should be taken with them, came into the place of mine aboad at Northampton, ransacked my study, and tooke away with him all such printed books and written papers as he him self thought good, *what they were as yet I cannot justly tel.* And not contented to keepe him self within the immoderate limits of a larger commission, then as I thinke can be warranted by lawe, he offered violence vnto diuers persons, and threatened not only to breake open doores (hauing noe such commission) but also to vntile houses, vnlesse he could find me *where in deed I was not.* At his departure he charged the Maior of the towne, who then attended vpon him, *to apprehend me as a traitor,* giuing out that he had found in my study both printed books and also writings, which conteined treason in them. Whereas the bookes and writings of greatest disgrace (euē in the sight of his master) which he could there finde, were, one printed coppy of the demonstration of discipline, and *an answere vnto Master D. Some in writing,* both which he caried away with him. The treason conteined in either of those books, is no other then that which Amasiah the high priest at Bethel, found in Amos the prophet, euen the cleare words of truth not to be abidden in a corrupt state of a churche I graunt.

The second clue is a reference to an order given by the High Commission, presumably about the same time as the raid, to arrest Henry Sharpe:

From this insolency of theirs it is, that of late they haue in their mandatory letters, enjoined the Maior of Northampton, to surcease the execution of his office in the gouernment of that towne vnder hir maiestie, and either to become their pursiuant, in apprehending one of his neighbours, or else personally to appeare before them at London, and not to departe their court without special leave, his affaires in her maiesties seruice, and the distance of Place betweene Northampton & London, nothing considered. And yet required they of him that which he coulde not bring to passe, because the party whome he was to apprehend ["M. Sharpe book binder of Northampton"—marginal note], being wel known to be a dutiful subiect, *and for the loue he beareth vnto Gods truth to haue bene heeretofore so cruelly dealt with at some of their hands, by long imprisonment, and so euil dealt with, as his cause comming to be heard before the Ll. of her maiesties priuy counsel, their Hh. judged the bishops proceeding against him, to be against lawe and conscience, and so were the meanes of his deliuery,* the party I say, nowe fearing the like injustice, *that hee sometimes tasted of,* was compelled with the hinderance of his family *to absent himself from his calling.*[26]

On the basis of these two passages Arber concludes that the *Appellation* was published on March 7, 1590.[27]

At first accepting Arber's conclusion, McKerrow states that "in January 1589–90, an attempt was made to apprehend Penry at Northampton, but he escaped to Scotland, where he was well received by the Presbyterian clergy."[28] Before the edition of Nashe was completed, however, Wilson had dated the raid on Northampton on January 29, 1588–89, the dedication to the

Appellation on March 7, 1588–89, and—following Sutcliffe's statements unsupported by any evidence—its printing on Walde-grave's press at La Rochelle the following summer.[29] Accordingly, McKerrow in his "Errata and Addenda" at the end of his final volume of Nashe, repudiates his earlier dating of the raid and hence of the pamphlet, but as though not entirely satisfied he adds, "There appears, however, to have been a later raid on the house of Henry Godley, Penry's father-in-law, in the autumn of 1589." [30] Yet he gives no reasons for postulating this second raid. Pierce, on the assumption that Penry's defense of Sharpe preceded what he terms "Sharpe's betrayal," follows Wilson in dating the pamphlet March, 1589.[31]

As Wilson and Pierce interpret these two passages in the *Appellation*, Penry and Sharpe were in hiding from January to March, 1589; furthermore, Penry's answer to Some was already composed; most important of all, Sharpe had been imprisoned, had been tried before the Privy Council, and had abandoned his "calling" as bookbinder. Wilson, indeed, writes that "for some reason unconnected, as far as I can tell, with the Marprelate business," Sharpe "was in disfavor with the authorities" and "for the greater part of 1589" was "in hiding." [32] Commenting on Penry's defense of Sharpe, Pierce comes to the same conclusion as Wilson: "Sharpe, we have seen, was at this time in hiding at his wife's relations *at Wigston*, having had intimation of what was likely to happen to him. So that when Walton arrived in the town and summarily ordered the Mayor to arrest him, the pursuivant was asking an impossibility." [33] Pierce's misprint of "Wigston" for "Wolston," where Mrs. Wigston lived, perhaps results from a misreading of Sharpe's statement that "within a fortnight after Midsommer," 1589, he was "drawn by necessity to leave North-ampton" and "went to dwell at Wolston with his wives mother." [34] Regarding the possibility of a previous imprisonment for Sharpe, Pierce adds that "already because of his love of God's truth he had at the hands of some of them, suffered long imprisonment, and was 'so evill dealt with,' that at last the lords of the Privy Council took up his case, and judging the action of the bishops 'to be against lawe and conscience,' they set him free." [35]

Yet in the depositions there is no indication whatsoever that either Sharpe or Penry was under any restraint during these months. In fact, Sharpe recounts the delivery *at his home* of some copies of the *Epitome* "by Master Penrys appointment," also Newman's unimpeded visit to Northampton in order to pick up these copies, and before March 9, 1589, Sharpe's refusal to bind a thousand copies of Penry's *Supplication at Wolston, where he was visiting,* and his insistence upon having them brought *to his home at Northampton,* where he bound them and turned them over to Newman. In addition, Sharpe states that on March 23, 1589, he was in Northampton, where he bound seven hundred copies of *Hay any worke for Cooper* brought him by Newman. And again, about Midsummer Sharpe was visited *at his home* by Hodgkins. Sharpe's casual reference to an enforced visit to his mother-in-law's home in Wolston could hardly be the absence referred to in the *Appellation,* for if, as Wilson and Pierce maintain, this pamphlet had been completed by March 7, 1589, Penry could not then have foreseen what Sharpe would be forced to do "after Midsommer," 1589.

Penry's uncertainty in his *Appellation* as to what "printed books and written papers," beyond "one printed coppy of the demonstration of discipline and an answere unto master D. Some in writing," were seized by the pursuivants in the raid suggests that at the time of writing he was not near enough to Northampton to find out. Yet between January 20 and March 23, 1589, he was at Coventry, less than thirty miles away. As far as the projected *More worke for Cooper* is concerned, the first reference to it in the depositions, made early in May by Penry to Sharpe, indicates that this reply "at length" to Some had not yet been printed, perhaps not even composed.[36]

Finally, if Wilson and Pierce were correct in dating the raid on Northampton in January, 1589, certainly in the *Supplication*, published in February, 1589, Penry would have mentioned losing the manuscript. Yet in that pamphlet his only reference to a reply to Some also indicates that it had not yet been written:

Neyther is any man to maruell, that I being charged of late, by M. Doct. Some in publike writing, to be not onely a defender of many blasphemous errors, but also an vnderminer of the ciuill State, durst presume to become a sutor vnto the high Court of Parliament, before I had first cleared my selfe of those crimes. For my purpose being to haue published an answere to M. D. Some, before this cause should be made known; I was drawne whether I would or no, to take the opportunity of setting out this, which I thought to be most waighty [the *Supplication*]; least that if I had deferred it vntill th'other had come forth, I might haue bin preuented of the means to publish it in any due time. Besides the 185. page, line 2. & 30. of M. D. Somes booke, wherein he hath freely graunted me the contro[ver]sie between vs; which is, that vnpreaching ministers, are no ministers, and consequently, not to be communicated with: do euidently shew, that he did not well know himselfe what he did in charging me, so far beyond christian modesty, for defending nothing els in these points, but that which his owne writings do publikely witnes against him to be Gods truth. So that of al other causes, his bare (and by his owne witnes for the most part false) accusations, ought least of all to diswade me from this labour, though I never ment to aunswere him. *But by the grace of God he shalbe answered, and that very shortly.*[37]

Little did Penry foresee what obstacles fate would place in the path of his projected answer to Some before it would appear in print.

Perhaps the most convincing evidence that the *Appellation* was completed in 1590, while Penry was a fugitive in Scotland, is its general tone of desperation. On the first page he announces his purpose in appealing to Parliament, namely, "the care of pro-curing" his safety "from the dangerous attempts of those that seek nothing els" but his "vtter ouerthrowe and vndoing." He laments that for his attempted intercessions to expose the "spiritual bondage" of his Welsh "countrimen" he is "tossed from post to piller, and permitted to haue no assurance of quiet aboade *in any of her majesties territories and dominions*"—an indication that he is not dwelling in England proper. Then he admits that he is a hunted man, which he became only after Sharpe's confession: "Nowe may it please your honors to demaund of the high com-mission, *why they account me to be a disturber of the peace of our church, and a seditious person.* Either they wil think them selues not bound to giue any reason of their accusation, because against those that seeke the wealth of Ierusalem, any vntrueth wilbe ad-mitted, or their reason wilbe *because I hold in vnlawful for them to liue in popishe callings, to be Lords ouer their brethren, to smother the trueth, to rob Christ of his honor, and his church of her libertie, or to speake in their owne wordes, because I dislike the gouernment of the church by L. Archb. and Lord Bb. estab-lished by the prerogatiue of hir majestie* and parliament." Although he thus is aware that his hatred for the episcopacy has made him an enemy to the State, he seems hurt to learn that he is accused of "treason" and is being sought for by the "pursiuants."

Throughout the *Appellation* he makes no pretense of seeking reformation only in the Church of Wales but frankly states his in-tention to overthrow the entire episcopacy: "And because I doe not conceile that which in conscience I am bound to lay open: namely, that the blindess and ignorance of our blind & ignorant guides, the tiranny, vnlawful bondage, and vnjust oppression of Gods church *by vngodly, and tiranical Lord Bishops, with the rest of th'vnlawful church gouernoures* (who euen by vertue of their places cannot chuse but oppresse the church of God) are the ready and direct waie, *not only to kepe my countrimen from eternal life, but also to bringe the Lords wrath vppon vs, our prince, maiestrats, people, and the whol kingdome.*"

Another reason for being "molested" by the pursuivants, as he himself acknowledges, is his published statement "that our Sauiour lefte an externall gouernement of his Church, and so is equall with Moses: and such a gouernement as cannot be changed by any but himselfe, and is superior vnto Moses." His delineation of this "externall gouernement" is about the only theological principle contained in this more or less personal document: "I am driuen to confesse this vnchangeable forme of externall church gouernement ordained by him [Christ], to be a gouernment, th'execution whereof, is committed to these 4. officers: namely, *Teaching Pastors & Doctors, gouerning Elders, & ministring Deacons,* because I finde non other officers or offices, either expressed or included in the Newe Testament. Apostles, Prophetes and Euangelistes onely excepted, which being remooued out of the Churche by the Lorde himselfe, the boldnes of our Bishops & their defenders is intolerable, in demanding why Pastors, Doctors, Elders and deacons, should be permanent: seeing Apostles, Prophets and Euangelists were but temporarie." This "confession" of presbyterian doctrine shows that in spite of Penry's impatience with his fellow Puritans he still is in their camp.

Though he protests that the pursuivant Richard Walton has "ransacked" his study and appropriated "an answere vnto master D. Some in writing," he promises that "ere it be long" he will publish another "answere," in which he will defend himself against Some's accusation that Penry maintains "her maiestie with many thousandes of hir best subiects to be vnbaptized." [38] Shortly thereafter appeared the unsigned *M. Some laid open in his coulers,* which has every appearance of being this "answere."

In addition to being linked by type and date of composition with Penry's *Appellation, M. Some laid open in his coulers,* according to H. M. Dexter, shares "a common authorship" with the seven

Martinist tracts. From its signature, "I.G.," however, Dexter supposes that "there can be no reasonable doubt of the truth of the common judgment [in 1880, when Dexter was writing] that John Greenwood [the separatist] was its responsible author." Yet, recognizing that its "style" is "so different from that of other books of his [Greenwood's]—notably his replies to [George] Gifford, which involve subjects inviting like treatment," Dexter suspects that Greenwood's separatist companion, Henry Barrowe, was "a silent partner in this authorship and that to his slashing pen are due these caustic outbursts." On this basis and also on what he considers "remarkable similarities of style" between Barrowe's writing and that of Martin, Dexter concludes that Barrowe was Martin.[39] Though Arber felt that he owed Dexter the courtesy of inserting his opinion into the *Introductory Sketch to the Martin Marprelate Controversy* because of Dexter's "long acquaintance with the Controversy," Arber nevertheless differs "totally" from him.[40] Similarly, Pierce entirely rejects Dexter's hypothesis on the ground not only of style but also of theology. Indeed, states Pierce, "Greenwood certainly did not write alone, or with the aid of Barrowe, *M. Some in his Coulers,* although it bears the undeciphered initials I.G." [41]

Rather than accepting these initials as evidence, of authorship, we should examine the statement on the title page, "Done by an Oxford man to his friend in Cambridge." "Greenwood," Pierce informs us, "was a cleric who had studied for his calling at Cambridge, a graduate of Corpus Christi College." [42] Penry, on the contrary, could claim either university as his alma mater since, after graduating from Cambridge, he had transferred to Oxford for his M.A. Like the various subterfuges practiced by Martin to confuse and to mislead the curious reader, this statement might merely signify the whimsicality of being "written by me for myself."

The main topic in this tract, too, is the one that Penry had promised to discuss in his answer "at large" to Some, namely, whether the baptisms administered by "Popish and dumb ministers" are sacraments. Just as hitherto Penry had tried to sidestep a direct denial of the validity of the sacraments in the Church of England, so the author of *M. Some laid open in his coulers* seems to aim at implanting doubt in the mind of his reader without actually taking a stand on the issue. Can we be assured, he asks, that we have been baptized if we were baptized by "popish shauelings" or "dumb ministers" or by a midwife or other layman outside of the church?

Just as in discussing baptism in the *Exhortation* Penry resorts to ambiguity, so the author of this tract becomes almost unintelligible in defending Penry's doubts concerning the Anglican sacraments:

Then marke first what M. Penri setts downe to be the question, for these I take it be his owne words. *The question therefore is not* (saith he) *whether the one or th'other of them* ["popish shauelings" and "dumb ministers"] *haue deliured a Sacrament in respect of th'action don, but whether a christian going vnto them for these holy seales, may be assured that he can receiue the same at their hands* &c. This you see is plaine enough; yet M. Some in his preface tels vs far otherwise, *that the question is, whether such as were and are baptized by popish priests and ignorant ministers haue & doe receiue a Sacrament &c.* his aduersarie layeth downe in flat terms *that it is not the question,* and yet your D. blusheth not to say, *that it is the question.*[43]

The anonymous author here seems to interpret Penry's ideas with too much authority for a man who on the spur of the moment has decided to publish this pamphlet upon hearing of the "taking away of M. Penries book by the Pursiuant." Similarly, with reference to whether or not a person must give credit to the holy word of God, he writes, "First it is cleare M. Penri speaketh here (*as he doth in the whole course of his booke*) of that which is ordinary & not extraordinary." Another indication of Penry's hand is the personal pique in the author's repetition of M. Some's "poore ignorant Welchman." [44]

Assuming with Arber that Sutcliffe's unsubstantiated charges leveled at Throckmorton were based on evidence now unobtainable, Pierce accepts Sutcliffe's designation of Throckmorton as the author of *M. Some laid open in his coulers.* Yet, at the same time, Pierce is puzzled by Sutcliffe's assertion that Waldegrave could have taken an oath to this effect since the printer never was arrested by the English authorities after the publication of the Martinist tracts. But he resolves his doubt by guessing that "it must have been in Scotland," perhaps "when he was made the King's Printer for Scotland." In spite of accepting Throckmorton as the author, Pierce cannot help remarking that the style of the pamphlet "strongly reminds us" of the style of Martin Marprelate, for the author "wanders away from his text to deal with Dean Bridges and his *Defence* of the Church as established, the book which was the primary target of Marprelate"—and likewise, we might add, of Penry in his addition to the second edition of the *Exhortation.*[45]

Nevertheless, it must be admitted that the attacks on Bridges in *M. Some laid open in his coulers* are written not as a Welsh jeremiad, as in Penry's *Exhortation,* but rather in the tarletonizing vein of Martin's *Epistle:* "Now if you aske me what should be the reason why so many things out of question, shoulde be thus jumbled & enterlaced as it were, in one rolle, with things of question and controuersie indeede, let this suffize you, that there is a misterie in it, yea and such a misterie as peraduenture euerie one seeth not, & I beleeue I could go neer to gesse where M.D. learned it, I pray you what cal you him, that giueth in his coat *An asse with a tippet about his necke,* and writes vnderneath, *Come and see?* He should sure be some ancient gentleman by his coate: I meane that proper scholler that could speake Englishe before I was borne: he that hath giuen Caluine and Beza suche a blowe, as they could neuer speake word of good Irish since: I meane him that sucked so long, till he could carie his mother a stoole, and that phisitions say, is a shrewde thing for the brain."

Like Penry in the *Exhortation* and like Martin in the *Epistle*, he next ridicules the huge size of Bridges' *Defence of the Government Established*: "That pretie pigeon that wrote the 16. great volumes in defence of the Hierarchie of Bb. [Martin's satirical abbreviation] but as he hath handled it, it may serue aswell for the foule cawsey betwixt Glocester and Bristow: I doe not meane Tarleton man, Tushe no, I meane that musicall Poet that can so ingeniously translate rime into prose, and prose into rime againe: That patch of S. Maries pulpit, what should I call him? Bridges, Bridges, a shame on him, I shal hit on his name anon: This is he I feare me, that taught M. Some this tricke, and yet when it is looked into, it wil be found but a sluttish tricke neither I beleeue." Beginning with these excellent examples of "martinizing," the author of *M. Some laid open in his coulers*, while professing to reply to Some, never misses an opportunity to strike at Bridges: the "bignes" of his book, "a sluttish tricke of M. Bridges, liker a great deale, to begrease his fingers, then to bring any grace or credite to his penne," "a proper short declamation (but truly it is a sweet on) of the lerned Bridges," "M. Deane of Salisburies buttery booke," "brother Bridges . . . no learning . . . sot," and so on.[46] The only similar attacks on Bridges, ridiculing his book and hurling personal insults at him, were those of Penry and Martin.

Using Martin's technique, the author of *M. Some laid open in his coulers* introduces bits of gossip and gratuitously attacks Dr. Perne, with particular emphasis on Perne's inconstancy in his religious affiliations:

What will M. Some say to this? He that was last B. of Norwitch and is nowe (if I be not deceiued) either of Peterborough or of Worcester, calling once before him a godly minister of Suffolke, one M. Swette, about some small breach

of the booke in the administration of baptism when the saide
M. Swette for his just defense, had brought forth the iudgment
of M. Beza, the good B. in his angrye moode replied thus,
what tellest thou me of Beza? Beza I tell thee is but a brabler.
In like manner my L. of Cant. [Martin's favorite punning
abbreviation] hauing once before him one Thomas Settle a
preacher, about some doctrine that he had taught of Christs
descending into Hell, when the said M. Settle alleadged for
himselfe, that the doctrine taught by him, had not only the warrant of the holy scriptures, but also the approbation & testimony
of the best writers of our age, as namely, of M. Caluin and
others: *What tellest thou vs of Caluin?* (Quoth the B. in very
disdainful sort,) *I tel thee there are here that can teach Caluin.*
At which time, there satte in commission, th'Archb. himselfe,
the Deane of Westminster, D. Pearne and Cousins, a proper
band of musitians to teach Caluin. *But belike he meant it only
by his old Patrone and benefactor, D. Pearne, for whoe but
he could teach Caluin to fetch a turne, and a retourne?* [47]

Again he directs his aim at the favorite targets of both Penry and
Martin: "And therein I appeal to the flowre of your own vniuersitie: I do not mean D. Copquot for we count him but of the
middle sort, *as we set D. Bridges and D. Pearne in the seuen-
teenth fourme behind him:* No I meane the very ornaments of
your Vniuersitie in deed, whose very names and liues doe cary
with them an estimation to be reverenced: D. Fulke, D. Goad,
D. Whytaker, & M. Chaterton." [48]

Finally, echoing Penry, the author of *M. Some laid open in his
coulers* under the protection of anonymity is even more outspoken
in his attack on the Queen as the supreme governor of the Church.
Asserting that, whether or not Penry likes it, the argument between Some and Penry must be whether or not a sacrament delivered by "popishe or dumb ministers" can be a sacrament and
admitting that the next logical step will bring into question the

legality of the baptism of "her majestie and a number of excellent men mo," Penry's "friend" in rebuttal quotes Some's statement that "a godly prince may not suffer any religion but the true religion, either publikely or priuatly in his dominions." And slyly noting that the Queen allows certain ambassadors from other countries to have "their Masse, (which shee must needs knowe to be Idolatrie) within her dominions," he asks whether or not she is "in that regard vngodly." [49]

In consideration of the commonly accepted evidence connecting this pamphlet not only with the Martinist tracts but also with Penry's acknowledged writings, its generally uncompromising tone suggests an inherent sympathy with the separatist movement, to which all nonconformists, who, like Browne, weary of "tarying," were beginning to turn. Indeed, Pierce, in the section of his biography of Penry entitled "Penry and his Advocate are heading for Brownism," points out as much in his statement that "the Clerk of Oxenford [that is, the author of *M. Some laid open in his coulers*], writing on behalf of Penry, is in no better case" than "Barrowe and all his friends," who, refusing to recognize the validity of the Anglican sacraments, will not admit that the Queen is truly baptized. [50] But before Penry was ready to take this final step, he had at least one more strictly Puritan pamphlet to write.

Chapter XIV

Penry's Final Puritan Pamphlets

Although Waldegrave seems to disappear from the Martinist circle immediately after his departure from Coventry in April, 1589, he reappears in 1590 in Scotland, where he and Penry again collaborated in the printing and publishing of at least two pamphlets and probably more. Accordingly, since the evidence presented in the preceding chapter dates both the *Appellation* and *M. Some laid open in his coulers* in 1590 and since both of these pamphlets were printed with type identified as Waldegrave's, they may or may not have been printed by Waldegrave himself.

Indeed, much of the confusion concerning the similarity in typography between these two pamphlets and *Martins Junior* and *Senior*, all of which, as far as can be determined, were printed during Waldegrave's absence, and the three editions of Penry's *Exhortation* and his *Supplication*, which were printed while Waldegrave was actively associated with the Martinist press, seems to stem from the fact that no careful distinction has been made between pamphlets printed by Waldegrave himself and those printed with what, as Pierce phrases it, "was known to the printers of the time as Waldegrave's 'letter.' "

Waldegrave's name again serves as a common bond among the last four pamphlets associated with Penry's Puritan period—his

Reformation No Enemie, and the three anonymous pamphlets, the *Briefe Discovery of the Untruthes and Slanders,* the *Humble Motion with Submission,* and the *Dialogue wherin is plainly laide open.* Pierce designates Waldegrave as the printer both of Penry's pamphlet and the first two anonymous pamphlets.[1] Of the *Dialogue wherin is plainly laide open* Pierce remarks that "so far as the typographical evidence can determine the question of its origin, the *Dialogue* came from Waldegrave's press" and that "the type appears to be that used in *M. Some in his coulers,*" as well as in several pamphlets signed both by Penry and Martin.

In addition to sharing a common typographical history, these four pamphlets seem to be products of the same pen. *Reformation No Enemie* presents no problem since it bears Penry's signature. The first scholar to attempt to identify the author of the *Briefe Discovery of the Untruthes and Slanders,* Dexter, attributes it to Penry. Though Pierce at first casually dismisses Dexter's opinion with the comment, "Dr. Dexter . . . attributes the volume to Penry—without evidence and no doubt wrongly," [2] several years later in his biography of Penry he confidently states that "the book has always been assigned to Penry."

Also in his biography of Penry, Pierce in a lengthy note states that the *Humble Motion with Submission* "is written from Penry's general standpoint, and here and there follows very closely his line of argument," that "it is formally addressed 'To the LL. of Hir Maiesties Counsell' " (and here Pierce reminds his reader that "hir is a regular spelling of Penry's"), and finally that "the type (pica rom.) is that used in *A Briefe Discoverie* [*of the Untruthes and Slanders*] and in *Reformation No Enemie.*" [3]

As for the *Dialogue wherin is plainly laide open,* Pierce calls it "the only additional publication following heartily the lines laid down by Martin Marprelate," but he maintains that "it is not from Martin's pen," not because it is not witty enough but because it seems to come short in "serious religious purpose" of what should be expected from Martin.[4] Perhaps what Pierce senses is the loss of fervor for presbyterianism experienced by Penry during those two years before he became a separatist.

Considering first Penry's *Reformation No Enemie,* we note that the author's many jibes at the English clergy as well as at the Welsh further strengthen the impression that his attack on the episcopalian government in Wales was merely a front for his attack on episcopalianism anywhere. Personifying England, he has her tell the Lord's servants: "As for the gospel, and the ministeries of it, I haue already receaued al the Gospels, and al the ministeries that I meane to receaue. I haue receaued a reading Gospel, and a reading ministery, a pompous Gospel, and a pompous ministery: a Gospel and a ministery that strentheneth the hands of the wicked in his iniquity, and a ministery that will stoupe vnto me and bee at my beck either to speake or to be mute when I shal thinke good."

And this same writer, whose loyalty to the Queen is stressed by his biographer Pierce, adds that if "some Ieremy" were to come to England he might find a few—obviously the Puritans—who "as a cluster of grapes after the vintage" would be thankful for the Lord's blessings. But "as for the general state *either of the magistracy,* of the ministerye, or of the common people," he would behold "nothing els, but a multitude of conspirators against God, against his truth, against the building of his house, against his Saints and children: and consequentlie against the wealth of their owne soules, and the publike peace and tranquillity of this whole kingdome."

With all of Martin's rash vigor, then, he terms the episcopalian clergy "a troup of bloody soule murtherers, sacriligious church robbers, and suche as haue made them selues fatte with the bloude of mens souls, and the vtter ruine of the Church." Among the subscribers of the warrant out for him as "enemie of the state" he names only the Archbishop of Canterbury, whom, echoing Martin, he defiantly calls "John Cant." Indeed, he makes no attempt whatsoever to conceal his hatred for Whitgift, of whom he writes: "Whome both in respecte of his Antichristian Prelacye ouer Gods Church, and for the notable hatred which he hath euer bewrayed towardes the Lord and his truth, I thinke one of the dishonorablest creatures vnder heauen, and accordingly doe account of him."

Though Penry defies even the devil himself to accuse him of "attempting anything against her maiesties person," he again, as in his *Appellation,* expresses his full awareness that he is being accused of treason because "by publicke writing" he has sought to bring into the church "that vniforme order of church regiment, which our Sauiour Christ hath ordained in his word, to continue perpetually therein"—in other words, the presbyterian discipline— and also because he has "endeuored to seek the vtter ruine and ouerthrow of that wicked hierarchye of lorde Bishops, *together with whatsoever corruption dependeth therevpon,*" part of which, as he has already stated in his other pamphlets, is the power of the civil magistrate in the church, that is, the English sovereign's claim to be supreme governor.

The main theme of *Reformation No Enemie* is the familiar presbyterian demand initiated by Cartwright, namely, the removal of the episcopalian hierarchy and the substitution of the presbyterian officers and discipline. In order to effect this change, Penry reiterates, it is necessary to root out "al dumb and vnpreaching ministers, all nonresidents, Lord Archbishops and bishops, commissaries, officials, chancellors and all the rest of the wicked offices that depend vpon that vngodly and tyrannous hierarchie of Lord Byshops, together with their gouernment." The episcopalian hierarchy, he asserts, "are no more able to teach vs what belongeth to the pure worshipp of god [that is, presbyterianism], then can many a childe of six yeres old."

In order that his reader no longer will think that he is writing only of Wales, he is completely inclusive: "In the most congregations, not of miserable Wales and Ireland onely, but euen of England it self: we want not some necessary member, but euen all vitall partes, as the heart, lyfe blood, yea and soule of true religion: namely, the word preached, euen the very seed without which men can neyther be begotten vnto, nor nourished in the hope of aeternall blisse and happiness." Lest the reader miss the change in direction of his attack, he here inserts the marginal note "the lamentable state of religion *in England*."

As if recalling the futility of his appeal to the "LL. of the Covnsel" in the second edition of his *Exhortation*, he censures the "Hh. of hir Majesties priuie counsell" for upholding "our ignorant ministerie" and not furthering the advancement of presbyterianism. In his allusion to Whitgift's severe criticism of him at his trial before the High Commission for insisting "the ordinarie meanes to beget fayth and saluation, to be onely the word preached," he boldly echoes Martin's punning epithet "that notable seducer of your people, *the Arch. of Cant.*," whom he compares to Satan.

Following the standard Puritan line of argument, he labels as "ignorance" all opposition to his doctrines. In his own words, all persons, whether "dumb minister" or privy councillor, who refuse to admit that Christ in the Word left a perfect plan for his church, namely, presbyterianism, are "vpholders of . . . ignorance," or, episcopalianism. Lacking compassion "towardes the miserable dispersion of poore sheep that wander without a guyde [any one of the presbyterian officers]," these stubborn persons thus consent "vnto ignorance and blindness." If the people of England are to be saved, they must abolish "the offices of Ll. Archb. and Bb.," which belong "vnto the regiment of the beast and his Idolatrie" and "receaue the religion of Christ, together with government by pastors, doctors, elders, & deacons, which he hath appointed in his word." [5]

In spite of the extensive external evidence in favor of assigning all three of the anonymous pamphlets to Penry, the *Briefe Discovery of the Untruthes and Slanders* is the only one that Pierce finally accepts. Evoked by a sermon which had been delivered by

Richard Bancroft on February 8, 1589, at Paul's Cross and entered in the Stationers' Registers on March 3, 1589, it was termed by its author a "short answer" to "serve for the clearing of the truth, vntill *a larger confutation* of the Sermon be published." This promise—or threat—recalls Penry's similar description of his *Defence of that which hath bin written in the questions of the ignorant ministerie,* written in the summer of 1588, which he termed a temporary answer to Dr. Some until a refutation "at large" could be prepared.

Also like Penry in his *Aequity,* the author cleverly puts his own ideas in the mouths of his opponents and places on these men the responsibility for their expression: "[Bancroft] affirmeth that one of our reasons whie wee holde the established gouernment of the church of England to be Antichristian, is because the ciuil Magistrate is made a Pope amongst vs, and that we call her maiesties supremacie vnto question. Wherevnto wee answere no otherwise, then Nehemiah did Sanballat: It it not done according vnto these words that thou sayest, but thou fainest them of thine owne hart." Similarly he quotes Martin's assertion that "our Bishops" are "petty Popes and vsurpers" and calls attention to the fact that Bancroft does not deny Martin's accusations.

Further evidence of Penry's hand is the author's protest of loyalty to the Queen, both in civil and religious affairs, along with his expressed conviction that she surely will not support the bishops who "intrude their subscriptions, aduertisements, and cannons vpon the subiectes, whereas no such things can be warrāted by statute." Likewise characteristic of Penry's style is the immediate qualification of this patriotic sentiment, as though it had never been expressed, by the brusque demand that the supreme governor be subservient to the presbytery: "We say that the true gouernors of the church [the elders] are meetest to direct her majesty what lawes and ceremonies are most lawfull, expedient, & necessary, for the right gouernment of the church. And we say, that as her majestie in worldly matters, is to giue eare vnto the Lawiers which haue skil in that facultie: so, *in the matters of God is she to establish nothing in the church, but that which the true ministers and true gouernors (if they may bee had) shall shew vnto her to be according vnto the worde of GOD.*"

The author's complaint, "Yet notwithstanding, it is too well knowen, what a straunger, the sauiour of mankinde is to the most parte within our lande, because the voyce of his gospell is neuer effectually heard among them," echoes Penry's oft-repeated lament over the dearth of godly ministers in Wales. But in this pamphlet "our lande" is no longer just Wales, but the entire Anglican territory "vnder ye jurisdiction of our Bishops."

Even while denouncing Robert Browne, the leader of the separatist movement, as "a knowne Scismatike" and "a proud vngodly man," the author of *A Briefe Discovery of the Untruthes and Slanders* reveals his leaning toward separatism in his statement, "The visible church of God wheresoeuer it bee hath the power of binding and loosing annexed vnto it." And he attributes to episcopalian tyranny the refusal of the bishops to "grant that the visible congregations in England, ought to haue this power of binding and loosing." Accordingly, instead of condemning the separatists with the usual Puritan severity, he requests prayers for "any of our poore brethren" who may stumble into the error of "Scisme and Donatisme," forced upon them by the "Prelates."

A final possible link with Penry is the reference to *An Almond for a Parrat* as "that vile and scurrilous Palmphlet, late[l]y suffered to come a broad." As will be explained in the next chapter, this anti-Martinist pamphlet made Penry its principal target. The author of *A Briefe Discovery of the Untruthes and Slanders* angrily condemns it along with all other retaliatory episcopalian writings: "The strength which they get by such leud and filthie stuffe, & the discredit which thereby they worke either vnto the cause, or the men and women whome they suffer to bee so vnworthilie traduced, is noe other then it were to bee wished (that seeing they will needs be filthy) they would publish such another booke euery day: That then it might appeare indeede whose sonnes they are. And this is all the confutation that I thinke, so godles & leud a scrole to deserue." With this feigned shudder that his opponents would indulge in such bad taste as the Martinists had taught them, the author of *A Briefe Discovery of the Untruthes and Slanders* dismisses Nashe's pamphlet.[6]

The second anonymous tract, the *Humble Motion with Submission* opens with an ominous threat that "Gods vengeance" is "not far off," strongly reminiscent of similar threats in Penry's *Supplication*. The author hits upon a clever bit of sophistry, which only a writer with a keen wit like Penry's would attempt. In order to overcome episcopalian prejudice he states that the ministers, "ordinary and perpetual," are "in general termes" called "Bishops & deacons" and that the "two sorts" of bishops, "Pastors and Teachers," possess the power of "prophesie." Thus he cleverly interweaves the two ecclesiastical systems for the purpose of catching the wavering episcopalian.

Then, after setting forth the duties of the presbyterian officers, he advances Penry's customary reason why the "milde" Queen, "so highlye honored of God, so tenderly beloued of hir subiects," delays in displacing the bishops. Someone, presumably the "Archb.," is keeping her in ignorance of the "discipline." After protesting his own admiration and gratitude "for the rare and honorable vertues of wisedome and magnanimity, in hir most excellent Majesty, and the constant, faithfull, and diligent prouidence and labour of hir most honorable and graue counsellors," the author of the *Humble Motion with Submission* contradicts this conventional obeisance to the supreme governor by demanding the abolition of the episcopacy as well as repeating Penry's and Martin's assertion that "the ordinarie means of God to instruct and bring into the way of truth, is the preaching ministery." As for the Queen, she can still act as head of a presbyterian church if she desires. Comparing the bishops to the abbots of Henry VIII's day, he suggests that each bishop be put in charge of a congregation and his livings divided among the "learned," or presbyterian, ministers.[7]

The third anonymous pamphlet is connected with Penry only through his *alter ego*, Martin. Termed by Pearson an "interesting auxiliary pamphlet" to Martin's writings,[8] *A dialogue wherin is plainly laide open* consists of a conversation involving a Puritan, a Papist, Jacke of both sides, and Idoll Minister, the purpose of which is to justify the presbyterian demand for equality of ministers and a government by pastors, teachers, elders, and deacons. Interspersed throughout are such scathing references to personalities as Martin had made, including a sneer at Whitgift's supposed defeat by Cartwright and several scandalous stories of Bishop Elmer, which had already appeared in the Martinist tracts. Particularly suggestive of a Welsh pen is the charge of bigamy directed against the Bishop of St. David's in Wales. Likewise in the Penry-Martin vein are allusions to Bridges' resentment at not being made bishop, to Cooper's alteration of his text in his *Admonition to the People of England* at Whitgift's command, and to Perne's reputation as a turncoat. Especially indicative of a softening attitude toward the cause of separatism, the author of *A Dialogue wherein is plainly laide open* unquestionably still Puritan in doctrine, groups together the Puritans and the Brownists as fellow sufferers from episcopalian tyrrany.[9]

With these four pamphlets—one signed by Penry and the other three closely associated with him—his career as a Puritan controversialist draws to a close. His last publication in Scotland, his *Propositions and Principles of Divinitie* (1591), a translation of the so-called *Genevan Theses*, a Latin work published in 1586, Pierce terms "a more or less neutral work." [10] During the final two years of his life Penry abandoned presbyterianism and became actively involved in the separatist movement.

Chapter XV

The Most Important Anti-Martinist Replies

While the Martinist tracts were following one another off the secret presses operated first by Waldegrave, later by Hodgkins and his men, but always with Penry in the background, the episcopalians were not idle. At first the audacity of Martin's satire completely floored them. When they began to revive, they made several ineffectual attempts at reprisal. The first of these was the publication of Bishop Thomas Cooper's *Admonition to the People of England*. It is a serious pamphlet written somewhat in the manner of Whitgift's *Defense of the Aunswere* and, as McKerrow describes it, "in the main a sound and soberly reasoned defense of the Church of England." McKerrow adds, however, "It is quite evident that a work of this character would be almost totally ineffective as a reply to the Martinist *Epistle*." In fact, he is convinced that the *Admonition to the People of England* "was not originally composed with the purpose of answering" the first Martinist tract but instead "written, and at least partly printed, before it was determined that it should include an answer to Martin— perhaps indeed before the *Epistle* appeared." [1] Cooper's heavy-handed theological reasoning served to invoke one of Martin's brightest pamphlets, *Hay any worke for Cooper*.

Doubtless Cooper inserted the word "Admonition" in his title in order to associate his pamphlet with the notorious first Puritan tract, the *Admonition to the Parliament;* furthermore, instead of signing his full name on the title page, at the end of his epistle to the reader he merely used the initials "T.C.," with which Cartwright had signed his original *Reply* to Whitgift in defense of the Puritan *Admonition.* These obvious attempts to capitalize on the popularity of the Puritan writings infuriated Martin, and feigning bewilderment, he queries: "But Thomas Cartwright shal I say that thou madest this booke against me because T.C. is sett to it[?]" Accordingly, in order to distinguish between the Puritan and the Bishop, Martin addresses the following explanation to Cartwright: "The distinction then between you both shall be this: he shalbe profane T.C. because he calleth Christ Iesus by whom the gouernment by Pastors, Doctors, Elders & Deacons was commanded to be he knowes not whom: and thou shalt be simple T.C." Throughout *Hay any worke for Cooper,* then, Martin ostentatiously distinguishes between the two "T.C.'s." [2]

Unfortunately for Cooper, in the first edition of his *Admonition to the People of England,* which apparently was rushed to the press, two emendations were made by means of printed slips clumsily pasted over the original text. In the first of these, with reference to Martin, Cooper had originally written, "The Libeller doth but dreame, let him and his doe what he dare"; this challenge was corrected to read "The Libeller doth but dreame, let him and his doe what they can." [3] In reply, Martin mockingly asks, "Why brethren, what wisedome is this in you to dare your betters?" In a confidential aside to his readers he adds: "And here I pray thee mark how I haue made the bishops to pull in their hornes. For whereas in this place they had printed the word *dare,* they bethought themselues y[t] they had to deale with my worship which am fauoured at the Court, and being afraide of me they pasted the word *can* vpon the word *dare,* and so where before they bad me and mine doe what we durst: now they bid vs do what we can, hoping thereby to haue a frinde in a corner whoe woulde not suffer vs to doe what wee ought and durst: and so our abilitie shoulde not be according vnto their demerit." After thus taking advantage of Cooper's seeming timidity, Martin taunts the bishops for their cowardice: "Marke now, ye bishopps of the Diuell, whether you be not afraide of me." [4]

Also in the original text of the *Admonition to the People of England*, Cooper had made the following concession: "They [the Martinists] will say, the Apostles afterward, and the Primitive Church did practice the same [the presbyterian "discipline"]. *I will not deny it*." [5] Cooper, it seems, had not yet realized how clever his opponent was. It is not at all difficult to imagine the startled reaction of an experienced controversialist like Whitgift at the bishop's blunder in thus playing into the hands of his opponent. At any rate, according to Martin, when the *Admonition to the People of England* finally appeared, over the apologetic "I will not deny it" was pasted the more positive and likewise provocative statement, "That is not yet proved." This alteration Martin ridicules in a series of brilliant puns: "Hauing said that they wil not denie the discipline to haue bene in the Apostles time, they haue now pasted there vpon that That is not yet proued. So that although their consciences do tell them that the discipline was then, yet they will beare the world in hand that that is not yet proued. Here you see that if *this patch* T.C. had not used *two patches* to couer his *patcherie* the bishops woulde haue accounted him to be as very a *patch* as Deane Iohn [Bridges]." [6] Then when a second edition of Cooper's *Admonition to the People of England* came out with the challenge "That is not yet proved" properly inserted in the text, Penry in his *Appellation* again strikes out at episcopalian "impudencie": "It is alleaged, that this gouernment by Pastors, Doctors, Elders and Deacons, was inuented by, they know not whom, and *that it is not yet proued*, that any such gouernment was in the primitiue Church. Why this is more then shamelesse impudencie, Is not that prooued in the 31. yeare of the raigne of Queene Elizabeth, to haue bene at all in the primitiue Church, which our booke of common prayer, in the beginning of her Majesties raigne, testified to haue been therein, and to shewe the necessitie thereof, declareth that we are to wishe for the discipline then practized?" [7] Cooper's emendations, perhaps prompted by his superior, Archbishop Whitgift, thus became grist for Martin's mill.

The next anti-Martinist effort came in the form of a sermon delivered by Dr. Richard Bancroft on February 9, 1589, at Paul's Cross. In this sermon, entered in the Stationers' Registers on March 3, 1589, Dr. Bancroft, later Bishop of London and eventually Archbishop of Canterbury, taunts the nonconformist clergy with greed for the episcopal livings and church revenues. Deploring their demand for a return to the primitive church of the Apostles, he strongly objects to any unauthorized exposition of the Scriptures by laymen. The Puritan interpretation of *Dic ecclesiae* as meaning "to establish in the church for ever the same plat and forme of ecclesiasticall government, to be erected in every parish, which Moses by Jethroes counsel appointed in mount Sinaie," he terms the statement of false prophets. He likewise dismisses the Puritan analogy of their presbyterian system of pastors, doctors, elders, and deacons with Jewish counterparts. With reference to the Puritan attacks on the civil magistrate, he quotes their statements in favor of bypassing the Queen in order to establish presbyterianism. And he specifically accuses one unnamed nonconformist, doubtless Browne, of writing "when he was of that humor" that "if this reformation . . . be not hastened forward by the magistrate, the subjects ought not any longer to tarie for him, but do it themselves." [8] He also mentions the threats both in the *Second Admonition,* which he implies was written by Cartwright, "the chiefe ringleader in this crue," [9] and in the Martinist tracts.[10]

As far as strictly literary replies to the Puritan attacks were concerned, after the dismal failures of Bridges and Cooper—the one evoking the Martinist fusillade, the other merely increasing the size of the target—the bishops attempted, first, to satirize Martin on the stage,[11] and then to reply in kind. The stratagem of using plays, none of which is extant, was doubtless suggested by the similarity between Martin's patter and that of the celebrated clown Dick Tarleton. In addition to a few none too successful efforts to ridicule Martin in verse,[12] a series of satirical pamphlets appeared just about the time Martin was winding up his career. The most important of these were the three Pasquil tracts—the *Countercuffe giuen to Martin Iunior*, the *Returne of the renowned Caualiero Pasquill*, and the *First parte of Pasquils Apologie*—also *Pappe with an hatchet* and *An Almond for a Parrat*.

At first believed by modern scholars to be the work of Thomas Nashe, the Pasquil tracts, as McKerrow suggests, more likely were written by an older man. It is possible, indeed, that one of the churchmen may have tried his hand at "martinizing"—perhaps even Bancroft himself, who is credited with the original suggestion for replying in kind to Martin.[13] In the second of these tracts, dated October 20, 1589, the author promises to assemble in print some notes gathered "in an assemblie of the brotherhood at Ashford in Kent," where he went "with a Student of Cambridge to a sollemne exercise"—doubtless one of the presbyterian "prophesyings," particularly objected to by the Queen. In short, the episcopalian defenders were setting out to collect as much personal gossip about the Puritans as Field through the years had gathered about the bishops. Since the nonconformists referred to their congregations as gatherings of the saints, the episcopalian counterpart to the Martinist tracts was to be called "The Liues of the Saints."

But by far the most informative of these three tracts is the final one, which, dated July 2, 1590, is expressly an answer to Penry's last signed Puritan tract, *Reformation No Enemie*. By this date, of course, all of the information that we now have—the depositions of the suspects, the government reports, and so on—was available for perusal by the author. In the third Pasquil tract Penry is expressly charged with the responsibility for publishing the Martinist tracts: "Who had the ouersight of the Libell at Fawslie [the *Epitome*]? Iohn of Wales: Who was corrector to the Presse at Couentrie? Iohn of Wales: Who wrote the last treatise of Reformation so full of slaunders, but Iohn of Wales?" Even though Penry is not specifically named as the author of the Martinist tracts, Pasquil's detailed analysis and rebuttal of the arguments in *Reformation No Enemie* show that its author is at last recognized as the most formidable adversary of the bishops.[14]

The other two anti-Martinist tracts—*Pappe with an hatchet*, published about October, 1589, and *An Almond for a Parrat*, published about March, 1590—deserve mention for widely different reasons. The earlier tract is interesting, not for its literary quality, which is abusive rather than clever, but because it was written by John Lyly. The later pamphlet is vastly superior to the earlier and probably is the work of Nashe.[15] Although Wilson concedes that *An Almond for a Parrat* is "much more closely reasoned and well-informed than any other anti-Martinist production," he regards its "literary merits" as small.[16] Yet to the student of the Marprelate Controversy these merits are anything but small. Historically it was the first pamphlet to publish an authentic account of the Martinists; in fact, it preceded the *First parte of Pasquils Apologie* by about six months. Not only does the writer know of the printers Hodgkins, Tomlyn, and Symmes, he also mentions Sharpe, who bound some of the pamphlets, Newman the cobbler, who distributed them, Udall, to whom Field had given the scandalous stories, and finally Penry, whom he names as Martin. Indeed, here for the first time in print is Martin identified as Penry.

What is more important from a literary point of view is that the author of *An Almond for a Parrat* was the first of the anti-Martinist writers successfully to imitate Martin's invective. He actually out-Martins Martin. No other known Elizabethan pamphleteer until this time had attained to this distinction. The only other examples of "martinizing" at all comparable with it are to be found in Nashe's *Pierce Penilesse* and his attacks on Gabriel Harvey. It may well be that it was *An Almond for a Parrat* that won Nashe the reputation for stopping Martin's mouth, for it is the only anti-Martinist pamphlet that can with any certainty be ascribed to him.[17] Perhaps, too, it was in this pamphlet that he developed the satirical style that earned him the title of the young "Iuvenall" of the University Wits, that Greene gave him before *Pierce Penilesse,* the first signed pamphlet in which he demonstrated this style, was published.

In a series of passages filled with epithets the author of *An Almond for a Parrat* gleefully makes good his boast that he, too, can play at the game of "martinizing":

> Much good do it you, M. Martin, how like you my stile, am not I old *Ille ego qui quondam* at ye besleeuing of a sichophant? Alas, poore idiot, thou thinkest no man can write but thy selfe, or frame his pen to delight except he straine curtesie with one of thy Northren figures; but if authority do not moderate the fiery feruence of my enflamed zeale, ile assaile thee from terme to terme, with Archilochus, in such a compleat armour of Iambicks as the very reflexcye of my fury shall make thee driue thy father before thee to the gallows, for begetting thee in such a bloody houre.

In payment for Martin's ringingly alliterative "tearms" describing the bishops, which the author of *An Almond for a Parrat* repeats with evident admiration—"wicked Priests, presumptuous Priests, proude Prelates, arrogant Bishops, horseleeches, butchers, persecutors of the truth, Lamhethical whelps, Spanish Inquisitours" —he tosses back "seely sophister," "good munckie face Machiuell," "good hedge-creeper," "olde Martin of Englande," "brother Timothie," "his welchnes," "Masse Martin," "sweete M. sauce malapert."

In addition, he tries to match Martin's stories of the bishops with equally irreverent allusions to "a good fellow in Cambridge," who, "hearing all thinges might be obtained by prayer, prayed two dayes and two nightes for visions," the "zealous sheepebyter" of Martin's "owne edition in Cambridge," and more specifically to Cartwright's and Penry's activities at the university. In a mocking allegory he personifies the alleged Puritan "pride of singularity" in Cartwright and Puritan hypocrisy in Penry. To Cartwright, indeed, is attributed all the dissension in the Church. The author also scoffs at the Puritan writer Philip Stubbes, who is accused of dicing with one of his Puritan brethren.

Of Penry the author of *An Almond for a Parrat* invents a mock biography with an account of the supernatural events surrounding the Welshman's birth and describing his supposedly deformed appearance: "Neither was this monster of Cracouia unmarkt from his bastardisme to mischief: but as he was begotten in adultery and conceiued in the heate of lust, so was he brought into the world on a tempestuous daie, & borne in that houre when all planets wer opposite. Predestination, y^t foresaw how crooked he should proue in his waies, enioyned incest to spawne him splayfooted. Eternitie, that knew how aukward he shoulde looke to all honesty, consulted with Conception to make him squint-eied, & the deuill, that discouered by the heauens disposition on his birthday, how great a lim of his kingdom was comming into the world, prouided a rustie superficies wherein to wrap him as soone as euer he was separated from his mothers wombe." Thus, in this one pamphlet the anti-Martinists achieved Bancroft's goal, at least to outdo Martin in that element of his style that made it an effective weapon in the hands of the Puritan writers, namely, the use of satirical invective.[18]

Since the last two important opponents of separatism, George Gifford and Matthew Sutcliffe, were only incidentally concerned with Martinism, their relation to Penry will be taken up in subsequent chapters.

Chapter XVI

Penry's "Separatist Manifesto"

Penry's last important pamphlet, which was not printed until 1609, sixteen years after his death, was his *Historie of Corah, Dathan, and Abiram,* which Pierce calls his "Separatist Manifesto." In order to understand the final stages of Penry's conversion from presbyterianism to congregationalism, it is necessary to examine the writings of Henry Barrowe, whom Pierce calls "the great personality in London Separatism," and those of his prison companion, John Greenwood, both of whom, like Robert Browne, in their impatience to get on with the work of reformation had determined no longer to tarry for the magistrate. Both Barrowe and Greenwood spent their last five years in prison, and both were executed on April 6, 1593, a few weeks before Penry was led to the gallows. While in prison, both men did considerable writing which was circulated outside by their followers.

The first of these tracts was Barrowe's *Brief Discoverie of the False Church,* which as Pierce points out,[1] must have been of great interest to Penry both because of its "fresh exposition of the Separatist principles of Church polity" and because Barrowe therein discusses the treatment of the sacrament of baptism in the Penry-Some controversy. Since Some in 1589 had brought out a third *Godly Treatise* directed against Barrowe and Greenwood "and other of the Anabaptisticall order," Barrowe's *Brief Discoverie of the False Church* serves as an indignant reply to Some and

also as a more fraternal rebuke to a Puritan already showing signs
of wavering in his faith in presbyterianism as a means of reform,
namely, Penry.

Barrowe's chief criticism of the Church of England is its failure
to separate sinner from saint, at first through baptism, later
through excommunication. Indeed, he writes, the Church of England receives "all without exception or respect of person . . . not
denying baptisme to the seed euen of whores and witches." He
ironically scoffs at Elizabeth's establishment of Protestantism after
the death of Catholic Mary: "All this people, with all these manners, were in one daye, with the blast of Q. Elizabeths trumpet, of
ignorant papistes and grosse idolaters, made faithfull Christianes,
& true professors." The real fault in the Established Church, insists Barrowe, is that it bases its authority on the presence of a
Christian prince who follows Calvin's interpretation of the scriptural definition of the Church as including both saint and sinner.
Contradicting this doctrine, Barrowe asserts, "The seruantes of
God can neither build the Church, nor ioine in any spiritual actiō
with the profane."

Continuing beyond episcopalianism to presbyterianism, Barrowe
condemns the later doctrines of Cartwright just as Cartwright
earlier had condemned Whitgift. With reference to the teaching
of Calvin, that "where the word of God is sincerely taught, and
the sacramentes rightly administred, there vndoubtedly is still the
true Church of Christ," Barrowe asks "how yt is possible for the
ministers of the Church, either to preach the word sincerely, or
administer the sacramentes rightly, where there is no regard had
to the faithfull practise of the word, no care to redresse thinges
amisse, no power to shut out or excommunicate the vnworthy."
Since "yt is vnpossible to haue the word sincerely taught, and the
sacramentes purely administered, where any open sinne or sinner
is maintained or reteined," the church may on occasion be "for a
season" without sacraments. Thus he implies that it would be
better for a person to go unbaptized than to receive the sacrament

from a "false" minister—a doctrine that Penry, quite independently, had suggested in his advice to the Welsh people who might live too far from a presbyterian community.

That in discussing baptism Barrowe is addressing himself to Penry becomes evident when he refers to the "solution" of the Clerk of Oxenford "in the behalf of M^r. Penry," in other words, *M. Some laid open in his coulers,* which, as has been pointed out, has every appearance of being the product of Penry writing in his Martinist style.[2] Although Barrowe is willing to play along with the fiction of the pamphlet's being written by Penry's friend, he directs his remarks to Penry himself.

Particularly significant to the student of the Marprelate Controversy is the subtle identification of Penry with Martin, as though Barrowe himself were aware of the secret. For instance, in contending that the Queen is kinder to foreigners holding the reformed faith than to her "owne natural & true hearted subiectes," he cites as evidence "their owne complaintes & *supplications to the Parliamētes, their protestations* & new deuised scoffing libells." This passage, according to Pierce, is a direct allusion to Penry's *Supplication* and to Martin's *Protestation.* Furthermore, Barrowe suggests that their "Theses," which Pierce glosses as Martin's *Theses Martinianae* or *Martin Junior,* may well be applied to themselves.[3] Slyly Barrowe insinuates that "if Mr Penry prouide not better stuffe for his owne defence then his friend of Oxenford hath as yet brought," he and his companions "must become Brownists."

In the course of his remarks he deplores Penry's unwillingness to state flatly that the Queen is unbaptized. What particularly disturbs Barrowe is Penry's concession that since Elizabeth is persuaded in her conscience that she has received the true sacrament in the "popish" church, she is baptized and needs no further outward sign of baptism. Since Barrowe holds that she and all the other members of the Church of England, which has no true ministry, are unbaptized, he urges Penry to reconsider: "No mid-

dle course (as you affirme) may heere be taken; we must either
make yᵉ tree good or euill, these ministers of the Church of England, true or false: yf false then deliuer they no true sacramentes,
then is all their administration, sacramentes, sermons accursed,
how holy soeuer, or neere the truth in outward shew: then are
they the minister of Sathan or Antichrist." Hence, these "false"
ministers have no right to administer the sacrament of the Lord's
Supper, nor the Queen to receive it. By rationalizing that she is
"baptised with the inward baptisme of the Spirit," then, Penry's
"friend" is encouraging her to remain unbaptized and, at the same
time, is legitimizing not only the ministry of the Church of England but also that of Rome. Penry's only way out of his dilemma,
as Barrowe sees it, is either to grant the Queen and the Church
of England special immunities from the obligation to proceed from
baptism and to permit them to continue with their "english mass"
and their "english Popes" or else to gather a church, make a fresh
start, and erect a new ministry qualified to administer the sacraments.

Also important to Penry's conversion are Barrowe's views on
church government. Agreeing with the presbyterians that the
ministry of the church of Christ consists of two kinds of elders—
first, the pastor and the teacher, and second, the governor—and
also of deacons, he nevertheless expresses his conviction that "the
execution of Christs gouernment and iudgments" belongs to "the
whole bodie of the Church." Ironically to the student of Protestantism, Barrowe, echoing Cartwright's condemnation of bishops,
turns his fire not only against the episcopacy but also against "the
other sect of these Priests, *the counterfait Reformists*," who
"would exclude the church from this & al other ecclesiastical
cēsures, assuming thē wholy into their owne hādes, either into
the Priests hāds with *his silly presbitery or eldership*, which he
ouerruleth at his pleasure in euerie particular congregation, or els
into their synodes and councels." On the contrary, writes Barrowe, every member of the church has the power "publikely to

reprove any publike transgression of anie member of the Church, or of the whole Church," including the pastors and the teachers.

With Barrowe's extension of the interpretation of *Dic ecclesiae* to include the entire congregation, the attack on episcopalian authority begun by Cartwright reaches its logical conclusion. And Cartwright's doctrine of the illumination of the ignorant man by an inner light in the Scriptures plays an important part in the process. "The people of Christ," according to Barrowe, "are all inlightened with that bright morning star, that sonne of righteousnes." Consequently, "the eye of their faith is single, and the whole bodie is light" so that they are able to discern truth from falsehood. Accordingly, "prophesying," or the private interpretation of the Scriptures, should not be restricted to the ministers alone but should be the privilege of any member of the congregation. In Barrowe's opinion, the cause of this restriction heretofore has been the insistence upon university training for the episcopalian clergy.

Indicative of the lengths to which the anti-intellectualism inherent in this doctrine of the "inner light" has finally driven its exponents is Barrowe's contempt for acquiring the knowledge of "the latine or greeke tongue from lasciuious Poets & heathenish philosophers." From his point of view "these vniuersitie colledges are a misseline [miscellaneous?] rowte of very young men for the most part & boies together, leading their liues in idolatrie, confusion, disorder; spending their liues in vanitie, follie, idlnes, liuing neither in the feare of God, nor in any well established order of his Church, neither in any lawful calling in the cōmon wēlth." Considering, in addition, their "popish & idolatrous beginning," Barrowe demands the abolition of both Oxford and Cambridge.[4]

Again, in his *Collection of certaine sclaunderous Articles*, Barrowe denounces the Church of England and its liturgy as "false, superstitious, popish," and "antichristian," and the sacraments of baptism and the Lord's Supper administered therein as likewise false and not to be recognized. Although he condemns as "forged positions" Bishop Elmer's report of disloyalty in the points of view of the various imprisoned nonconformists, yet his own statements, both in this pamphlet and in his *Brief Discoverie of the False Church,* strongly suggest that the bishop may have been both accurate and fair.

For example, his assertion in Article 8 that "all true Christians within her Maiesties dominions acknowledg her Maiestie to be the supreame maiestrate & gouernesse of all persons with in the Church, & without the Church, yea ouer all causes ecclesiasticall & ciuill," is immediately contradicted by the heading of Article 9, "That the lawes ecclesiasticall alreadye established by the aucthoritie of the Queene or Realme, be not lawfull." Indeed, he makes it abundantly clear that he believes that the Queen should not be regarded as the supreme governor but should be liable to excommunication if she were to disobey his blueprint for reform.[5]

In 1590 George Gifford, a presbyterian clergyman, undertook to reply to these increasingly vociferous demands for separation from the Church of England. To this end he wrote two pamphlets, in each of which he likens the Brownists to the Donatists, with whom St. Augustine contended. In his *Plaine Declaration that our Brownists be full Donatists* he refutes the separatist doctrine that the presence of sinners in the congregation renders the service invalid. Gifford points out that in St. Augustine's time sinners were present in the church and yet that St. Augustine did not demand separation; also that even Calvin declares that the good cannot separate from the wicked without great cause. In defending the ordination of the ministers of the Church of England by "Antichristian," that is, Catholic, bishops, Gifford asserts that the guilt or innocence of the ordainer no more affects the validity of the ordination than the worthiness or unworthiness of the minister affects the efficacy of the sacrament.[6]

In his *Short Treatise against the Donatists of England* Gifford replies to the arguments originally formulated by Browne and repeated by Barrowe against the inclusion not only of sinners but even of their children in the congregation of the saints. Pointing out that the sins of good men like David, Solomon, and Samson did not pollute the church, Gifford insists that the Brownists are preaching heresy in maintaining that "where corrupt manners breake foorth in those that professe the Gospell, they be not onely vtterly voide of faith which offend, but also, that all they which worship together with them, though neuer so much greeued at their sinnes, are fallen from the couenant most cruelly by this meanes, thrusting downe all the weake, and casting foorth all poore babes." Furthermore, writes Gifford, a minister may be reprobate "touching his owne person," but at the same time a minister of Christ "touching his ministerie." In his *Short Treatise against the Donatists of England* the author also takes occasion to assert the validity of the ministry of the Church of England and its liturgy, particularly the use of prescribed prayers and homilies.[7]

Gifford's invidious comparison of separatism with Donatism evoked an immediate reply from Barrowe, entitled *A Plaine Refutation of M. G. Giffordes reprochful booke,* most of which is merely a repetition and elaboration of the doctrines set forth in his *Brief Discoverie of the False Church.* In his *Plaine Refutation of M. G. Giffordes reprochful booke* the author specifically addresses himself not only to Gifford's "two reprochfull blasphemous Bookes" but also to Dr. Some's third *Godly Treatise.* Indignantly protesting that Some and Gifford are "two special instruments" employed by the bishops to "accuse & blaspheme" him, Barrowe again condemns the Church of England for permitting "prophane multitudes" to mingle in worship with the "saints."

Though declaring baptism in "the false church" an invalid sacrament, he, like Penry, does not demand its repetition; thus he does not open himself or his followers to the charge of anabaptism. Instead, again like Penry, he advises them not to "offer & bring their children vnto the false church to be baptized," but instead to ignore the "outward baptisme." They should "seeke out & re-paire vnto the true Church of Christ," to which their children already belong through their parents' covenant with God. If Gifford, as he implies, recognizes the Church of Rome as a true church, then, Barrowe points out, the Church of England must be schismatic. If, in addition, Gifford recognizes the validity of the baptism of the Roman Church, Barrowe asks how he can condemn as "blasphemous and execrable" any other sacrament in that Church—for instance, the sacrament of holy communion.

Repeating his earlier statement in his *Brief Discoverie of the False Church,* that every member of the true church has the power to excommunicate every other member, Barrowe develops his theory of congregationalism as the church polity prescribed by Christ and distinguishes it *from presbyterianism* as well as from episcopalianism. In his own words, the phrase *Dic ecclesiae* means "the whole Congregation," not only the pope nor "the Lord Archbishops grace" nor "the Lord Bishops" nor even *"the companie of Elders* aparte, from, and without the people, *which companie they cal the Consistorie."* Indeed, the separatist scoffs at the idea that "our Sauiour Christ would fetch his patterne for the Elders of his Church . . . from that corrupt degenerat Sanedrion of the Iewes." In his opinion, the elders "are of God set ouer the flocke, to watche, to instruct, admonish, exhort, rebuke, &c.: yet not to pluck awaye the power & liberty of the whole Church or to translate and assume the publicke actions of the whole Church into their owne handes alone," for "they are men and may erre." On the contrary, "they themselues euen for al their doctrines and actions are subiect to the censure of the Church, or of the least members of the Church, if in any thing they be founde to erre or transgresse." While protesting that he himself is not a Brownist, in defending the followers of Browne he tacitly admits his sympathies with the followers of the first separatist. Like Browne, he maintains that since all communicants are one in the Church, the

· 189 ·

Body of Christ, a person known to be evil will infect the entire congregation.

Of course, he reiterates all of the usual strictures on the anti-Christian nature of the episcopacy and their "reading ministry." But he now denounces both episcopalian and presbyterian ministries as anti-Christian: "Here hence ariseth these schismes and sectes in the Church of England, some holding *with these Preachers, which make shewe as though they sought a sinceare reformation of all thinges according to the Gospell of Christ,* and yet both execute a false ministrie themselues, and they, together with all their hearers and followers, stand vnder the throne of Antichrist, the Bishops, their Courtes, and accomplices, and all those detestable enormities which they would haue vtterly remoued & not reformed: And these are herevpon called Precisians, or Puritanes, and now lately Martinistes." In short, just as the early reformers —Hugh Latimer, John Jewel, and even Cartwright—accused the Catholics of abandoning the teachings of the Apostles, so Barrowe accuses the episcopalians and presbyterians of deserting the principles of the "blessed Martyres that suffered in Q. Maries daies."

A final proof of Barrowe's Brownist sympathies is his demand that "priuate men," the few faithful banded together against "Antichrist," must at once *separate* from the false church and set up a congregationalist church government according to the Scriptures. The duty of "euerie particular Congregation," then, will be "to practize Christes Testament, either in erecting his officers and ordinances, or in reforming or correcting anie faulte or abuse that ariseth amongst them, without staying for the Princes license: yea though the Prince should vpon the paynes of death forbid," for each congregation has Christ's "sacred power and aucthoritie to binde and to loose in earth."

To this separatist document Greenwood adds an epilogue in which he asks Gifford how he can deny the Catholic sacrament of holy communion and yet accept their baptism, both of which must be false or else neither. Yet, like Barrowe, he does not require rebaptism for a person baptized in a "false" church.[8] And in a separate pamphlet, *An Answere to George Giffordes Pretended Defence of Read Praiers,* he reveals that his chief concern is not with baptism but with the old complaint, first mentioned in the *Admonition to the Parliament,* against the use of prescript prayers and homilies, both of which he labels "idolatry": "Much more odious yt is to bring in mens writings into the publique assemblies, proued vnlawfull in the first argument; and then to cōmit Idolatrie with them by reading them instead of praying." [9] It is not Greenwood's theology, however, that interests the student of the Marprelate Controversy, but rather his literary style. After reading his dull, frequently ambiguous, sentences, no one would ever think of attributing the sprightly tract *M. Some laid open in his coulers* to his pen. Indeed, only the knowledge that he was Barrowe's companion in suffering makes him worthy even of this brief consideration.

The final word in the "separatist" controversy went to Gifford, who in 1591 published his *Short Reply unto the last printed books of Henry Barrow and Iohn Greenwood.* In this pamphlet Gifford scoffs at Barrowe's hair-splitting distinction—which, incidentally, is similar to Penry's—between true baptism by a nonconformist minister and the sacrament administered in the Roman and Anglican Churches, which, while not a "true" sacrament in the opinion of the separatists, is nevertheless a true baptism "concerning the outwarde washing." "I pray you M. Barrow, is not the outward washing the whole Baptisme, and the whole seale of Gods couenant?" asks Gifford. As he sees it, the "inward grace is no part of the Sacrament" but rather "the thing represented and sealed by the Sacrament." Finally, he utterly repudiates Barrowe's assertion that the laws of the prince, or civil magistrate, in things indifferent are not binding on the conscience, which is concerned only with good and evil, upon which the minister, not the prince, must legislate.[10]

But Gifford was not the only writer strongly moved by Barrowe's ideas. Pierce comments that though Penry in his earlier years took pains "to disavow Brownism," he "moved continually towards Browne's ideals and towards liberty." Then, coming under the influence of Barrowe, Penry completed his conversion to separatism. When he returned from Scotland, he joined the London separatists and actively participated in their life and fellowship.[11] From this experience came the last of his controversial writings, his *Historie of Corah, Dathan, and Abiram*, in which he calls upon "every member of CHRIST . . . to *separate himself* vnder paine of Gods everlasting wrath" from "the whole parish-assemblies of this land, and the members thereof."

Based on the account of the rebellion of Corah, Dathan, and Abiram against the divinely appointed rule of Moses, this pamphlet excoriates the ministry of the Church of England, symbolized by these rebels in the Old Testament, for failing to adopt the presbyterian system supposedly set forth in the Scriptures. Using his favorite method of argument, the syllogism, Penry condemns the episcopalian heirarchy as "Anti-christian." Finally arriving at a decision concerning baptism, in no uncertain terms he declares it unlawful to "communicate in any action of religion, as in hearing trueth taught, in receiving the Sacraments, praying &c., within any of the publik meetings of the Land, as now they stand by law."

Aware, as always, that he must take into account the power of the supreme governor, he tries to separate her "Civill Authoritie," which in itself is ordained by God, from "the Ecclesiastical jurisdictiō of these Corahs, these Dathans, these Abirams." Not exactly satisfied with this resolution of his dilemma, he makes a second attempt to rationalize Elizabeth's position in religious affairs. Since her authority comes from God, he reasons, it embraces all causes, ecclesiastical and civil, public and private. Her only restriction in the civil sphere is that of law; her only restriction in the ecclesiastical sphere is the Word of God. Accordingly, she has no power to establish "either false Religion" or "false & Antichristian ordinances." [12]

Thus he never really clearly commits himself on this painful issue of the position of the supreme governor in the church. But as far as the episcopalian hierarchy is concerned, his decision, unlike that of Cartwright, was separation from the Church of England.

Chapter XVII

The Epilogue to
the Marprelate Controversy

The last episcopalian champion to ride into the lists during the reign of Queen Elizabeth was Matthew Sutcliffe, who took on all Puritan challengers and wrote the epilogue to the Marprelate Controversy, as well as to nonconformist pamphleteering in general for the sixteenth century. His first pamphlet, his *Remonstrance or Plaine Detection,* is mainly directed at John Udall, whose trial was a prominent event in 1590. Like the anti-Martinist imitations of "martinizing," Sutcliffe's pamphlet in abusiveness closely resembles Martin's style. Frequently referring to Whitgift's *Defense of the Aunswere,* he names Cartwright as "the Bel-weather of this bande," [1] whose "stuffe" Udall in his *Demonstration of Discipline* has taken "on trust" in his contention that the perfect plan for the Christian church is set forth in complete detail in the Scriptures. As might be expected, then, Sutcliffe's pamphlet is as repetitious of the episcopalian line as Udall's is of the Puritan.

In 1591, in his *Treatise of Ecclesiasticall Discipline,* Sutcliffe continues his attack on Cartwright. Again, in condemning the presbyterian orders as defined by Cartwright, he seems merely to be reworking Whitgift's arguments. Yet, in view of the events that had occurred in the almost twenty years since the publication of Whitgift's *Defense of the Aunswere,* Sutcliffe clearly sees that separatism is the logical endpoint of Cartwright's doctrines: "If their [the Puritans'] discipline be a part of the Gospell; then are not they the true Church of Christ, that refuse the same; then haue the *Barrowistes* iust cause to depart, and seperate themselues from vs."

And concerning Cartwright's belated—and illogical—defense of the Church of England against the first of the separatists, Robert Harrison, Sutcliffe adds the following warning: "I maruell with what face he [Cartwright] durst take vpon him the defence of our cause, handling the same so weakely and vnfaithfully. it was an error vntollerable, to make discipline a part of the Gospel: but hauing laid downe that for a position, it was more absurd and sencelesse to defend our Church that refuseth his discipline. therefore, if he will heare good counsell, let him lay hand off our cause, which we are by Gods grace able to defend, as wel against him, as against the *Barrowistes;* both which consent together alike, in defacing the Church of England." [2] But the major part of Sutcliffe's *Treatise of Ecclesiasticall Discipline* is but a repetition of the standard episcopalian counterarguments.

Sutcliffe's literary activity was partly responsible for the appearance of the anonymous *Petition directed to her most excellent Maiestie*, in which appear certain disparaging rejoinders directed at "one Matthewe Sutcliffe." [3] Accordingly, the episcopalian polemicist brought out his *Answere to a Certaine Libel*, in which he makes a number of sweeping charges as though he hoped that at least one of them might find a target. One of these was his identification of Martin with "I. Penry, I. Vd[all]., I. F[ield]., and I. Thr[ockmorton]." In this pamphlet he also, more specifically, attributes to Throckmorton "all his Libels, and scoffes published vnder the name of *Martin,* as namely his theses, protestations, dialogues, arguments, laying men out in their colours [*M. Some laid open in his coulers*]—in short, all of the literary products printed with "Waldegrave's 'letter' " so-called, and hence associated with the Martinist press. [4]

Consequently, in 1594 Throckmorton, the only living member of the quartet of "I.'s," issued a brief letter entitled the *Defence of Iob Throkmorton,* in which, taking cognizance of the fact that Sutcliffe in his second reference attributes all of the Martinist tracts to him, Throckmorton indicates his own awareness that these tracts were the product of only one pen: "And so to speake the trueth, he [Sutcliffe] may as well [attribute to Throckmorton] all as one." Yet, denying that his was that pen, he points out that Sutcliffe, "when, it may be, hee had slept better all night," had brought him "in at the later end [after the other three "I.'s"] as a candle holder," and thus had both cleared and disburdened him of the charge of Martinism. At the same time Throckmorton takes occasion to issue a forthright denial of his own complicity in the Marprelate Controversy: "I will for my finall clearing heerein (when so euer it shall be thought so good by the State) willinglie take this oth, as I haue heeretofore offered, to witte, *That I am not Martin, I knewe not Martin, And concerning that I stande endighted of, I am as cleare as the childe vnborne.*" [5]

This firm denial was all that Sutcliffe needed, and without further ado he launched a blistering attack, his *Answere unto Iob Throkmortons Letter,* in which he seems determined to send to the gallows the last of the three men named in the depositions as actively connected with the publication of the Martinist tracts, the other two, Penry and Udall, having already died. By thus setting out to prove Throckmorton's guilt, however, Sutcliffe succeeded in confusing the entire issue for posterity. First, he repeats his earlier accusation: "Iohn Penry, say I, Iohn Vdall, Iohn Fielde, all Iohns, and Iob Throkmorton, all concurred in making Martin." Then he adds an amplifying statement that is a masterpiece of ambiguity: "Which words are so farre from clearing him [Throckmorton], that they doe clearely conuict him, euen as these wordes cleare him, so let him, of those matters whereof he would purge himselfe be cleared. Nay he confesseth in the ende, that he is brought in for a candle holder. Vntrue then it is, that hee is left out, or cleared. The trueth is, that he is brought in as a principall agent in all these libels. Next to Penry that was hanged for libelling against the state, M. Throkmorton deserueth the first place." [6] However, as the depositions clearly indicate, "the truth is" that Throckmorton's association with the Marprelate press did not begin until after the publication of the first four Martinist tracts. Furthermore, it should be noted that in this indictment of Throckmorton, Sutcliffe does not name him as "principall agent" *instead of Penry* but "next to Penry."

Although Arber and Pierce cite this fragment of Sutcliffe's testimony as their strongest argument for identifying Throckmorton as Martin, in all fairness to both scholars it must be admitted that neither of them seems entirely convinced. As though detecting inconsistencies in Sutcliffe's account, Arber concludes that the episcopalian writer must have had access to documents now lost. [7] And though likewise skeptical of Sutcliffe's accuracy and apparently recognizing that this indictment of Throckmorton is just about the only evidence for naming him instead of Penry as Martin, Pierce eventually falls back on Arber's unsupported assumption that Sutcliffe had access to documents no longer extant: "The value of Sutcliffe's indictment for our present inquiry lies in the use he was able to make of the depositions of a number of implicated persons under legal examination, and the collections of notes, made by the prosecution for the use of their counsel; all of which was *apparently* placed at his disposal. *It is only from his pages that several of these persons are known to have made depositions, as the documents used by Sutcliffe are not, for the most part, known to exist today. . . . It is possible, it is highly probable, in some cases, that* these scraps of evidence concerning Penry were given after his execution when they could do him no harm." [8] In the face of this wild speculation Throckmorton's denial, supported as it is by the *extant* information in the hands of the Government during and immediately after the publication of the Martinist pamphlets, must outweigh Sutcliffe's statement, at least until the "lost documents" turn up.

Although the *Defence of Iob Throkmorton* was Sutcliffe's main target, he seizes this opportunity again to attack Cartwright. Among the Puritan leader's many offenses against the Establishment, Sutcliffe declares that "M. Cartwright vpō the cōming forth of Martin is reported to haue said, that it was no matter, if the Bishops were so handled, seeing they would take no warning." [9] Accordingly, in 1596 the accused man decided to write a *Brief Apologie* in order to clear his name: "For me, I am able to produce witnesses, that the first time that euer I heard of Martin Marprelate I testified my great misliking & grief, for so naughtie, and so disorderly a course as that was. And therefore where . . . he asketh when I will condemne th'vnlawfull and vnciuill practice of Martin and Penry? I aske againe what office or charge I haue to publishe condemnation vpon euery vnlawfull and vnciuill writing that cometh abroad. And yet I haue witnesses, that euen publikely when I was alowed to preach, I condemned all dealing in that kinde." [10]

This explanation, however, did not in the least placate Sutcliffe, who in his *Examination of M. Thomas Cartwrights late apologie* repeats his allegation that Cartwright had approved of Martin's course and actually names the place where Cartwright was supposed to have expressed his approval: "in olde M. Bodleyes house." Furthermore, adds Sutcliffe, Cartwright "by his scoffes and flowers of railing traced out a way for Martin," and while "the libels of Martin went currantly thorow euery mans hands without all answere, or opposition," Cartwright "and his confraternitie of disciplinarians" gave their silent approval.

Not content with thus implicating Cartwright in the Marprelate Controversy, Sutcliffe asks him whether "Barowes erroneous conclusions" had not resulted from his doctrines and whether Cartwright's demand that the prince be subjected to excommunication was not an outright attack on the power of the supreme governor.

In connection with this accusation of disloyalty Sutcliffe accuses Cartwright of the same kind of equivocation that has already been pointed out in Penry's pamphlets and in the Martinist publications: "True it is, that you offer to sweare to the supremacie . . . it may be, you will acknowledge her Maiesties authoritie in generall termes, and yet wil not acknowledge the seuerall points of her authoritie. You doe also offer to sweare to the supremacie, but you haue a preuerse interpretatiō, by which you ouerthrow all the chiefe points of it in effect." [11] This "preuerse interpretation" is undoubtedly a reference to the oft-repeated Puritan doctrine that the civil magistrate should be subject to the elders and should willingly submit to the discipline of excommunication. Thus, in Sutcliffe's opinion, Cartwright takes the oath but interprets the law according to his own thinking.

No one who has delved to any considerable depth in the Puritan literature of the sixteenth century would question Sutcliffe's estimate of Cartwright's position of leadership among the nonconformists. His attacks on the episcopalian hierarchy were mainly responsible for the rise of presbyterianism, and the logical working out of his theories of church government tended toward a congregational, rather than a strictly presbyterian, polity, which could not possibly be contained within the Church of England and would ultimately lead to separation. This separatist trend is epitomized in the career of Penry, who, according to tradition, was born a Catholic but died a martyr to the cause of congregationalism. If Cartwright best typifies the spirit of nonconformity during the first half of Elizabeth's reign, then Penry holds that place during the second.

Under the circumstances Penry's decision to separate was far more logical than Cartwright's backing down on his original program of reform and remaining in the Church of England. Both men regarded the episcopacy as anti-Christian, but Cartwright was willing to compromise at the expense of his own convictions. Whether or not either man was "right" in condemning the bishops is not the question; at least both men were convinced that they were on the side of the angels. As Hamlet says, "There is nothing either good or bad but thinking makes it so." Penry, thinking himself "right" and Whitgift and the bishops "wrong," acted.

A far more talented writer than Cartwright, Penry, even in his signed writings, presents an adequate picture of the movement toward separatism. Commenting on his literary ability, Pierce speculates whether or not "if, under another star, a kindly providence such leisure had granted him," Penry might "have shown an urbane and erudite appreciation of the writings of his great literary contemporaries." [12] Yet, if Pierce is looking for "sugared sonnets" or heroic epics, he could hardly expect them from the pen that wrote the *Exhortation,* much less the *Epistle* and *M. Some laid open in his coulers.* Penry's fiery phrases, frequently as staccato as the rattling of rifles on a battlefield, were composed for the purpose of arousing the English reading public to the spiritual dangers that their creator believed he found in the "ecclesiastical polity" controlled by "arch-Bb. and Ll. Bb."

In addition to the vast amount of circumstantial evidence pointing to Penry as author, proofreader, compositor, and publisher, the fact that these tracts, though presbyterian in content, were separatist in spirit at a time when Penry himself was turning from presbyterianism to separatism forces the conclusion that to him alone belongs the title of Martin Marprelate. If his admirers in Wales and elsewhere accept this attribution of the authorship of the Martinist pamphlets to him, Pierce's dream of a place for him in the great circle of Elizabethan writers will be realized. To Penry, then, will be awarded the title already given Martin, namely, that of "the great prose satirist of the Elizabethan period." [13]

Why anyone at this late date would wish to deny him this signal honor is a baffling problem involving both religious and patriotic sentiments. But since attributing these supposedly infamous pamphlets to the "pilgrim martyr," as his biographer John Waddington calls him, continues to arouse resentment in certain circles, it may be fitting to conclude this discussion of

Martin Marprelate with the statement of Dexter, whose scholarly history of Congregationalism, though published in 1880, remains a storehouse of information for the student of sixteenth-century Puritanism:

In my judgment, there is absolutely nothing in the seven tracts for which Martin is properly responsible, of which anybody— Churchman, or Dissenter—need be ashamed, or for which apology need be made. Surely there is no word in anything of Martin's own that is blasphemous or obscene; nothing which indicates either a brutal head or beastly heart. Of course they run—that kind of writing in that day must always have done so—often very near to the perilous edge of that precipice whose feet are washed by the sea of words that cannot be spoken; they often employ terms which would now seem extreme in violence, and sometimes lay hold of an epithet from which the taste of our age would shrink. But Martin was writing in and for the sixteenth, and not the nineteenth century; and was, of set purpose, launching out into a style of rough and rollicking satire new to his time, with the intent to seize and hold the convictions of the more intelligent masses of the English people as he knew them to be.[14]

These reassuring words from a reputable Congregationalist historian may help to convince the venerators of Penry, who hitherto have resented identifying him with Martin, that the pamphlets contain nothing that might sully the moral reputation of their martyred hero.

Chapter XVIII

The Significance of
the Controversy

Pierce closes his biography of Penry with an "Epilogue," in which he pays tribute to his "illustrious countryman, John Penry, saint and hero, patriot and Martyr," who, as the biographer writes, "inspired" him "to believe in a day, that is ever on its way, when tyranny, ecclesiastical and political, of priest and kaiser, shall darken men's lives no more." In view of the great industry of this Welsh scholar, it may seem uncharitable to enlarge upon the extravagances to which his enthusiasm frequently carried him. Yet, since his exaggerations have tended to confuse our understanding of the Marprelate Controversy and its significance both in its own time and afterward, it becomes necessary to write another epilogue, in which some of these are corrected.

Today his picture of Penry or of any other Puritan as an apostle of freedom of thought seems almost ludicrous. Sometimes, indeed, Pierce writes almost as though he had never read the pamphlets that he is discussing. Noting that "Penry never forsakes his grave religious manner of dealing with religious affairs," his biographer paints a completely sentimentalized picture: "Yet in the exigency of the conflict, unfairly matched and unequally equipped with literary apparatus and convenience for writing against his antagonists, he uses no word, employs no device, which for his fair fame, as his biographer, I am tempted to regret. . . . Writing during the primacy of Whitgift, harried by the intrigue and espionage of Bancroft, his pages are free from brutality; on the contrary *he is a chivalrous antagonist. He can be courteous even to a wordy and irritating old egotist, like Dr. Robert Some.*"

But who, we might ask, would look for either chivalry or courtesy in a Savonarola? Surely Penry's hatred of the episcopacy, which, in his opinion, had blocked the reformation of the English Church, was scarcely less violent than that of the great Italian reformer for what he considered the religious abuses among the Florentines. Indeed, in a rare moment of objectivity Pierce himself accurately expresses the true spirit of Penry's writing: "Fire and indignation redden and glow in some of his pages." Rather than a "great lover," as Pierce somewhat romantically terms him, he is more accurately depicted by the same biographer as a single-minded religious enthusiast: "During the six years in which he [Penry] claims our attention we discover in his life one interest only. Religion so completely filled his thought that it left no place for any companion enthusiasm." [1] And as we read the pages of his several pamphlets, we become aware of his intense determination to press his reforms of the Church of England even at the expense of his own life.

McKerrow, with his customary common sense, places the English Puritans, among which Penry for the greater part of his career was one of the most vociferous, in their proper perspective: "The Puritan movement has on the whole tended to religious toleration—partly, if not mainly, by reason of the number of sects to which it has given rise—but it must not be thought that in the sixteenth century it in any way favoured individual interpretation or greater liberty of thought. The purpose of the Puritans was not to found a separate Church governed according to their own views, but to change the government of the existing Church. They wished to worship in their own way, *but they wished also, and perhaps quite as much, to prevent others from worshipping in any different way. . . . It is important that this fact should be clearly borne in mind, that the Puritan ideal was no more favourable to liberty of thought than was the Anglican view,* for there has been much loose writing upon the subject. That upon either side we find comparatively few references to the necessity of all men belonging to the same Church is simply because this was fully accepted by both parties, and there was therefore no necessity for insisting upon it." [2] In other words, the idea of "pluralism" in religion is a strictly mid-twentieth century intellectual and spiritual achievement.

The Presbyterian historian Scott Pearson likewise points out that the Puritans, like many other religious and political rebels against despotism, unconsciously helped to hasten the realization that if one group is to be free from molestation it must permit others the same freedom: "By their claim to liberty of conscience the Puritans prepared the way for that toleration which allowed both State and Church to be free. This they did, *not because they believed in toleration for all* but because, like other dissenting minorities, they showed that peace in a realm can only be achieved if the rights of conscience are recognized. . . . The Puritans were allied with Jesuits, Huguenots, and Dutchmen in the struggle against the forces of absolute monarchy and the tyranny of civil power, *and in spite of themselves they contributed to the furtherance of both civil and religious liberty*." Hence, when Penry, writing either under his own name or under the pseudonym of Martin Marprelate, is described as an enemy of tyranny, his contribution to religious and intellectual freedom must be regarded as purely fortuitous.

Everything, too, that Pearson specifically has to say of Cartwright, the presbyterian, is applicable to Penry, presbyterian and separatist. Premising "that God has decreed Presbyterianism as the only perfect and perpetual polity of the Church" and "that God is a Presbyterian," Cartwright, according to Pearson, required universal acceptance of the "discipline." This insistence upon enforced conformity, continues Pearson, "implies that a Puritan Presbyterian Church should be established, that uniformity should be enforced, that Puritan ministers are the best judges, and that the evils of intolerance would continue, the victims and the oppressors changing places."

Had Cartwright and the Puritans attained their national presbyterian church, Pearson is convinced that the inevitable result would have been a far greater intolerance than that practiced by the episcopacy: "It is obvious that the Puritans did not believe in toleration. They could not conceive of more than one true religion, and held that their duty to God bade them seek the furtherance of it and simultaneously the suppression of all that was incompatible with it. . . . If in power, the Elizabethan Puritans would doubtless have excelled in intolerance the authorities whose regime they denounced. . . . For the Puritan freedom of conscience means in general liberty to act according to his own interpretation of the word of God, and in particular liberty to set up a Puritan Church with a Presbyterian polity. But what of others whose interpretation of divine law differs from theirs? All are wrong, for there is only one true religion." [3] As Cartwright's most zealous disciple, Penry sought to carry out his presbyterian program of reform within the Church of England until 1590, when he began to realize that this program was incompatible with the episcopalian Establishment. Then he joined Barrowe, Greenwood, and the other separatists.

Moreover, it is incontestable that Penry's separation from the Established Church was not a move toward greater tolerance. Placing the power to excommunicate in the hands of every member of the congregation, as Browne and his followers had recommended, caused the break up of several Brownist communities. [4] Apparently the zeal of some of the saints to ferret out the sinners in their midst resulted in even greater intolerance than that experienced under the bishops or the presbytery.

The first attempt to heal the breach between the nonconformists and the Church of England was Bishop Bancroft's *Survey of the Pretended Holy Discipline* (1593). But Bancroft, to whom credit is given for spearheading the counterattack on the Martinists, was too pugnacious to spread oil on the troubled waters. The most tolerant attitude displayed in the Elizabethan period toward the religious strife was that of Richard Hooker, whose *Ecclesiastical Polity* was written for the purpose of restoring peace to the Church of England. Since Martin had loudly accused Whitgift of tacitly admitting defeat in failing to answer Cartwright's last two *Replies*, the Archbishop, probably too preoccupied with his duties as ecclesiastical head of the Church, assigned the task to Hooker. Book V of Hooker's famous work, therefore, is dedicated to the Archbishop. Hooker's analysis of the struggle between the nonconformists and the Established Church was in its own time generally regarded as both honest and impartial.[5]

In the Preface to the *Ecclesiastical Polity* Hooker reviews all of the arguments directed against the Establishment since the beginning of Elizabeth's reign. Adopting Whitgift's scholarly technique, Hooker throughout his argument quotes large sections from the Puritan pamphlets, particularly from those of Cartwright, and answers them in a spirit of candor and tolerance that places his work above and beyond what might be termed purely controversial. In a complete reversal of policy among English Protestants he renounces Calvin, whose standing had hitherto been questioned only by Whitgift.[6] While conceding that the Genevan reformer was "incomparably the wisest man that ever the French church did enjoy, since the hour it enjoyed him," Hooker clearly portrays him as a political opportunist who had set up in Geneva an ecclesiastical system based on expedience and not on the Scriptures, which Hooker concedes to be one that "the wisest at that time living" could not have bettered. Noting, however, that "some of the chiefest place and countenance amongst the laity" had expressed the opinion that Calvin's discipline was little better than "Popish tyranny disguised and tendered unto them under a new form," Hooker reminds "the present inhabitants of Geneva" that he has used "their books and writings" as his sources for his present account of the planting of the "discipline" among them.

In order to soften his denial of Calvin's claims for scriptural authority for the Genevan church government, Hooker remarks that "that which Calvin did for establishment of his discipline, seemeth more commendable than that which he taught for the countenancing of it established." Then he proceeds to label all Calvin's claims the product of the reformer's rationalization: "Wherefore a marvel it were if a man of so great capacity, having such incitements to make him desirous of all kind of furtherances unto his cause, could espy in the whole Scripture of God nothing which might breed at the least a probable opinion of likelihood that divine authority itself was the same way somewhat inclinable. And all which the wit even of Calvin was able from thence to draw, by sifting the very utmost sentence and syllable, is no more than that certain speeches there are which to him did seem to intimate that all Christian churches ought to have their elderships endued with the power of excommunication, and that a part of those elderships every where should be chosen out from amongst the laity, after that form which himself had framed Geneva unto." The result, as Hooker explains, is that both in France and in Scotland Calvin's scriptural interpretations have become "almost the very canon to judge both doctrine and discipline by."

Turning to Calvin's influence in England, Hooker traces the development of nonconformity from the return of the Marian exiles through the Vestiarian Controversy to the Admonition Controversy. Before discussing Cartwright's defense of the two *Admonitions*, he invokes a spirit of understanding as though well aware that he is about to present the crucial points in his argument: "Concerning the Defender of which Admonitions [Cartwright], all that I mean to say is but this: *there will come a time when three words uttered with charity and meekness shall receive a far more blessed reward than three thousand volumes written with disdain-*

ful sharpness of wit." After thus attempting to mollify Cartwright himself, Hooker appeals to the nonconformists in general to attend to the pronouncements of learned theologians even while disagreeing with them.

Then he plunges into an analysis of the various techniques used by the Puritan writers to promulgate their presbyterian doctrines: first, their sharp criticism of persons in power in order to win themselves "a great good opinion of integrity, zeal, and holiness"; second, the imputation of "all faults and corruptions, wherewith the world aboundeth, unto the kind of ecclesiastical government established"; third, their proposal of their own form of church government "as the only sovereign remedy of all evils"; fourth, "fashioning the very notions and conceits of men's minds in such sort, that when they read the Scripture, thay may think that every thing soundeth toward the advancement of that discipline, and to the utter disgrace of the contrary," so that "the simple and ignorant" will find the presbyterian regiment of pastors, elders, doctors, and deacons in every line of Scripture; fifth, their insistence that they have discovered this system of government through "the special illumination of the Holy Ghost"—a claim that implies that they alone are the chosen people of God and that all others are "worldlings, time-servers, pleasers of men not of God, with such like."

Regarding the discipline that the nonconformists profess to find in the Scriptures, Hooker comments as follows: "A very strange thing sure it were, that such a discipline as ye speak of should be taught by Christ and his apostles in the word of God, and no church ever have found it out, nor received it till this present time; contrariwise, the government against which ye bend yourselves be observed every where throughout all generations and ages of the Christian world, no church ever perceiving the word of God to be against it."

Hooker likewise fails to discover the "primitive church" that Cartwright and his followers claim as their model: "Many things out of antiquity ye bring, as if the purest times of the Church had observed the selfsame orders which you require; and as though your desire were that the churches of old should be patterns for us to follow, and even glasses, wherein we might see the practice of that which by you is gathered out of scripture." Moreover, asserts Hooker, no sooner have the Puritans set up the apostolic church as the model "primitive church" than as authoritative they cite persons and customs existing either before or after the days of the Apostles; in other words, they fail to limit the scope of the so-called "Apostolical times." As a matter of fact, Hooker points out, "what was used in the Apostles' times the Scripture fully declareth not." Conversely, certain specific customs of the Apostolic Church, like the *oscula sancta* and the feasts of charity, are no longer recognized. Consequently, since the Puritans cannot convincingly demonstrate that their presbyterian orders existed in apostolic times, they are driven to cite the opinions of whatever contemporary reformers may happen to agree with them. Regarding these reformed churches, too, Hooker notes that they themselves are not in agreement on the titles and functions of the ecclesiastical orders.

Replying to the Puritan demand for a "public disputation," Hooker first suggests "the schools in universities," where at "their yearly acts and commencements, besides other disputations both ordinary and upon occasion" any of the controversial matters may be debated. Otherwise Hooker would have these matters taken up "by solemn conference in orderly and quiet sort," for which he would set down the following rules of procedure: first, that since the Puritans are attacking the established order, they should consider themselves as plaintiffs who must prove that the present order should be abolished and the new accepted; second, that before descending to particulars they take up, one by one, the general points of difference, each of which must be fully understood by both sides; third, that the Puritans select a speaker whose views will represent their consensus, a copy of which should be duly notarized and presented to the Anglicans, who, in turn, would be given sufficient time to draw up a reply under similar rules of procedure; fourth, that at the outset each side should agree to publish only "that very book and no other," in which the "present authorized notaries" have written down these matters.

A final requirement for a peaceful conference, according to Hooker, is a mutual agreement that once the final judgment has been pronounced, no one, no matter what his private opinion may be, shall continue to dispute. For, as Hooker expresses it, "So full of wilfulness and self-liking is our nature, that without some definitive sentence, which being given may stand, and a necessity of silence on both sides afterward imposed, small hope there is that strifes thus far prosecuted will in a short time quietly end."

By setting forth the episcopalian view that the laws of the Established Church are rational and therefore worthy of obedience and respect, Hooker in the main text of his book is taking the first step toward a council such as he envisions. In his argument, which is to follow, he intends to examine "the nature, kinds, and qualities of laws in general" and then to investigate the "first and chiefest principle" on which the nonconformists build, namely, whether the laws for which they strive are actually to be found in the Scriptures and, indeed, whether "in Scripture there must of necessity be found some particular form of Polity Ecclesiastical, the Laws whereof admit not any kind of alteration." Turning then to rebuttal, Hooker next plans to reply to the accusations that the Church of England retains "manifold popish rites and ceremonies," that its liturgy is corrupt, that the episcopacy should be replaced by the presbytery, and that the power of the civil magistrate should be eliminated.

In the conclusion to his Preface he utters an eloquent appeal to charity and common sense: "The best and safest way for you therefore, my dear brethren, is, to call your deeds past to a new reckoning, to re-examine the cause ye have taken in hand, and to try it even point by point, argument by argument, with all the diligent exactness ye can; to lay aside the gall of that bitterness wherein your minds have hitherto over-abounded, and with meekness to search the truth. Think ye are men, deem it not impossible for you to err; sift unpartially your own hearts, whether it be force of reason or vehemency of affection, which hath bred and still doth feed these opinions in you. If truth do any where manifest itself, seek not to smother it with glossing delusions, acknowledge the greatness thereof, and think it your best victory when the same doth prevail over you." With this fraternal approach, Hooker temporarily elevated the argument between nonconformist and conformist from the low level of name calling and character assassination to which it frequently had descended.[7]

Unfortunately, however, though not openly condemned by the nonconformists, his ecumenical efforts were unavailing. The dissension between those in favor of the Establishment and those against it festered for almost half a century until the Puritans with Oliver Cromwell as their leader rose up, took over the Government, and executed both the religious and the civil heads of the Church of England—the Archbishop and the Supreme Governor. In this time of conflict an edition of Martin's *Hay any worke for Cooper* again made its appearance, along with four other pamphlets written under the pseudonym of "young Martin Marpriest." [8] And in Penry's footsteps in attacking the episcopacy followed one of England's greatest poets, John Milton.

Until the present day, indeed, Hooker's plea for a peaceful solution to the controversies among the warring Protestant sects has fallen on deaf ears. The studies of the Marprelate Controversy made in the nineteenth and early twentieth centuries, notably the strongly pro-Anglican editions of William Maskell and the equally strongly pro-Puritan writings of Arber and Pierce, merely continued the religious strife. The presbyterians and the episcopalians still differ in their theories of church government. The evangelical sects continue to protest against the episcopalian liturgical customs. It may be, however, that the movement for church unity begun by Pope John XXIII in Rome will draw together not only the "separated brethren" and the Mother Church but also the separated brethren among themselves. The personal encounters in recent years between the Pope and the heads of the English and the Scottish Churches respectively would suggest that a new spirit abroad in Britain—and, indeed, throughout Christendom—may be ushering in an era of tolerance entirely foreign to the writers of Elizabethan England.

A Note on Previous Bibliographical Studies of Penry's Exhortation

Designating the *Exhortation* "one of the most important of all Penry's writings," Pierce makes the following reference to its publication:

It [the secret printing press] was soon at work, wherever located, and *strangely enough* it was occupied in publishing two further editions [the second and the third] of the *Exhortation,* which are not only to be distinguished from the first edition by difference in type, but from each other, in spelling, capitals, italics and other orthographical peculiarities. The second and third editions are enlarged, each by an appendix special to itself, and each has its own note to the Reader. The difficulty of producing any edition was so great, and one would suppose the difficulty of vending copies to be equally great, *even if there were a public demand for this kind of contraband religious controversy; which could hardly be the case with a tractate on the evangelisation of Wales, with divagations on the complexities of Penry's and Some's theories of baptism, and of the status of ministers; that the appearance of these two later editions under the circumstances stated, raises several questions which cannot at present be answered.*

If instead of presuming that there was no "public demand for this kind of contraband religious controversy," Pierce had analyzed the additions and alterations made during the process of publishing these three editions, he might have been able to answer some of the "several questions" thus raised.

Of all of Penry's fiery pamphlets the *Exhortation* is probably the most revolutionary. The first edition, printed by the Puritan printer Robert Waldegrave, was published some time before April 16, 1588, when Waldegrave's shop was raided, for no copies were reported as seized there.[1] On or about May 6, 1588, appeared a second edition with a slightly lengthened title and a greatly expanded text. Following the first forty pages, which except for three marginal notes are identical with the first edition, are two new sections: the first, pp. 41–65, consisting of fifty-three syllogisms supporting Penry's claim that "dumb"—that is, episcopalian—"ministers" are no true ministers; the second, pp. 65–110, an appeal directed "To the LL. of the Covnsell," to which is appended a closing note "To the Reader," beginning "Master D. Somes booke was published this day, I haue read it." Dr. Robert Some's *First Godly Treatise*, to which Penry here refers, is dated May 6, 1588. Furthermore, a reference to the impending threat of attack by the Spanish Armada places the second edition of the *Exhortation* well before August 9–12, when the Armada was dispersed.[2]

Although the third edition also is undated, the closing note beginning, "I haue read Master D. Somes booke, the reasons he vseth in the questions of the dumbe ministerie, and communicationg with them, I had answered (as you may see in this booke) before he had written," [3] would indicate that Penry is still referring to Some's *First Godly Treatise* rather than his *Second*, published September 19, 1588. Evidently, then, the third edition of the *Exhortation* came out during the summer of that year. In addition to the revision of the concluding note "To the Reader," the third edition differs from the second in omitting the appeal "To the LL. of the Covnsell."

As well as failing to exlain why Penry within a few weeks published these three different editions of ostensibly the same tract, Pierce presents a faulty bibliographical description of both the second and the third editions. After correctly describing the first edition he writes of the second:

> Title as above. . . . Similar to the 1st ed. in all particulars, but without the signature. Then follows an addition, "To the LL. of the Covnsell," pp. 65–110. This is signed "John Penri," and appears later as the separate tract known as the *Supplication*.

Pierce's initial error in this description occurs in his reference to the title of the second edition. The startling addition to the original title, "There is in the ende something that was not in the former impression," he ignores. Indeed, according to him, this subtitle appears only in the third edition.[4]

His next descriptive comment, "similar to the 1st ed. in all particulars," is likewise incorrect. Yet Penry himself calls attention to what at first glance might seem only a slight change in the original text: "Thus I haue set downe the exhortation, word for word, as it was in the former impressiō, without the altering or deminishing of any one thing, (*three marginall notes added*) sauing the faults escaped in the printing." [5] These seemingly unimportant "marginall notes," thus overlooked by Pierce, all occur at the point in the essay where Penry is wrestling with the problem of the validity of the sacrament of baptism in the Roman and English Churches and hence are closely related to his eventual conversion to separatism, which had much to do with the publication of the Martinist tracts.

Much more extensive than these brief notes, but omitted from

Pierce's description, is the section of twenty-four pages containing the fifty-three syllogisms. Though he mentions the second section, the appeal "To the LL. of the Covnsell," his inaccurate statement that this addition "appears later as the separate tract known as the *Supplication*" is termed a "strange error" by David Williams, recent editor of the *Exhortation*. Williams also expresses astonishment at Pierce's description of the *Supplication* as "a 'reprint' of the former address 'with slight alterations and amplifications.' " On the contrary, writes Williams, "in the *Supplication* the address is amplified to twice its length, and is prefaced by a long 'Epistle to the Reader.' " [6]

Likewise inaccurate is Pierce's description of the third edition of the *Exhortation*. Along with the incorrect implication that the expansion of the original title occurs only in this edition, he refers to the section, pp. 41–65, as "*the* addition," as though he means the "addition, 'To the LL. of the Covnsell,' " mentioned in his description of the second edition. [7] Actually the addition in the third edition is merely a reprint of the fifty-three syllogisms attacking the "dumb ministers," also pp. 41–65 as in the second edition but omitted from his description of that edition. In the third edition, indeed, the highly inflammatory address "To the LL. of the Covnsell" never appears.

Although Williams to some extent repairs Pierce's bibliographical commentary, in his own "Bibliographical Note" his statement that "the *Exhortation* was printed in a first impression, of which there is no copy in B.M. [British Museum] or N.L.W. [National Library of Wales]" would suggest that he is unaware of, or at any rate has not examined, the copy at the Huntington Library, to which reference is made in this study. In reporting Penry's statement in the second edition (to which Williams, adopting Penry's Elizabethan vocabulary, inaccurately refers as a "second impression"), that he is reprinting the *Exhortation* "word for word, as it was in the former impressiō," Williams, like Pierce, neglects to mention Penry's "three marginall notes added," the significance of which has been pointed out.

Moreover, while commenting on the "twenty-four pages of syllogistic argument" not mentioned by Pierce, Williams incorrectly states that this is what is "referred to in the title-page, 'There is in the ende something that was not in the former impression,'" rather than the "forty-five page address 'To the LL. [Lords] of the Counsel,' that is, to the Privy Council," which actually comes at the end of the second edition of the *Exhortation* and which Penry himself, who revised and expanded it as the *Supplication,* must have considered especially important. Even though Williams questions Pierce's description of the *Supplication* as a mere reprint of this address, Williams himself apparently considers it so unimportant that he omits it in his own reprint on the ground that "it was superseded by a separate treatise *A viewe of . . . such publike wants,* addressed not to the Privy Council but to Parliament, and generally known from its running title as the *Supplication.*"

Further indication that Williams was not completely familiar with the address "To the LL. of the Covnsell" is that in summarizing the contents of the *Supplication* (1589) he writes, "There had now appeared *A Defence of the Government established in the Church of England* by John Bridges, dean of Salisbury," as though Bridges had just published.[8] As a matter of fact, Penry's most scathing denunciation of Bridges and his book is an important part of the address appended to the second edition of the *Exhortation,* published some nine months earlier; moreover, in the *Supplication* the criticism of the Dean is much toned down. Hence, the publication of the *Defence of the Government Established* antedates not only Martin Marprelate's *Epistle* (October, 1588), which also attacks it, but the second edition of the *Exhortation* (May, 1588) as well. The date on the title page of Bridges' volume, indeed, is 1587.

Notes

CHAPTER I: THE YEAR OF DECISION

1. For much of the historical background in this introductory chapter I am indebted to Garrett Mattingly's *The Armada* (Cambridge, Massachusetts, 1959).
2. Mattingly, *The Armada*, p. 184.
3. *Ibid.*, p. 63.
4. *Ibid.*, pp. 397 ff.
5. Donald J. McGinn, *The Admonition Controversy* (Rutgers University Studies in English, No. 5, New Brunswick, New Jersey, 1949), pp. vii–viii.

CHAPTER II: THE RISE OF PURITANISM

1. For a detailed account of these events see McGinn, *Admonition Controversy*, pp. 20, 467 ff., 23, 23 n., 278, 322, 511, 52, 45, 49–50.
2. W. H. Frere, *The English Church in the Reigns of Elizabeth and James I (1558–1625)* (London, 1911), p. 182.
3. *Hay any worke for Cooper*, sig. A 2ᵛ.
4. McGinn, *Admonition Controversy*, pp. 301, 401 ff., 521–22, 480–81, 529, 115, 420, 431, 459, 464, 182, 189–92, 169, 171, 176–77, 181. (The italics are mine.)
5. William Haller, *The Rise of Puritanism* (New York, 1938), pp. 169–70.
6. Pearson, *Church and State*, p. 37.

CHAPTER III: THE FIRST SIGNS OF SEPARATISM

1. Albert Peel and Leland H. Carlson, eds., *The Writings of Robert Harrison and Robert Browne* (London, 1953), pp. 152 ff., 164, 335, 267. (The italics are mine.)
2. McGinn, *Admonition Controversy*, p. 152.

3. Peel and Carlson, *Harrison and Browne*, pp. 106, 98, 91, 121. (The italics are mine.)
4. McGinn, *Admonition Controversy*, pp. 205, 206, 207–08.
5. Albert Peel and Leland H. Carlson, eds., *Cartwrightiana* (London, 1951), p. 51.
6. Peel and Carlson, *Harrison and Browne*, pp. 460, 275, 276, 160, 155, 254–55. See also McGinn, *Admonition Controversy*, p. 492.
7. *Ibid.*, pp. 115, 100. As Peel and Carlson point out, however, Browne admits that the "joining and partaking of manie churches together, and of the authority which manie haue, must needes be greater & more waightie, then the authoritie of anie single person" (*ibid.*, p. 21). And he outlines plans for synods comparable to those described by Cartwright (McGinn, *Admonition Controversy*, pp. 455–56). In other words, Browne did not entirely repudiate the presbyterian organization.
8. Peel and Carlson, *Harrison and Browne*, pp. 465, 443, 487 ff., 12, 11–12.
9. Peel and Carlson, *Cartwrightiana*, pp. 51–52, 52–53, 54, 56, 51, 74, 72.
10. McGinn, *Admonition Controversy*, p. 80.
11. Peel and Carlson, *Cartwrightiana*, p. 104.
12. Peel and Carlson, *Harrison and Browne*, pp. 21, 491, 452, 471–72. (The italics are mine.)

CHAPTER IV: LAST ATTEMPTS AT PEACEFUL REFORM

1. John Strype *The Life and Acts of John Whitgift, D.D.* (Oxford, 1822), I, 267.
2. William Pierce, *An Historical Introduction to the Marprelate Tracts* (London, 1908), pp. 76–77.
3. *Abstract of Certain Acts of parliament*, pp. 2, 88, 21, 8, 105.
4. *Demonstration of Discipline*, ed. by Edward Arber (The English Scholar's Library of Old and Modern Works, No. 9, London, 1880), pp. 8, 65–66.
5. *Answer to the Abstract*, sigs. A 3ᵛ, A 3, pp. 2, 122, 105, 194, 209, 175, 123 ff.
6. *Counter-poyson*, sigs. A 6ᵛ–A 7, pp. 9, 149 ff.
7. *Defence of the Reasons of the Counter-poyson*, sigs. A 5, A 5ᵛ, A 4.
8. *Defence of the godlie Ministers*, p. 56.
9. *Learned Discourse*, p. 2, sig. A 4ᵛ.

10. Pierce, *Historical Introduction*, pp. 135–43.
11. *Defence of the Government Established*, p. 2; see also McGinn, *Admonition Controversy*, pp. 78–86.
12. *Defence of the Government Established*, p. 204; see also McGinn, *Admonition Controversy*, pp. 65–74.
13. *Defence of the Government Established*, pp. 1289, 934, 77, 83, 101, 43, 1279.
14. Pierce, *Historical Introduction*, p. 144.
15. *Defence of the Ecclesiastical Discipline*, pp. 5, 22, 57 ff., 48, 68. See also Pierce, *Historical Introduction*, p. 144.

CHAPTER V: THE WELSH LITERARY WIZARD

1. R. B. McKerrow, *Works of Thomas Nashe* (London, 1903–1910), III, 366.
2. William Pierce, *John Penry, His Life, Times and Writings* (London, 1923), pp. 7, 8, 3. (The italics are mine.)
3. David Williams, *Three Treatises Concerning Wales* (University of Wales Press, Cardiff, 1960), p. x.
4. Pierce, *John Penry*, pp. 63, 22.
5. McKerrow, *Works of Thomas Nashe*, III, 366–68. (Except for the proper names the italics are mine.)
6. Williams, *Three Treatises Concerning Wales*, pp. xiv, xv.
7. Pierce, *John Penry*, p. 154.
8. Williams, *Three Treatises Concerning Wales*, p. xiv.
9. *Aequity*, pp. 39–41. See also Edward Arber, *An Introductory Sketch to the Martin Marprelate Controversy, 1588–1590* (The English Scholar's Library of Old and Modern Works, No. 8, London, 1875), pp. 55–56. (The italics are mine.)
10. Pierce, *John Penry*, p. 159.
11. *Aequity*, pp. 45, 51.
12. McGinn, *Admonition Controversy*, pp. 556–57.
13. *Aequity*, p. 54.
14. Pierce, *John Penry*, pp. 169–70.
15. *Aequity*, pp. 37–38, 22, 9. (The italics are mine.)
16. Pierce, *John Penry*, p. 437. Pierce also denies the charge against Penry that he desired "the overthrow of religion and the destruction of the honour of the Queen, by whose care it had been established." Pierce's denial is based on his own assumption that "all this [the charge] must not be supposed to have any necessary rela-

tion to the facts as we know them and least of all are they in agreement with Penry's utter aversion from all insurrectionary movements" (*ibid.*, p. 448).

17. *Ibid.*, pp. 30, 15, 19–20, 24, 38. (The italics are mine.)
18. Pierce, *John Penry*, p. 482.
19. *Aequity*, pp. 54, 24–25.

CHAPTER VI: PENRY AND THE SECRET PRESS

1. Arber, *Introductory Sketch*, pp. 84, 86.
2. Pierce, *John Penry*, p. 181.
3. *Exhortation* (1st ed.), pp. 22, 27, 11, 16, 23–24, 13, 14, 31 (incorrectly numbered 29).
4. Albert Peel, ed., *The Notebook of John Penry, 1593* (Camden Third Series, LXVII, London, 1944), p. xiii.
5. *Exhortation* (1st ed.), pp. 4, 38 (incorrectly numbered 36), 15, 40. (The italics are mine.)
6. McGinn, *Admonition Controversy*, pp. 50, 419.
7. Arber, *Introductory Sketch*, p. 71.
8. *Exhortation* (1st ed.), pp. 42, 50–51, 51–52.
9. McGinn, *Admonition Controversy*, pp. 228 ff.
10. *Exhortation* (1st ed.), pp. 52, 55, 56, 57, 63–64, 65. (The italics are mine.)
11. *Second Godly Treatise*, pp. 67–68.
12. *First Godly Treatise*, pp. 17, 18, 20, 20–21, 22, 23, 24, 28, 31 ff.
13. *Second Godly Treatise*, p. 67.
14. *First Godly Treatise*, p. 34.
15. *Exhortation* (2nd ed.), pp. 110, 41. (The italics in the postscript are mine.)
16. *Ibid.*, pp. 31–32; see also *Exhortation* (1st ed.), pp. 50–52.
17. *Exhortation* (3rd ed.), p. 31.
18. *Exhortation* (2nd ed.), p. 66. (The italics are Penry's.)
19. *Ibid.*, p. 67. (The italics are mine.)
20. *Ibid.*, pp. 68–69, 70, 71–72, 72, 72–73, 73–74, 79, 83, 85, 86. (The italics are mine.)
21. McGinn, *Admonition Controversy*, pp. 68 ff.
22. *Exhortation* (2nd ed.), pp. 87–88, 89.
23. For example, H. M. Dexter, as quoted by Arber, *Introductory Sketch*, p. 188. See also Pierce, "That Penry was not Marprelate is obvious enough to those who are familiar with their respective

writings. Their styles are as distinct as the poetic styles of Tennyson and Browning" (*John Penry*, p. 222).

24. *Exhortation* (2nd ed.), pp. 91, 91–92, 93, 94, 96–98, 98, 100, 109.

25. *Exhortation* (3rd ed.), p. 65.

26. Williams, *Three Treatises Concerning Wales*, p. xxviii. (See also Appendix.)

27. William Pierce, *The Marprelate Tracts* (London, 1911), pp. 13, 15, 113, 115. Similarly, Martin's first imitator, Thomas Nashe, in *Pierce Penilesse*, pretends to misspeak for comic effect. For example, addressing Richard Harvey, he writes: "Thou hast a Brother [John], hast thou not, student in Almanacks? Go too, Ile stand to it, he fathered one of thy *bastards* (*a book I meane*) which, being of thy begetting, was set forth vnder his name" (McKerrow, *Works of Thomas Nashe*, I, 196). (The italics are mine.)

CHAPTER VII: PENRY'S FIRST REPLY TO SOME

1. Pierce, *John Penry*, p. 200.

2. *Defence of that which hath bin written in the questions of the ignorant ministerie*, pp. 40, 44–45; see also McGinn, *Admonition Controversy*, pp. 42 ff.

3. *Defence of that which hath bin written in the questions of the ignorant ministerie*, pp. 1, 2, 6–7, 8, 9–10, 10, 11, 15, 22–23, 24, 27–28. (The italics are mine.)

4. *Ibid.*, p. 28. In fact, in denying that the pronunciation of "the wordes of institution with the deliuerie of the element" is sufficient, he clearly states that to sever the preaching of the Word from "the deliuery of the element" is "a breach of God's ordinance" (*ibid.*, pp. 48–49).

5. *Ibid.*, pp. 31, 32, 43–44, 45, 47, 48, 52, 52–53, 5–6. (The italics are mine.)

6. Pierce, *John Penry*, p. 200.

7. *Second Godly Treatise*, pp. 73, 102, sigs. F 2–F 2ᵛ.

8. McGinn, *Admonition Controversy*, pp. 65–66.

9. *Defence of that which hath bin written in the questions of the ignorant ministerie*, p. 3.

10. *Second Godly Treatise*, pp. 67–68, 77.

11. *Defence of that which hath bin written in the questions of the ignorant ministerie*, p. 23.

12. *Second Godly Treatise*, p. 172.
13. McGinn, *Admonition Controversy*, pp. 127 ff.
14. *Second Godly Treatise*, pp. 175, 180, 164.

CHAPTER VIII: THE FORMATION OF THE MARTINIST CONSPIRACY

1. Pierce, in an appendix attached to his *Historical Introduction*, adds two more depositions: "The Examinations of (1) John Hodgkins, the printer of *Theses Martinianae* and *The Just Censure and Reproofe;* also of (2) his assistants Valentine Simms and Arthur Thomlyn," both of which appear to be more detailed accounts of what was summarized in certain of Arber's documents.
2. Arber, *Introductory Sketch*, pp. 11, 6, 183, 193 ff., 175 ff. The inconsistencies and bias in Sutcliffe's arguments have previously been pointed out in my article "The Real Martin Marprelate," in which Arber's assumption that important documents are missing also is discussed.
3. Pierce, *Historical Introduction*, pp. 285, 163, 201, 155. (The italics are mine.)
4. John Waddington, *John Penry, the Pilgrim Martyr* (London, 1854), pp. 222, 223.
5. Pierce, *Historical Introduction*, pp. 334–35. (The brackets were added by Pierce.)
6. See also McGinn, "The Real Martin Marprelate," pp. 96–97.
7. Pierce, *Historical Introduction*, pp. 336, 337, 338. (The brackets were added by Pierce.)
8. Arber, *Introductory Sketch*, p. 182.
9. *Appellation*, p. 46.
10. Arber, *Introductory Sketch*, pp. 103–04.
11. McKerrow, *Works of Thomas Nashe*, V, 188–89 n.
12. J. Dover Wilson, "The Marprelate Controversy," *The Cambridge History of English Literature*, III, 443.
13. J. Dover Wilson, "Did Sir Roger Williams Write the Marprelate Tracts," *The Library*, 3rd series, IV (1913), 92–104.
14. J. Dover Wilson, "A Date in the Marprelate Controversy," *The Library*, New Series, VIII (1907), 348, 341–42. (The italics are mine.)
15. Arber, *Introductory Sketch*, pp. 55–56, 94, 194.
16. *Epistle*, pp. 29–30. See also Arber, *Introductory Sketch*, pp. 68–74.

17. Arber, *Introductory Sketch*, pp. 90–93, 83, 81, 82, 88, 85, 94, 123, 124. (The brackets were added by Arber.)

18. Pierce, *Historical Introduction*, pp. 152–53; John Penry, pp. 179–80.

19. Arber, *Introductory Sketch*, p. 100. See also Pierce, *John Penry*, p. 193. McKerrow considers that the "type which Waldegrave carried away has acquired an altogether undue importance in the accounts of the press," so that "it has even been supposed that it formed the bulk of the type afterwards used by the Martinists," and that "in fact, save the 'Dutch letter,' it was their whole stock." He inclines to agree with Wilson's opinion "that it was probably merely a small quantity of pica, which at most might be of use to add to what Waldegrave already possessed" (*Works of Thomas Nashe*, V, 185 n.).

20. Pierce points out that "contemporary writers, especially those writing in the interests of the reformers, knew nothing of the private resolutions of the Stationers' Court of Assistants" and that therefore "contemporary references to the defacing of Waldegrave's type must be taken as allusions to the events of April 16" (*Historical Introduction*, p. 152 n.) and not "after 13th May 1588," as dated by Arber (*Introductory Sketch*, p. 86).

21. *Ibid.*, p. 86. McKerrow expresses uncertainty as to whether the type was removed "one month or three months" after it was deposited with Mrs. Crane (*Works of Thomas Nashe*, V, 187). Tomkins, in his first deposition on February 15, 1588, had said "a Month together." In colloquial Elizabethan English the addition of *together* to an interval of time seems to make it indefinite; see also Hamlet's "four hours together," II.ii.160 (*Hamlet*, ed. by J. Q. Adams [New York, 1929], p. 54 n.). In his second deposition on November 29, 1589, here quoted, Tomkins is more specific than in the first. (The brackets were added by Arber.) Concerning Mrs. Crane see M. M. Knappen, *Tudor Puritanism* (Chicago, 1939), p. 295 and note.

22. Arber, *Introductory Sketch*, p. 86; see also *ibid.*, pp. 95, 104, and Pierce, *John Penry*, p. 193.

23. Regarding Tomkins' deposition, McKerrow writes as follows: "It should be noted that Tomkins was with his mistress in London and does not appear to have been at Molesey at all while the printing was going on, and could therefore only speak from hearsay

as to the visits of Penry and Waldegrave. They must surely have spent more time there than he was aware of" (*Works of Thomas Nashe*, V, 187 n.).

24. Pierce, *John Penry*, p. 192. McKerrow suggests that "at the first establishment of the press at Molesey it is probable that Penry only had the type which had previously been used by Waldegrave at his press in London." This type, "a Roman letter in four sizes," was used, at least in part, in "each of the books printed in roman" (*Works of Thomas Nashe*, V, 187).

25. Arber, *Introductory Sketch*, pp. 121, 87, 89, 85, 123, 124, 87. (The italics are mine; the brackets were inserted by Arber.)

26. Pierce, *Historical Introduction*, p. 155. See also Pierce, *John Penry*, p. 209.

27. Arber, *Introductory Sketch*, p. 87.

28. *Ibid.*, p. 77. See also Pierce, *Historical Introduction*, p. 156.

29. Arber, *Introductory Sketch*, pp. 129, 87.

30. *Ibid.*, pp. 129–30, 126. (The italics are mine; the brackets are Arber's.) See also Pierce, *Historical Introduction*, pp. 158–59.

31. Arber, *Introductory Sketch*, pp. 127, 130, 95.

32. *Ibid.*, pp. 125, 130. See also Pierce, *Historical Introduction*, p. 162, and *John Penry*, p. 211.

33. Arber, *Introductory Sketch*, pp. 125, 129, 125.

34. *Ibid.*, pp. 127, 130. See also Pierce, *John Penry*, p. 212. Moreover, Giles Wigginton was examined on December 6, 1588, "about the 'second Martin'" (Pierce, *Historical Introduction*, pp. 164–65).

35. Arber, *Introductory Sketch*, pp. 169–72, 96, 130.

CHAPTER IX: THE ROLE PLAYED BY HENRY SHARPE

1. Arber, *Introductory Sketch*, p. 94.

2. *Ibid.*, pp. 107–08. See also Kydwell's deposition, *ibid.*, pp. 81, 82; Pierce, *Historical Introduction*, pp. 160–61; McKerrow, *Works of Thomas Nashe*, V, 188 n.

3. Arber, *Introductory Sketch*, p. 95. (The brackets are Arber's.)

4. Pierce, *Historical Introduction*, pp. 149, 314, 324.

5. Arber, *Introductory Sketch*, p. 94.

6. McKerrow, *Works of Thomas Nashe*, V, 188–89 n.

7. Arber, *Introductory Sketch*, p. 94.

8. *Ibid.*, pp. 94–95. While naming Waldegrave as the printer of the first two Martinist tracts, Penry himself concedes that the *Epistle* was printed on *his own* press and that he had shared the profits of its sale with Waldegrave; moreover, both revealing and concealing his close contact with these tracts, he implies that he had served as the "Corrector" for the *Epitome*, which was printed by Waldegrave.

9. *Ibid.*, pp. 87, 95, 129–30, 95, 129, 126, 129, 95, 116, 95, 97, 130, 96, 95, 130, 96, 97, 96, 130, 97. (The brackets are Arber's.)

10. *Ibid.*, p. 98. Rather than being a downright lie, Penry's evasive remark may represent the equivocation characteristic of Puritan "confessions." Since the first two Martinist tracts were being widely circulated among the dissenters in London, among whom the two most prominent were John Greenwood and Henry Barrowe, it is possible that Penry may have received suggestions from them. Both Greenwood and Barrowe, separatist in persuasion, were acquainted with the Martinist tracts (Pierce, *John Penry*, pp. 351 ff.). On January 1, 1589, Barrowe was examined at Fleet Prison regarding his notes written in the margin of one of Some's *Godly Treatises*, which Penry had undertaken to answer in both the second and third editions of his *Exhortation* and also in his *Defence of that which hath bin written in the questions of the ignorant ministerie*, all of which were written and published in the summer of 1588 (Pierce, *Historical Introduction*, p. 315).

11. Arber, *Introductory Sketch*, p. 98. Without giving any reason for contradicting Sharpe, Pierce writes that this broadside "was issued about March 20, 1589" (*John Penry*, p. 216).

12. Arber, *Introductory Sketch*, pp. 94, 98, 97.

13. *Ibid.*, p. 102. See also *John Penry*, p. 248 n.

14. Arber, *Introductory Sketch*, p. 98.

15. Pierce, *Historical Introduction*, p. 165.

16. Arber, *Introductory Sketch*, pp. 99, 97, 99.

17. *Ibid.*, pp. 99, 100. (The brackets are Arber's.) Symmes, who later assisted in printing *Martins Junior* and *Senior*, was told by Hodgkins that Waldegrave "had played the knave notably wth the brethren in that hauing gotten the copy of Cartwrights book agaynst the Rhemish testament he was gone to print that for his comoditye and had giuen the brethren ouer" (Pierce, *Historical Introduction*, p. 339).

CHAPTER X: EXIT SHARPE, ENTER THROCKMORTON

1. Arber, *Introductory Sketch*, p. 100. (The brackets are Arber's.)
2. *Ibid.*, p. 100. See also McGinn, "A Perplexing Date in the Marprelate Controversy," *Studies in Philology*, XLI, 2 (April, 1944), 169 ff. for further clarification of the ambiguity of the pronouns in this passage from Sharpe's deposition. (The brackets identifying the pronouns are mine.)
3. Arber, *Introductory Sketch*, pp. 100–01. (Arber incorrectly identifies "one Hoskins" as William. The reference obviously is to the master printer, John Hodgkins.)
4. McKerrow, *Works of Thomas Nashe*, V, 190 n.
5. Arber, *Introductory Sketch*, pp. 102, 129, 131, 102–03, 131, 102, 103. (The italics are mine.)
6. *Ibid.*, p. 102.
7. *Ibid.*, p. 103. Regarding the confusion concerning the presses, McKerrow makes the following observation: "The press which they had at Manchester does not seem to have been the same as that they had been using at Wolston, which Hodgkins said that he misliked. There must at one time have been two presses at Wolston, for immediately after Whitsuntide (May 18, 1589), Hodgkins sent from that place to Warrington, a printing-press [that is, "the press which he told Sharpe, about Midsummer, that he had sent into the North" (Arber, *Introductory Sketch*, p. 101)], two boxes of type, a barrel of ink, a basket, and a brass pot. As when Hodgkins and his men were arrested at Manchester there was still a press and type remaining at Wolston, it seems probable that it was this first press which, sent from Warrington, was used for printing *More Work for the Cooper*" (*Works of Thomas Nashe*, V, 191 and notes).
8. Pierce, *John Penry*, p. 228.
9. Arber, *Introductory Sketch*, p. 175.
10. McGinn, "The Real Martin Marprelate," pp. 98 ff. See also Pierce, *John Penry*, pp. 231–32; *Historical Introduction*, p. 235.
11. Arber, *Introductory Sketch*, pp. 127, 134–35. Disregarding Hodgkins' explicit statement in Puckering's brief that he took Penry's letters to Mrs. Wigston, Sutcliffe apparently selected Symmes' testimony, wrung from him with torture and obviously conjectural: "When this examinate Simes mett wth Hodgkins first at

warwick he showed him as they were going to Wolston a letter w^ch *he thinketh* was written from m^r Throckmorton. It was directed to m^rs Wigston *as he supposeth* for theyr intertaynement" (Pierce, *Historical Introduction*, p. 339). (The italics are mine.)

12. Arber, *Introductory Sketch*, pp. 127, 134. (The italics are mine.) See also Pierce, *Historical Introduction*, p. 333.

13. Arber, *Introductory Sketch*, p. 127. Sutcliffe, however, inaccurately writes that "the books came to Hodgskin's hands by the *appointment of* Throkmorton, being laid in the way betwixt his and Mistress Wigstons house, ready for Hodgskin to take up" (*ibid.*, p. 177). (The italics are mine.)

14. *Ibid.*, pp. 102–03. (The brackets are Arber's.)

15. Pierce, *Historical Introduction*, pp. 336–37, 339, 338.

16. Arber, *Introductory Sketch*, p. 177.

17. *Ibid.*, p. 134. (The brackets are Arber's; the italics are mine.) See also Pierce, *Historical Introduction*, p. 336.

18. Arber, *Introductory Sketch*, p. 127. (The brackets are Arber's; the italics are mine.)

19. Pierce, *Historical Introduction*, p. 339. (The brackets are Pierce's.)

20. Arber, *Introductory Sketch*, p. 127. (The brackets are Arber's; the italics are mine.) Whereas "chamber" in Puckering's brief seems to mean "room," Sutcliffe, in addition to substituting Throckmorton's name for the names of Penry and Newman, evidently took the word to mean "chamber pot": "Lastly, it is deposed both by Hodgskin and Simmes, that Throkmorton while *Martin senior* and *Martin junior* were in printing, should say unto Hodgskin 'that *More work for Cooper* should come to his handes shortly.' And so it did, being dropped out of a chamber into a room where then Hodgkin was. If he [Throckmorton] were not the Author or at least an Actor in it, how could he know how the book should come to his hands? Could he prophesy that the book would drop out of the chamber, if he had not been privy to the dropping [of] it? An unhappy drop for poor Hodgskin! who, if her Majesty had not been gracious to him, had dropped off the gibbet for it" (*ibid.*, pp. 178–79). Furthermore, in none of the depositions did Throckmorton even allude to *More worke for Cooper*.

21. *Ibid.*, p. 117. (The brackets are Arber's.) Arber here notes that "Matthew Sutcliffe stated in 1595 that this other man's handwriting, was that of Job Throckmorton."

22. Peel, *Notebook*, p. xxiv.
23. Arber, *Introductory Sketch*, pp. 127, 135.
24. McKerrow, *Works of Thomas Nashe*, V, 192.
25. Arber, *Introductory Sketch*, p. 181.
26. McKerrow, *Works of Thomas Nashe*, V, 192.
27. Arber, *Introductory Sketch*, p. 175.
28. Pierce, *Historical Introduction*, p. 235.

CHAPTER XI: PENRY'S HAND IN THE MARTINIST TRACTS

1. *Epitome*, sig. B 2ᵛ, e.g.
2. *Epistle*, p. 4, e.g.
3. *Epitome*, sig. B 2ᵛ, e.g.
4. *Epistle*, pp. 1, 6, 9, 16, 2, 12, 16, 19, 31, 2–3, 3, 4 ff., 8–10, 19–21, 36–37.
5. See Wilson, "The Marprelate Controversy," *The Cambridge History of English Literature*, III, 425–52; Pierce, *Historical Introduction*.
6. *Epistle*, pp. 1, 12–13, 10, 12, 18, 13, 22.
7. *Ibid.*, p. 23. This familiarity with Welsh literature fits in with Martin's comic use of *f* for *v*, the conventional English way of mimicking Welsh dialect (see Shakespeare, *Henry V*: Fluellen's "prerogatifes," IV.i.67, "falorous," III.ii.81, "aggrief'd," IV.vii.-170, "scurfy," V.i.23).
8. *Epistle*, pp. 30, 10, 13, 32, 51.
9. *Epitome*, sigs. B 1ᵛ, B 4ᵛ, A 2, C 4.
10. Peel, *Notebook*, p. xi.
11. *Epitome*, sig. E 1ᵛ.
12. Arber, *Introductory Sketch*, pp. 94, 98.
13. *Hay any worke for Cooper*, p. 37.
14. Arber, *Introductory Sketch*, p. 117.
15. *Hay any worke for Cooper*, p. 14.
16. Arber, *Introductory Sketch*, p. 99.
17. *Hay any worke for Cooper*, pp. 20, 21.
18. Pierce, *John Penry*, p. 248.
19. *Theses Martinianae*, sigs. A 1ᵛ, C 4, A 2, C 4ᵛ, C 3.
20. *Ibid.*, sig. C 4. See also Arber, *Introductory Sketch*, p. 117.
21. *Theses Martinanae*, sig. C 3ᵛ.
22. Arber, *Introductory Sketch*, p. 134.

23. *Just Censure,* title page, sigs. A 2ᵛ, B 2, B 2ᵛ, A 2, B 4, A 2ᵛ ff., C 2, C 2ᵛ, C 3, C 3ᵛ. (The italics are mine.)

24. Arber, *Introductory Sketch,* pp. 117, 135–36. (The italics are mine.) Contradicting the assertion that the serious parts in *More worke for Cooper* resemble passages in Penry's signed writings, Dexter, as quoted by Arber, states that in spite of the fact that "Penry's books show plenty of power, sometimes a rude and plaintive eloquence, sometimes a severe invective," they never reveal "that brusque, strong, coarse, homely wit and queer sarcasm with which Martin abounds" nor "Martin's most peculiar turns of expression and favorite epithets" (*ibid.,* p. 188). But Dexter fails to note that the government officials who viewed the captured manuscript were comparing it with Penry's own writings, which were not written in the "scoffinge veyne" of the Martinist tracts.

25. McKerrow specifically places the responsibility for the publication of the *Protestation* on Penry: "Penry managed to get one more book Printed, the *Protestation of Martin Marprelate.*" Moreover, he mentions Penry as the probable printer: "The execution of the work is so bad, at any rate in the first sheet, as to suggest that it was carried out by Penry himself, or at any rate by some one who was not a regular printer" (*Works of Thomas Nashe,* V, 192). Pierce, surprisingly enough, goes even further than McKerrow and implicates Penry in the composition of the tract, though always along with Throckmorton: "They [Penry and Throckmorton] combined, in the very defiance of Whitgift, to write another short tract [*The Protestation*], partly consisting of a fresh statement of their case and of their determined attitude of mind" (*Historical Introduction,* p. 192).

26. *Protestation,* pp. 3 ff., 12.

27. Pierce, *Marprelate Tracts,* p. 402 n.

28. *Epistle,* p. 5.

29. Arber, *Introductory Sketch,* pp. 90–91, 94.

30. *Protestation,* pp. 15–16.

31. Arber, *Introductory Sketch,* p. 97.

32. *Protestation,* pp. 24 ff.

CHAPTER XII: PENRY's *Supplication*

1. Pierce, *John Penry,* p. 217.

2. Williams, *Three Treatises Concerning Wales,* p. xxix.

3. *Supplication*, sigs. A 2, A 2ᵛ–A 3, A 4, A 4ᵛ–B 1, B 1–B 1ᵛ, B 2–B 2ᵛ. (The italics are mine.)
4. Pierce, *John Penry*, p. 222.
5. *Supplication*, sig. C 1.
6. *Supplication*, p. 9.
7. *Exhortation* (2nd ed.), p. 66.
8. *Supplication*, pp. 2, 26–27, 30, 39. (The italics are mine.)
9. *Exhortation* (2nd ed.), p. 71.
10. *Supplication*, pp. 19–20.
11. *Exhortation* (2nd ed.), p. 71.
12. *Supplication*, p. 20.
13. *Exhortation* (2nd ed.), pp. 72, 82 ff.
14. *Supplication*, pp. 31 ff., 45 ff., 47–49, 52. (The italics are mine.)
15. *Epistle* and *Epitome*, title pages.
16. *Supplication*, pp. 56–57. (The italics are mine.)
17. *Exhortation* (2nd ed.), p. 105.
18. *Supplication*, pp. 73, 74, 77, 78 ff.

CHAPTER XIII: PENRY's *Appellation* AND HIS ANSWER TO SOME

1. Arber, *Introductory Sketch*, pp. 117, 135–36.
2. *Protestation*, pp. 24 ff.
3. Arber, *Introductory Sketch*, pp. 114–15, 103. (Except for the first set, the brackets are Arber's; the italics are mine.)
4. McKerrow, *Works of Thomas Nashe*, V, 191–92.
5. Pierce, *John Penry*, p. 248. (Except for titles, the italics are mine.)
6. Pierce, *Historical Introduction*, p. 193.
7. McKerrow, *Works of Thomas Nashe*, V, 187, 191 n., 192. (Except for titles, the italics are mine; likewise the brackets.)
8. Arber, *Introductory Sketch*, p. 100. (The brackets are Arber's.)
9. Wilson, "A Date in the Marprelate Controversy," *The Library*, New Series, VIII (1907), 342.
10. *Introductory Sketch*, p. 100. (The brackets are Arber's; the italics are mine.)
11. *Ibid.*, p. 179.
12. Wilson, "A Date in the Marprelate Controversy," *The Library*, New Series, VIII (1907), 339. (The italics are mine.)
13. Pierce, *John Penry*, p. 232.
14. Pierce, *Historical Introduction*, pp. 183, 184. (Except for titles, the italics are mine.)

15. Pierce, *John Penry*, p. 247.
16. Pierce, *Historical Introduction*, p. 339. (The brackets and italics are mine.)
17. Arber, *Introductory Sketch*, p. 68.
18. McKerrow, *Works of Thomas Nashe*, IV, 55–56, 471.
19. Arber, *Introductory Sketch*, pp. 98, 125.
20. Pierce, *Historical Introduction*, p. 316.
21. *Supplication*, p. 1, sig. A 3ᵛ, pp. 11, 13. (The italics are mine.)
22. *Exhortation* (2nd ed.), pp. 99–100. (The italics are mine.)
23. *Supplication*, p. 67. (The italics are mine.)
24. Pierce, *John Penry*, p. 269.
25. *Reformation No Enemie*, sigs. A 2ᵛ, B 1ᵛ, H 3. (The italics are mine.)
26. *Appellation*, pp. 34, 8, 37, 6–7, 46–47. (The italics are mine.)
27. *Introductory Sketch*, pp. 173–74.
28. McKerrow, *Works of Thomas Nashe*, IV, 55–56.
29. Wilson, "A Date in the Marprelate Controversy," *The Library*, New Series, VIII (1907), 337–59.
30. McKerrow, *Works of Thomas Nashe*, V, 374.
31. Pierce, *John Penry*, pp. 241, 241 n.
32. Wilson, "A Date in the Marprelate Controversy," *The Library*, New Series, VIII (1907), 349.
33. Pierce, *John Penry*, p. 241. (The italics are mine.)
34. Arber, *Introductory Sketch*, pp. 101–02.
35. Pierce, *John Penry*, pp. 241–42.
36. Arber, *Introductory Sketch*, pp. 96, 98, 131, 99, 101–02, 100.
37. *Supplication*, sigs. A 2ᵛ–A 3. (The italics are mine.)
38. *Appellation*, pp. 1, 3, 24, 39, 16, 17, 17–18, 6–7, 19, 47–48. (The italics are mine.)
39. H. M. Dexter, *The Congregationalism of the Last Three Hundred Years as Seen in Its Literature* (New York, 1880), p. 234 n.
40. Arber, *Introductory Sketch*, pp. 187 ff.
41. Pierce, *Historical Introduction*, pp. 286–89.
42. Pierce, *John Penry*, pp. 358–59.
43. *M. Some laid open in his coulers*, p. 51. (The italics are the author's.)
44. *Ibid.*, sig. A 2, pp. 119, 14, 16, 19, 27, etc. (The italics are mine.)
45. Pierce, *John Penry*, pp. 231–32, 244, 246.
46. *M. Some laid open in his coulers*, pp. 30–31, 34, 51, 53, 69, 71. (The italics are mine.)

47. *M. Some laid open in his coulers*, pp. 35–36 (p. 36 incorrectly numbered 39). (Only the italics in the last sentence are mine.)
48. *Ibid.*, pp. 86–87. (The italics are mine.)
49. *Ibid.*, pp. 52–53.
50. Pierce, *John Penry*, p. 349.

CHAPTER XIV: PENRY'S FINAL PURITAN PAMPHLETS

1. Pierce, *John Penry*, pp. 247–48, 269 n., 264, 285–86. See also McKerrow, *Works of Thomas Nashe*, V, 187, 191 n.
2. Pierce, *Historical Introduction*, pp. 243, 176 n.
3. *John Penry*, pp. 264, 488–89, 286.
4. Pierce, *Historical Introduction*, p. 242.
5. *Reformation No Enemie*, sigs. A 2ᵛ, A 3, A 4, A 4ᵛ, B 2ᵛ–B 3, B 3ᵛ, B 4ᵛ–C 1, C 1, C 4, C 4ᵛ ff., E 1ᵛ, E 2, F 3, H 2ᵛ. (The italics are mine.)
6. *Briefe Discovery of the Untruthes and Slanders*, title page, pp. 39, 42, 39, 40, 40–41, 17, 43, 44, sigs. A 3ᵛ–A 4, A 4. (The italics are mine.)
7. *Humble Motion with Submission*, sig. A 3, pp. 17, 18, 39 ff., 47–48, 58, 94 ff.
8. Pearson, *Thomas Cartwright*, p. 284.
9. *A Dialogue wherin is plainly laide open*, sigs. A 4ᵛ, C 3ᵛ, B 1ᵛ, B 3, B 4, C 1ᵛ, C 2ᵛ ff., B 2ᵛ, C 3–C 3ᵛ, C 1, C 4ᵛ, A 4–A 4ᵛ.
10. Pierce, *John Penry*, p. 301.

CHAPTER XV: THE MOST IMPORTANT ANTI-MARTINIST REPLIES

1. McKerrow, *Works of Thomas Nashe*, V, 43, 42.
2. *Hay any worke for Cooper*, pp. 36, 37, 42.
3. *Admonition to the People of England*, p. 33. See also Pierce, *Marprelate Tracts*, p. 269 n.
4. *Hay any worke for Cooper*, pp. 37–38.
5. *Admonition to the People of England*, p. 105. See also Pierce, *Historical Introduction*, p. 169; *Marprelate Tracts*, p. 270 n.
6. *Hay any worke for Cooper*, p. 38. (The italics are mine.)
7. *Appellation*, p. 27. (The italics are mine.)
8. *Sermon Preached at Paules Crosse*, pp. 24 ff., 38 ff., 8, 9, 68 ff., 82.
9. *Ibid.*, p. 100. See also *ibid.*, p. 82: "The author of the second

Admonition (*against whom, as I thinke, there will no exception be taken. . . .*" (The italics are mine.)

10. *Ibid.*, pp. 82–83.

11. McKerrow, *Works of Thomas Nashe*, V, 45, 49; see also Pierce, *Historical Introduction*, pp. 221–23.

12. McKerrow, *Works of Thomas Nashe*, V, 54, 63; see also Pierce, *Historical Introduction*, pp. 223 ff.

13. McKerrow, *Works of Thomas Nashe*, V, 57, 44.

14. *Ibid.*, I, 88–90, 61, 100, 136, 115.

15. See McGinn, "Nashe's Share in the Marprelate Controversy," pp. 952–84.

16. Wilson, "The Marprelate Controversy," *The Cambridge History of English Literature*, III, 450–51.

17. McKerrow, *Works of Thomas Nashe*, V, 60.

18. *Ibid.*, III, 369, 347 ff., 376, 372, 359, 365 ff., 385 ff., 356–57, 365–66.

CHAPTER XVI: PENRY'S "SEPARATIST MANIFESTO"

1. Pierce, *John Penry*, pp. 386, 335–36, 300.

2. *Brief Discoverie of the False Church*, pp. 9, 10, 17, 22, 26, 34, 104.

3. *Brief Discoverie of the False Church*, pp. 108–09. See Pierce, *John Penry*, p. 351. (The italics are mine.)

4. *Brief Discoverie of the False Church*, pp. 105, 112, 108, 46, 223, 241, 167, 169 ff., 174 ff., 51, 175–76, 55. (The italics are mine.)

5. *Collection of certaine sclaunderous Articles*, sigs. A 4, B 1ᵛ, B 3ᵛ.

6. *Plaine Declaration that our Brownists be full Donatists*, pp. 11 ff., 46 ff., 41 ff.

7. *Short Treatise against the Donatists of England*, pp. 64, 67, 20 ff.

8. *Plaine Refutation of M. G. Giffordes reprochful booke*, sigs. ◊ 2ᵛ, A 2ᵛ, pp. 64–65, 68, 73 ff., 74, 75, 77, 93, 98, 134, 155, 96, 198, 215, 226. (The italics are mine.)

9. *Answere to George Giffordes Pretended Defence of Read Praiers*, p. 16.

10. *Short Reply unto the last printed books of Henry Barrow and Iohn Greenwood*, pp. 47–48, 90.

11. Pierce, *John Penry*, pp. 328–29, 362.

12. *Historie of Corah, Dathan, and Abiram*, pp. 5, 8 ff., 3, 27 ff., 30. (The italics are mine.)

CHAPTER XVII: THE EPILOGUE TO THE MARPRELATE CONTROVERSY

1. *Remonstrance or Plaine Detection*, p. 2.
2. *Treatise of Ecclesiasticall Discipline*, p. 165. (The italics are Sutcliffe's.)
3. *Petition directed to her most excellent Maiestie*, p. 7.
4. *Answere to a Certaine Libel*, pp. 78, 201–02.
5. *Defence of Iob Throkmorton*, sig. E 2.
6. *Answere unto Iob Throkmortons Letter*, p. 70^v.
7. Arber, *Introductory Sketch*, p. 175.
8. Pierce, *John Penry*, p. 296. (The italics are mine.)
9. *Answere unto Iob Throkmortons Letter*, p. 48.
10. *Brief Apologie of Thomas Cartwright*, sig. C 2^v.
11. *Examination of M. Thomas Cartwrights late apologie*, pp. 48, 48^v, 2^v–3, 10 ff., 42.
12. Pierce, *John Penry*, p. 482.
13. Wilson, "The Marprelate Controversy," *The Cambridge History of English Literature*, III, 451.
14. Dexter, *Congregationalism of the Last Three Hundred Years*, p. 191.

CHAPTER XVIII: THE SIGNIFICANCE OF THE CONTROVERSY

1. Pierce, *John Penry*, pp. 485, 482–83, 483, 483–84, 481.
2. McKerrow, *Works of Thomas Nashe*, V, 39–40.
3. Pearson, *Church and State*, pp. 115, 37, 106–07, 113–14.
4. Peel and Carlson, *Harrison and Browne*, pp. 424–29.
5. Richard Hooker, *Ecclesiastical Polity* (Everyman's Library, London, 1925), pp. xiv–xv, xvi.
6. McGinn, *Admonition Controversy*, pp. 137–38.
7. *Ecclesiastical Polity*, pp. 79, 84, 89, 90, 91, 93–94, 98, 99–101, 103, 107 ff., 114, 115, 116–17, 119, 122–23, 143. (The italics are Hooker's.)
8. Arber, *Introductory Sketch*, pp. 17–18.

APPENDIX: A NOTE ON PREVIOUS BIBLIOGRAPHICAL STUDIES OF PENRY'S *Exhortation*

1. Pierce, *John Penry*, pp. 180, 194, 180. (The italics are mine.)
2. *Exhortation* (2nd ed.), pp. 110, 103.

3. *Exhortation* (3rd ed.), p. 65.
4. Pierce, *John Penry*, p. 192 n.
5. *Exhortation* (2nd ed.), p. 41. (The italics are mine.)
6. Williams, *Three Treatises Concerning Wales*, p. xxix. See also Pierce, *John Penry*, p. 217.
7. *Ibid.*, p. 192 n. (The italics are mine.)
8. Williams, *Three Treatises Concerning Wales*, pp. xxviii, xx.

Bibliography

PRIMARY SOURCES

(In parentheses after each full title is the shortened title used for convenience in the main text.)

An Abstract, of Certain Acts of parliament: of certaine her Maiesties Iniunctions: of certaine Canons, Constitutions, and Synodalles prouinciall established and in force, for the peaceable gouernment of the Church, within her Maiesties Dominions and Countries, for the most part heretofore vnknowen and vnpractized. 1583. (*Abstract of Certain Acts of parliament*)

An answere for the tyme, to the Examination put in print, with out the authours name, pretending to mayntayne the apparrell prescribed against the declaration of the mynisters of London. 1566. (*An answere for the tyme, to the Examination*)

Antimartinvs, sive Monitio cuiusdam Londinensis ad Adolescentes vtriusque Academiae, contra personatum quendam rabulam, qui se Anglicè Martin Marprelat. 1589.

Bancroft, Richard, *Davngerovs Positions and Proceedings, published and practised within this Iland of Brytaine, vnder pretense of Reformation, and for the Presbiteriall Discipline.* London, 1593.

Bancroft, Richard, *A Sermon Preached at Paules Crosse the 9. of Februarie, being the first Sunday in the Parleament, Anno. 1588.* 1588 [i.e., 1589]. (*Sermon Preached at Paules Crosse*)

Bancroft, Richard, *A Svrvay of the Pretended Holy Discipline. Contayning the beginninges, successe, parts, proceedings, authority, and doctrine of it with some of the manifold and materiall repugnances, varieties and vncertaineties, in that behalfe. Faithfully gathered, by way of historicall narration, out of the bookes and writings, of principall fauourers of that platforme.* London, 1593. (*Survay of the Pretended Holy Discipline*)

Barrowe, Henry, *A Brief Discoverie of the False Chvrch. Ezek 16.44*

As the Mother Svch the Davghter is. 1590. (*Brief Discoverie of the False Church*)

Barrowe, Henry, *A Collection of certaine sclavnderovs Articles gyuen out by the Bisshops against such faithfull Christians as they now vniustly deteyne in their Prisons together with the answeare of the saide Prisoners therunto. Also the Some of Certaine Conferences had in the Fleete according to the Bisshops bloudie Mandate with two Prisoners there.* 1590. (*Collection of certaine sclaunderous Articles*)

[Barrowe, Henry], *A petition directed to her most excellent Maiestie, wherein is deliuered* 1. *A meane howe to compound the ciuill dissention in the church of Englande.* 2. *A proofe that they who write for Reformation, doe not offend against the stat. of 23. Eliz. c. and therefore till matters bee compounded, deserue more favour. Herevnto is annexed Some opinions of such as sue for Reformation: By which it may appeare howe vniustlie they are slaundered by the Bishops, etc. pag. 53. Togither with the Authors Epistle to the Reader, pag. 58. Also: Certayne Articles wherein is discouered the negligence of the Bishops, their Officialls, Fauourers and Followers, in performance of sundrie Ecclesiasticall Statutes, Lawes and Ordinancies Royall and Episcopall, published for the gouernement of the Church of Englande, pag. 60. Lastlie: Certayne Questions or Interrogatories drawen by a fauorer of Reformation, wherein he desireth to be resolued by the Prelates, pag. 74.* [1590.] (*A petition directed to her most excellent Maiestie*)

Barrowe, Henry, *A Trve Description ovt of the Word of God, of the visible Church.* 1589.

Barrowe, Henry, and Greenwood, John, *A Plaine Refvtation of M. G. Giffardes reprochful booke, intituled a short treatise against the Donatists of England. Wherein is discouered the forgery of the whole Ministrie, the confusion, false worship, and antichristian disorder of these Parish assemblies, called the Church of England. Here also is prefixed a summe of the causes of our seperation, and of our purposes in practice, which M. Giffard hath twise sought to confute, and hath now twise receiued answere, by Henrie Barrowe. Here is furder annexed a briefe refutation of M. Giff. supposed consimilitude betwixt the Donatists and vs. Wherein is shewed how his Arguments haue bene & may be by the Papists more iustly retorted against himself & the present estate of their Church by I. Gren. Here are also inserted a fewe obseruations of M. Giff. his cauils about read prayer*

& deuised Leitourgies. 1591. (*Plaine Refutation of M. G. Giffordes reprochful booke*)

Bridges, John, *A Defence of the Government Established in the Chvrch of Englande for Ecclesiasticall Matters. Contayning an aunswere vnto a Treatise called, The Learned Discourse of Eccl. Gouernment, otherwise intituled, A briefe and plaine declaration concerning the desires of all the faithfull Ministers that haue, and do seeke for the discipline and reformation of the Church of Englande. Comprehending likewise an aunswere to the arguments in a Treatise named The iudgement of a most Reuerend and Learned man from beyond the Seas, &c. Aunswering also to the argumentes of Caluine, Beza, and Danaeus, with other our Reuerend learned Brethren besides Caenalis and Bodinus, both for the regiment of women, and, in defence of her Maiestie, and of all other Christian Princes supreme Gouernment in Ecclesiasticall causes, Against the Tetrarchie that our Brethren would erect in euery particular congregation, of Doctors, Pastors, Gouernors and Deacons, with their seuerall and ioynt authoritie in Elections, Excommunications, Synodall Constitutions and other Eccleseasticall matters.* London, 1587. (*Defence of the Government Established*)

A briefe and lamentable consyderation, of the apparell now vsed by the Cleargie of England. (See *Whether it be mortall sinne to transgresse ciuil lawes.*)

A Briefe and plaine declaration, concerning the desires of all those faithfull Ministers, that haue and do seeke for the Discipline and reformation of the Church of Englande: Which may serue for a iust Apologie, against the false accusations and slaunders of their aduersaries. Printed by Robert Waldegraue. London, 1584. (*Learned Discourse*)

A briefe discourse against the outwarde apparell and Ministring garmentes of the popishe church: A declaration of the doings of those Ministers of Gods worde and Sacraments, in the Citie of London, which haue refused to weare the outward apparell, and Ministring garmentes of the Popes church. 1566. (*A briefe discourse against the outwarde apparell and Ministring garmentes of the popishe church*)

A briefe examination for the time of a certain Declaration. 1566.

Browne, Robert, *An answere to Master Cartwright His Letter for Ioyning with the English Churches: whereunto the true copy of his sayde letter is annexed.* 1585. (*Answere to Master Cartwright*)

Browne, Robert, *A Booke Which Sheweth the life and manners of all true Christians, and howe vnlike they are vnto Turkes and Papistes, and Heathen folke. Also the pointes and partes of all diuinitie, that is of the reuealed will and worde of God, are declared by their seuerall Definitions, and Diuisions in order as followeth.* 1582. (*A Booke Which Sheweth the life and manners of all true Christians*)

Browne, Robert, *A Treatise of reformation without tarying for anie, and of the wickednesse of those Preachers which will not reforme till the Magistrate commaunde or compell them.* [1582.] (*A Treatise of reformation without tarying for anie*)

Cartwright, Thomas, *A brief Apologie of Thomas Cartwright against all such slaunderous accusations as it pleaseth Mr. Sutcliffe in seuerall pamphlettes most iniuriously to loade him with.* 1596. (*Brief Apologie of Thomas Cartwright*)

[Cartwright, Thomas, translator], *A full and plaine declaration of Ecclesiasticall Discipline owt off the word off God and off the declininge off the churche of England from the same.* [1574.] See also Travers, Walter, *Ecclesiasticae Disciplinae*, etc. (*Full and Plaine Declaration of Ecclesiasticall Discipline*)

C[artwright]., T[homas]., *A Replye to an answere made of M. Doctor Whitegifte. Againste the Admonition to the Parliament.* 1573. (*Replye to an answere*)

Cartwright, Thomas, *The rest of the second replie of Thomas Cartwright: agaynst Master Doctor Whitgifts second answer, touching the Church discipline.* 1577. (*The rest of the second replie*)

[Cartwright, Thomas], *A second Admonition to the Parliament.* 1572. (*Second Admonition*)

Cartwright, Thomas, *The second replie of Thomas Cartwright: agaynst Maister Doctor Whitgiftes second answer, touching the Churche Discipline.* 1575. (*Second replie*)

C[ooper]., T[homas]., *Admonition to the People of England.* (The English Scholar's Library of Old and Modern Works, No. 15, Birmingham, 1882.)

C[ooper]., T[homas]., *An Admonition to the People of England: Wherein are answered, not onely the slaunderous vntruethes, reprochfully vttered by Martin the Libeller, but also many other Crimes by some of his broode, objected generally against all Bishops, and the chiefe of the Cleargie, purposely to deface and discredite the present state of the Church.* 1589. (*Admonition to the People of England*)

[Cosin, Richard], *An Answer To the two first and principall Treatises of a certeine factious libell, put foorth latelie, without name of Author or Printer, and without approbation by authoritie, vnder the title of An Abstract of certeine Acts of Parlement: of certeine hir Maiesties Iniunctions: of certeine Canons, &c.* 1584. (*Answer to the Abstract*)

Cosin, Richard, *Conspiracie for Pretended Reformation viz. Presbyteriall Discipline. A Treatise discouering the late designments and courses held for aduancement thereof, by William Hacket Yeoman, Edward Coppinger, and Henry Arthington Gent. out of others depositions and their owne letters, writings & confessions vpon examination: Together with some part of the life and conditions, and the two Inditements, Arraignment, and Execution of the sayd Hacket. Also An answere to the calumniations of such as affirme they were mad men: and a resemblance of this action vnto the like, happened heretofore in Germanie.* 1592.

A Dialogve Concerning the strife of our Churche: Wherein are aunswered diuers of those vniust accusations, wherewith the godly preachers and professors of the Gospell, are falsly charged; with a briefe declaration of some such monstrous abuses, as our Byshops haue not bene ashamed to foster. Printed by Robert Waldegrave. London, 1584.

The Examinations of Henry Barrowe, Iohn Grenewood and Iohn Penrie before the high commissioners and Lordes of the Counsel. Penned by the prisoners themselues before their deathes. [1593.]

[Fenner, Dudley], *A Covnter-poyson, modestly written for the time, to make aunswere to the obiections and reproches, wherewith the aunswerer to the Abstract, would disgrace the holy Discipline of Christ.* London, Printed by Robert Waldegrave. 1584. (*Counterpoyson*)

[Fenner, Dudley], *A Defence of the godlie Ministers, against the slaunders of D. Bridges, contayned in his answere to the Preface before the Discourse of Ecclesiasticall gouernement, with a Declaration of the Bishops proceeding against them. Wherein chieflie 1. The lawfull authoritie of her Maiestie is defended by the Scriptures, her lawes, and authorised interpretation of them, to be the same which we have affirmed, against his cauilles and slaunders to the contrarie. 2. The lawfull refusing also of the Ministers to subscribe, is mainteyned by euident groundes of Gods worde, and her Maiesties lawes, against his euident wresting of both. 3. Lastlie, the forme of Churchgouernement, which we propounde, is according to his demaunde Sillogisticallie proued to be ordinarie, perpetuall, and the best.* 1587. (*Defence of the godlie Ministers*)

[Fenner, Dudley], *A defence of the Reasons of the Counter-poyson, for maintenance of the Eldership, against an aunswere made to them by Doctor Copequot, in a publike Sermon at Pawles Crosse, vpon Psal. 84. 1584. Wherein also according to his demaunde is proued Syllogisticallie for the learned, and plainlie for all men, the perpetuitie of the Elders office in the Church.* 1586. (*Defence of the Reasons of the Counter-poyson*)

[Field, John, and Wilcox, Thomas], *An Admonition to the Parliament.* 1572. (first *Admonition*)

Gifford, George, *A Plaine Declaration that our Brownists be full Donatists by comparing them together from point to point out of the writings of Augustine. Also a replie to Master Greenwood touching read prayers, wherein his grosse ignorance is detected, which labouring to purge himselfe from former absurdities, doth plunge himselfe deeper into the mire.* 1590. (*Plaine Declaration that our Brownists be full Donatists*)

Gifford, George, *A short Reply vnto the last printed books of Henry Barrow and Iohn Greenwood, the chiefe ringleaders of our Donatists in England: Wherein is layd open their grosse ignorance, and foule errors: vpon which their whole building is founded.* 1591. (*Short Reply vnto the last printed books of Henry Barrow and Iohn Greenwood*)

Gifford, George, *A Short Treatise against the Donatists of England, whome we call Brownists. Wherein, by the Answeres vnto certayne Writings of theyrs, diuers of their heresies are noted, with sundry fantasticall opinions.* 1590. (*Short Treatise against the Donatists of England*)

Gilby, A., *A Pleasavnt Dialogve Betweene a Souldior of Barwicke and an English Chaplaine. Wherein are largely handled & laide open, such reasons as are brought in for maintenaunce of popishe Traditions in our Eng. Church. Also is collected, as in a short table, 120. particular corruptions yet remaining in our saide Church, with sundrie other matters, necessarie to be knowen of all persons. Togither with a letter of the same Author, placed before this booke, in way of a Preface.* 1581.

Greenwood, John, *An Answere to George Giffords Pretended Defence of Read Praiers and deuised Litourgies with his vngodlie cauils & wicked sclanders comprised in the first parte of his last vnchristian & reprochfull booke entituled A Short Treatise against the Donatists of England.* 1590. (*Answere to George Giffordes Pretended Defence of Read Praiers*)

Greenwood, John, *A Plaine Refvtation of M. G. Giffardes reprochfull booke*, etc. (see Barrowe, Henry)

H[arrison]., R[obert]., *A Little Treatise. vppon the firste Verse of the 122. Psalm. Stirring vp vnto carefull desiring & dutifull labouring for true church Gouernement.* 1583.

[Harvey, Richard], *Plaine Percevall the Peace-Maker of England. Sweetly indevoring with his blunt persuasions to botch vp a Reconciliation between Mar-ton and Mar-tother. Compiled by lawfull art, that is to say, without witch craft, or sorcery: and referred specially to the Meridian and pole Artichocke of Nomans Land: but may serue generally without any great error, for more Countries than Ile speake of.* [1590.]

[Harvey, Richard], *A Theologicall Discovrse of the Lamb of God and His Enemies: Contayning a briefe Commentarie of Christian faith and felicitie, together with a detection of old and new Barbarisme, now commonly called Martinisme. Newly published both to declare the vnfayned resolution of the wryter in these present controuersies, and to exercise the faithfull suiect in godly reuerence and dutiful obedience.* 1590.

Hooker, Richard, *Ecclesiastical Polity.* (Everyman's Library, Vols. I–II, New York, 1940.)

[Lyly, John], *Pappe with an hatchet. Alias, A figge for my God sonne. Or Cracke me this nut. Or A Countrie cuffe, that is, a sound boxe of the eare, for the idiot Martin to hold his peace, seeing the patch will take no warning.* [1589.] (*Pappe with an hatchet*)

Mar-Martine. [1589.]

Marprelate, Martin, *Certaine Minerall and Metaphisicall Schoolpoints to be defended by the reuerende Bishops and the rest of my cleargie masters of the Conuocation house against both the vniuersities and al the reformed Churches in Christendome. Wherin is layd open the very quintessence of all Catercorner diuinitie. And with all to the preuenting of the Cauils of these wrangling Puritans the persons by whom and the places where these miseries are so worthely maintayned are for the most part plainly set downe to the view of all men and that to the ternall prayse of the most reuerend Fathers.* [1589.] (*Minerall Conclusions*)

Marprelate, Martin, *Hay any worke for Cooper: Or a briefe Pistle directed by waye of an hublication to the reuerende Byshopps coun-*

selling them if they will needs be barrelled vp for feare of smelling in the nostrels of her Maiestie & the State that they would vse the aduise of reuerend Martin for the prouiding of their Cooper. Because the reuerend T.C. (by which misticall letters is vnderstood eyther the bounsing Parson of Eastmeane, or Tom Coakes his Chaplaine) to bee an vnskilfull and a deceytfull tubtrimmer. Wherein worthy Martin quits himself like a man I warrant you in the modest defence of his selfe and his learned Pistles and makes the Coopers hoopes to flye off and the Bishops Tubs to leake out of all crye. [1589.] (*Hay any worke for Cooper*)

Marprelate, Martin, *The iust censure and reproofe of Martin Iunior. Wherein the rash and vndiscreete headines of the foolish youth, is sharply mette with, and the boy hath his lesson taught him, I warrant you, by his reuerend and elder brother, Martin Senior, sonne and heir vnto the renowmed Martin Marprelate the Great. Where also, least the springall shold be vtterly discouraged in his good meaning, you shall finde, that hee is not bereaued of his due commendations.* [1589.] (*Just Censure* or *Martin Junior*)

Marprelate, Martin, *Oh read ouer D. Iohn Bridges for it is a worthy worke: Or an epitome of the fyrste Booke of that right worshipfull volume written against the Puritanes in the defence of the noble cleargie by as worshipfull a prieste Iohn Bridges, Presbyter, Priest, or elder, doctor of Diuillitie and Deane of Sarum. Wherein the arguments of the puritans are wisely preuented that when they come to answere M. Doctor they must needes say something that hath bene spoken. Compiled for the behoofe and ouerthrow of the Parsons, Fyckers, and Currats that haue lernt their Catechismes and are past grace: By the reuerend and worthie Martin Marprelate gentleman and dedicated to the Confocation house. The Epitome is not yet published but it shall be when the Bishops are at conuenient leysure to view the same. In the meane time let them be content with this learned Epistle.* [1588.] (*Epistle*)

Marprelate, Martin, *Oh read ouer D. Iohn Bridges for it is worthy worke: Or an epitome of the fyrst Booke of that right worshipfull volume written against the Puritanes in the defence of the noble cleargie by as worshipfull a prieste Iohn Bridges, Presbyter, Priest, or elder, doctor of Diuillitie and Deane of Sarum. Wherein the arguments of the puritans are wisely preuented that when they come to answere M. Doctor they must needes say some thing that hath bene spoken. Compiled for the behoofe and ouerthrow of the vnpreaching*

Parsons, Fyckers, and Currats that haue lernt their Catechismes and are past grace: By the reuerend and worthie Martin Marprelat gentleman and dedicated by a second Epistle to the Terrible Priests. In this Epitome the foresaide Fickers &c. are very insufficiently furnished with notable inabilitie of most vincible reasons to answere the cauill of the puritanes. And lest M. Doctor should thinke that no man can write without sence but his selfe the senceles titles of the seueral pages and the handling of the matter throughout the Epitome shewe plainely that beetleheaded ignoraunce must not liue and die with him alone. [1588.] (*Epitome*)

Marprelate, Martin, *The Protestatyon of Martin Marprelat Wherein notwithstanding the surprizing of the printer, he maketh it known vnto the world that he feareth, neither proud priest, Antichristian pope, tiranous prellate, nor godlesse catercap: but defiethe all the race of them by these presents and offereth conditionally, as is farthere expressed hearin by open disputation to apear in the defence of his caus aginst them and theirs Which chaleng if they dare not maintaine aginst him: then doth he alsoe publishe that he never meaneth by the assitaunce of god to leaue the a ssayling of them and theire generation vntill they be vterly extinguised out of our church.* [1589.] (*Protestation*)

Marprelate, Martin, *Theses Martinianae: That is, Certaine Demonstrative Conclusions, sette downe and collected (as it should seeme) by that famous and renowmed Clarke, the reuerend Martin Marprelate the great: seruing as a manifest and sufficient confutation of al that euer the Colledge of Catercaps with their whole band of Clergiepriests, haue, or canbring for defence of their ambitious and Antichristian Prelacie. Pvblished and Set Foorth as an after-birth of the noble Gentleman himselfe, by a prety stripling of his, Martin Iunior, and dedicated by him to his good neame and nuncka, Maister Iohn Kankerbury: How the yongman came by them, the Reader shall vnderstande sufficiently in the Epilogue. In the meane time, whosoeuer can bring mee acquainted with my father, Ile bee bounde hee shall not loose his labour.* [1589.] (*Theses Martinianae* or *Martin Junior*)

Marre Mar-Martin: Or Marre-Martins medling, in a manner misliked. [1589.]

Martins Months minde, That is, A certaine report, and true description of the Death, and Funeralls, of olde Martin Marre-prelate, the great makebate of England, and father of the Factious. Contayning the cause of his death, the manner of his buriall, and the right copies both of his Will, and of such Epitaphs, as by sundrie his dearest friends, and other of his well willers, were framed for him. 1589.

[Nashe, Thomas], *An Almond for a Parrat, Or Cutbert Curry-knaues Almes. Fit for the knaue Martin, and the rest of those impudent Beggers, that can not be content to stay their stomakes with a Benefice, but they will needes breake their fastes with our Bishops. Rimarum sum plenus. Therefore beware (gentle Reader) you catch not the hicket with laughing.* [1590.] (*An Almond for a Parrat*)

[Pasquil], *A Countercuffe giuen to Martin Iunior: by the venturous, hardie, and renowned Pasquill of England, Caualiero. Not of olde Martins making, which newlie knighted the Saints in Heauen, with rise vppe Sir Peter and Sir Paule; But latelie dubd for his seruice at home in the defence of his Countrey, and for the cleane breaking of his staffe vpon Martins face.* 1589. (*Countercuffe giuen to Martin Iunior*)

[Pasquil], *The First parte of Pasquils Apologie. Wherin he renders a reason to his friendes of his long silence: and gallops the fielde with the Treatise of Reformation lately written by a fugitiue, Iohn Penrie. Printed where I was, and where I will be readie by the helpe of God and my Muse, to send you the May-game of Martinisme for an intermedium, betweene the first and seconde part of the Apologie.* 1590. (*First parte of Pasquils Apologie*)

[Pasquil], *The Returne of the renowned Caualiero Pasquill of England, from the other side the Seas, and his meeting with Marforius at London vpon the Royall Exchange. Where they encounter with a little houshold talke of Martin and Martinisme, discouering the scabbe that is bredde in England: and conferring together about the speedie dispersing of the golden Legende of the liues of the Saintes.* 1589. (*Returne of the renowned Caualiero Pasquill*)

Penry, John, *Th'Appellation of Iohn Penri, vnto the Highe court of Parliament, from the bad and injurious dealing of th'Archb. of Canterb. & other his colleagues of the high commission: Wherein the complainant, humbly submitting himselfe and his cause vnto the determination of this honorable assembly: craueth nothing els, but either release from trouble and persecution, or just tryall. Anno Dom.* 1589 [1590]. (*Appellation*)

[Penry, John], *A Briefe Discovery of the Vntrvthes and Slanders (Against the Trve Gouernement of the Church of Christ) contained in a Sermon, preached the 8. of Februarie 1588. by D. Bancroft, and since that time, set forth in Print, with additions by the said Authour. This Short Answer may serve for the clearing of the truth, vntill a larger confutation of the Sermon be published.* [1590.] (*Briefe Discovery of the Untruthes and Slanders*)

Penry, John, *A defence of that which hath bin written in the questions of the ignorant ministerie, and the communicating with them.* [1588.] (*Defence of that which hath bin written in the questions of the ignorant ministerie*)

[Penry, John], *A Dialogve wherin is plainly laide open, the tyrannicall dealing of Bishopps against Gods children. with certaine points of doctrine, wherein they approue themselues (according to D. Bridges his judgement) to be truely the Bishops of the Diuell.* [1590.] (*Dialogue wherin is plainly laide open*)

Penry, John, *An exhortation vnto the Gouernours and people of her Maiesties countrie of Wales, to labour earnestly to haue the preaching of the Gospell planted among them.* [1588.] (first edition)

Penry, John, *An exhortation vnto the gouernours, and people of hir Maiesties countrie of Wales, to labour earnestly, to haue the preaching of the Gospell planted among them. There is in the ende something that was not in the former impression.* 1588. (second and third editions)

Penry, John, *Historie of Corah, Dathan, and Abiram, &c. Numb. 16. chap. Applied to the Prelacy Ministerie and Church-assemblies of England.* [Written in 1592.] 1609. (*Historie of Corah, Dathan, and Abiram*)

[Penry, John], *An Hvmble Motion With Svbmission vnto the Right Honorable LL. of Hir Maiesties Privie Covnsell. Wherein is laid open to be considered, how necessarie it were for the good of this Lande, and the Queenes Majesties safety, that Ecclesiasticall discipline were reformed after the worde of God: And how easily there might be provision for a learned Ministery. Anno 1590.* (*Humble Motion with Submission*)

Penry, John, *I Iohn Penry Doo Heare As I Shall Answere Before the Lord my God in that great day of Iudgement set down sumarily the Whole truth and nothing but the truth which I hold and professe at this hower eyther in regard of my faith towards my God and Dread Soueraigne Queene Elizabeth vnto whome only of all the potentas in the world I owe all reuerence, dutie and submission in the Lord.* [1593.]

[Penry, John], *M. Some laid open in his coulers: Wherein the indifferent reader may easily see, howe wretchedly and loosely he hath handeled the cause against M. Penri. Done by an Oxford man, to his friend in Cambridge.* [1590.] (*M. Some laid open in his coulers*)

Penry, John, *Propositions and Principles of Diuinitie, propounded and disputed in the vniuersities of Geneua, by certaine students of Diuinitie there, vnder M. Theod. Beza, and M. Anthonie Faius, professors of Diuinitie. Wherein is Contained a Methodical summarie, or Epitomie of the commonplaces of Diuinitie. Translated Ovt of Latine into English, to the end that the causes, both of the present dangers of that Church, and also of the troubles of those that are hardlie dealt with elswhere, may appeare in the English tongue.* 1591. (*Propositions and Principles of Divinitie*)

Penry, John, *To My Beloved Wife Helener Penry, partaker with me in this life of the suffrings of the Gospel in the kingdome and pacience of Iesus Christ: And resting with me in vndowbted hope of the glory that shalbe revealed: all strenght and comfort, with all other spirituall graces be multiplyed through Christ Iesus our Lord.* [1593.]

Penry, John, *A Treatise Containing the Aeqvity of an Hvmble Svpplication which is to be exhibited vnto hir Graciovs Maiesty and this high Court of Parliament in the behalfe of the Countrey of Wales, that some order may be taken for the preaching of the Gospell among those people. Wherein also is set downe as much of the estate of our people as without offence could be made known, to the end that our case (if it please God) may be pitied by them who are not of this assembly and so they also may bee driuen to labour on our behalfe.* Oxford, 1587. (*Aequity*)

Penry, John, *A Treatise Wherein is Manifestlie Proved, That Reformation and Those that sincerely fauor the same, are vnjustly charged to be enemies, vnto hir Maiestie, and the state. Written both for the clearing of those that stande in that cause: and the stopping of the sclaunderous mouthes of all the enemies thereof.* 1590. (*Reformation No Enemie*)

Penry, John, *A viewe of some part of such publike wants & disorders as are in the seruice of God, within her Maiesties countrie of Wales, togither with an humble Petition, vnto this high Court of Parliament for their speedy redresse. Wherein is shewed, not only the necessitie of reforming the state of religion among that people, but also the*

onely way, in regarde of substaunce, to bring that reformation to passe.
[1589.] (*Supplication*)

Rythmes against Martin Marre-Prelate. [1589.]

Some, Robert, *A Godly Treatise containing and deciding certaine questions, moued of late in London and other places, touching the Ministerie, Sacraments, and Church.* 1588. (*First Godly Treatise*)

Some, Robert, *A Godly Treatise containing and deciding certaine questions, mooued of late in London and other places, touching the Ministerie, Sacraments, and Church. Whereunto one proposition more is added. After the ende of this Booke you shall finde a defence of such points as M. Penry hath dealt against: And a confutation of many grosse errours broched in M. Penries last Treatise.* 1588. (*Second Godly Treatise*)

Some, Robert, *A Godly Treatise, Wherein are Examined and Confuted many execrable fancies, giuen out and holden partly by Henry Barrow and Iohn Greenewood: partly, by other of the Anabaptistical order.* 1589.

Sutcliffe, Matthew, *An Answere to a Certaine Libel Supplicatorie, or rather Diffamatory, and also to certaine Calumnious Articles, and Interrogatories, both printed and scattered in secret corners, to the slaunder of the Ecclesiasticall state, and put forth vnder the name and title of a Petition directed to her Maiestie. Wherein not onely the friuolous discourse of the Petitioner is refuted, but also the accusation against the Disciplinarians his clyents iustified, and the slaunderous cauils at the present gouernement disciphred by Mathew Sutcliffe.* 1593. (*Answere to a Certaine Libel*)

Sutcliffe, Matthew, *An Answere Vnto a Certaine Calumnious letter published by M. Iob Throkmorton, and entituled, A defence of I. Throkmorton against the slaunders of M. Sutcliffe, Wherein the vanitie both of the defence of himselfe, and the accusation of others is manifestly declared by Matthew Sutcliffe.* 1595. (*Answere unto Iob Throkmortons Letter*)

Sutcliffe, Matthew, *The Examination of M. Thomas Cartwrights late apologie, Wherein his vaine and vniust challenge concerning certaine supposed slanders pretended to haue bene published in print against him, is answered and refuted.* 1596. (*Examination of M. Thomas Cartwrights late apologie*)

Sutcliffe, Matthew, *A Remonstrance: or Plaine Detection of Some of the Favlts and Hideous Sores of Such Sillie Syllogismes and Impertinent Allegations, as ovt of sundrie factious Pamphlets and Rhapso-*

dies, are cobled vp together in a booke, Entituled A Demonstration of Discipline: Wherein also, The true state of the Controuersie of most of the points in variance, is (by the way) declared. 1590. (*Remonstrance or Plaine Detection*)

Sutcliffe, Matthew, *A Treatise of Ecclesiasticall Discipline Wherein that confused forme of gouernment, which certeine vnder false pretence, and title of Reformation, and true discipline, do striue to bring into the Church of England, is examined and confuted.* 1591. (*Treatise of Ecclesiasticall Discipline*)

Throckmorton, Job, *The defence of Iob Throkmorton, against the slaunders of Maister Sutcliffe, taken out of a copy of his owne hande as it was written to an honorable Personage.* 1594. (*Defence of Iob Throkmorton*)

To my louynge brethren that is troublyd abowt the popishe aparell, two short and comfortable Epistels. 1566.

[Travers, Walter], *A Defence of the Ecclesiastical Discipline ordayned of God to be vsed in his Church. Against a Replie of Maister Bridges, to a briefe and plain Declaration of it, which was printed An. 1584. Which replie he termeth, A Defence of the gouernement established in the Church of Englande, for Ecclesiasticall matters.* [1588.] (*Defence of the Ecclesiastical Discipline*)

[Travers, Walter], *Ecclesiasticae Disciplinae, et Anglicanae Ecclesiae ab illa aberrationis, plena e verbo Dei, & dilucida explicatio,* La Rochelle (?), 1574. [tr. by Cartwright as *A full and plaine declaration of Ecclesiasticall Discipline,* etc.]

T[urswell]., T., *A Myrror for Martinists, And all other Schismatiques which in these dangerous daies doe breake the godlie vnitie, and disturbe the Christian peace of the Church.* 1590.

[Udall, John], *A Demonstration of the truth of that Discipline, which Christ hath prescribed in His Word, for the government of his Church, in all times and places, until the end of the world.* Ed. by E. Arber. (The English Scholar's Library of Old and Modern Works, No. 9, London, 1880.) (*Demonstration of Discipline*)

[Udall, John], *The State of the Church of England laid open in a Conference between Diotrephes a bishop, Tertullus a Papist, Demetrius a Usurer, Pandochus an Inkeeper, and Paul a Preacher of the Word of God.* Ed. by E. Arber. (The English Scholar's Library of Old and Modern Works, No. 5, London, 1879.) (*Diotrephes*)

Whether it be mortall sinne to transgresse ciuil lawes, which be the commaundementes of ciuill Magistrates: The resolution of D. Hen.

Bullinger and D. Rod. Gualter, of D. Martin Bucer and D. Peter Martyr: A briefe and lamentable consyderation, of the apparell now vsed by the Cleargie of England: Set out by a faithful seruaunt of God, for the instruction of the weake. 1566. (*Whether it be mortall sinne to transgresse ciuil lawes, which be the commaundementes of ciuill Magistrates*)

A Whip for an Ape: Or Martin displaied. [1589.]

Whitgift, John, *An answere to a certen Libell intituled, An Admonition to the Parliament.* London, 1572. (*Answere to a certen Libell*)

Whitgift, John, *The Defense of the Aunswere to the Admonition, against the Replie of T.C.,* 1574. (*Defense of the Aunswere*)

Whitgift, John, *A Defence of the Ecclesiasticall Regiment in England defaced by T.C. in his Replie against D. Whitgifte.* London, 1574.

Wilcox, Thomas, *An Admonition to the Parliament* (see Field, John)

Wright, Leonard, *A Friendly Admonition to Martine Marprelate, and his Mates.* 1590.

SECONDARY SOURCES

According to the distinguished Elizabethan scholar R. B. McKerrow, "there is no thoroughly satisfactory account of the [Marprelate] controversy as a whole." William Maskell's *History of the Marprelate Controversy* he dismisses as "full of errors" and "written with a very strong anti-Martinist bias." Edward Arber's *Introductory Sketch to the Martin Marprelate Controversy* McKerrow terms "a very valuable collection of documents bearing on the subject . . . quite indispensable to the student," but adds that "it offers no connected account of the matter." William Pierce's *Historical Introduction to the Marprelate Tracts* is written, in McKerrow's opinion, "with a bias in favour of the Martinists no less strong than that of Maskell against them." Finally, J. Dover Wilson's chapter in *The Cambridge History of English Literature* "so far as it goes, is excellent," but "the author has, perhaps, failed to make it quite clear what the dispute was all about."

McKerrow thus summarized previous scholarship on the Marprelate Controversy in his monumental edition of the *Works of Thomas Nashe,* completed in 1910. His own brief account of the controversy in the last volume has remained the most lucid, the most concise, and the most unbiased treatment of the subject.

Arber, Edward, *An Introductory Sketch to the Martin Marprelate Controversy, 1588–1590* (The English Scholar's Library of Old and Modern Works, No. 8, London, 1875).

Bonnard, G., *La Controverse de Martin Marprelate, 1588–1590; épisode de l'histoire littéraire du puritanisme sous Élizabeth* (Geneva, 1916).

Carlson, Leland H., ed., *The Writings of Henry Barrow, 1587–1590* (Elizabethan Nonconformist Texts, Vol. III, London, 1962).

Carlson, Leland H., ed., *The Writings of John Greenwood, 1587–1590* (Elizabethan Nonconformist Texts, Vol. IV, London, 1962).

Dexter, H. M., *The Congregationalism of the Last Three Hundred Years as Seen in Its Literature* (New York, 1880).

Frere, W. H., *The English Church in the Reigns of Elizabeth and James I (1558–1625)* (London, 1911).

Haller, William, *The Rise of Puritanism* (New York, 1938).

Knappen, M. M., *Tudor Puritanism* (Chicago, 1939).

Maskell, William, *A History of the Martin Marprelate Controversy* (London, 1845).

Mattingly, Garrett, *The Armada* (Cambridge, Massachusetts, 1959).

McGinn, Donald J., *The Admonition Controversy* (Rutgers University Studies in English, No. 5, New Brunswick, New Jersey, 1949).

McGinn, Donald J., "Nashe's Share in the Marprelate Controversy," *PMLA*, LIX, 4 (December, 1944), 952–84.

McGinn, Donald J., "A Perplexing Date in the Marprelate Controversy," *Studies in Philology*, XLI, 2 (April, 1944), 169–80.

McGinn, Donald J., "A Quip from Tom Nashe," *Studies in the English Renaissance Drama* (New York, 1959), pp. 172–88.

McGinn, Donald J., "The Real Martin Marprelate," *PMLA*, LVIII, 1 (March, 1943), 84–107.

McKerrow, R. B., ed., *The Works of Thomas Nashe*, Vols. I–V (London, 1904–1910).

Neal, Daniel, *History of the Puritans* ed. by J. O. Choules (New York, 1844).

Pearson, A. F. Scott, *Church and State: Political Aspects of Sixteenth Century Puritanism* (Cambridge, 1928).

Pearson, A. F. Scott, *Thomas Cartwright and Elizabethan Puritanism 1535–1603* (Cambridge, 1925).

Peel, Albert, ed., *The Notebook of John Penry, 1593* (Camden Third Series, LXVII, London, 1944).

Peel, Albert, and Carlson, Leland H., eds., *Cartwrightiana* (London, 1951).

Peel, Albert, and Carlson, Leland H., eds., *The Writings of Robert Harrison and Robert Browne* (London, 1953).

Pierce, William, *An Historical Introduction to the Marprelate Tracts* (London, 1908).

Pierce, William, *John Penry, His Life, Times and Writings* (London, 1923).

Pierce, William, *The Marprelate Tracts* (London, 1911).

Strype, John, *The Life and Acts of John Whitgift, D.D.*, Vols. I–III (Oxford, 1822).

Waddington, John, *John Penry, the Pilgrim Martyr* (London, 1854).

Williams, David, *Three Treatises Concerning Wales* (University of Wales Press, Cardiff, 1960).

Wilson, J. Dover, "A Date in the Marprelate Controversy," *The Library*, New Series VIII (1907), 337–359.

Wilson, J. Dover, "Did Sir Roger Williams Write the Marprelate Tracts," *The Library*, 3rd Series, IV (1913), 92–104.

Wilson, J. Dover, "The Marprelate Controversy," *The Cambridge History of English Literature* (New York, 1939), III, 425–52.

Index

Monarchy: church authority and, 11–12, 18, 23, 24, 25, 26, 36, 38, 119, 168, 170–71, 172–73, 177, 183, 191, 192–93, 198–99; congregationalism and, 190; parliamentary power and, 127; Puritanism and, 5–6, 8, 42, 45, 56, 57, 62, 65, 141–42, 187, 204, 211

More worke for Cooper, 91, 111, 114, 115, 116; date of, 155; Penry authorship of, 125, 128, 129, 130, 132, 144; typography of, 112, 145, 147

Moses, 15, 158, 177, 192

Motley, John Lothrop, 5

Müller, Johann (Regiomontanus), 3, 4

Nashe, Thomas, xi–xii, 116, 153, 154, 178; Penry and, 48, 49–50, 170–71; style of, 50, 179–81

National Library of Wales, 68 (illustration), 216

Nehemiah, 24, 41, 170

Newcastle-on-Tyne, England, 99, 107

Newman, Humphrey, 94; secret press and, 106–107, 111, 113, 129, 155; tract distribution, 103, 104, 115, 179

New Testament, 15, 22, 66, 118, 158

Newton Lane, England, 112, 116

New World, 6, 58

Noah, 15

Nonconformism, *see specific sects*, e.g., Presbyterianism

Nonresidences, *see* Ministers, nonresident

Normandy, France, 4

Northampton, England: *secret press and*, 90, 98, 101, 102, 105, 107, 111, 129, 145; High Commission search in, 152, 153, 154, 155–56, 158

Norton, England, 103, 105, 133

Nowell, Alexander, 42

Oaths *ex officio mero*, vii, 37

Old Bailey Prison, vii

Old Testament, 28, 33, 119, 142, 192

Ordination: congregational voice in, 12, 25, 27–28; government by elders and, 14, 16; qualifications for, 18–21, 25, 36, 37–40, 45. *See also specific clerical orders*

Oscula sancta, 209

Oxford University: abolition proposal, 186; Penry at, vii, 49, 50, 51, 159

Pagett (Pagit), Eusebius, 127

Papacy, 4, 7, 72; canon law and, 39; magistrate authority and, 24; unequal ministers and, 139. *See also* Roman Catholicism; *and see specific popes*

Pappe with an hatchet (Lyly), 178, 179, 245

Parkes, William, 96

Parliament: Church reform and, 13, 18, 23, 25, 26, 36, 94, 135; episcopal appointments and, 139–40; Knightley in, 98; Penry's *Aequity* and, 51, 52,